Helping Bereaved Children

HELPING
BEREAVED CHILDREN
A Handbook for Practitioners

Edited by
NANCY BOYD WEBB, D.S.W.
Fordham University
Graduate School of Social Service

Foreword by Earl A. Grollman, D.D.

THE GUILFORD PRESS
New York   London

TO KEMPTON
For Love, Support, and Jokes
Past, Present, and Future
N. B. W.

©1993 The Guilford Press
A Division of Guilford Publications, Inc.
72 Spring Street, New York, NY 10012

Printed in the United States of America

This book is printed on acid-free paper.

Last digit is print number: 9 8 7 6 5 4 3 2 1

Library of Congress Cataloging-in-Publication Data

Helping bereaved children: a handbook for practitioners / edited by
 Nancy Boyd Webb.
     p.   cm.
 Includes bibliographical references and index.
 ISBN 0-89862-130-5
 1. Bereavement in children. 2. Grief in children. 3. Children
and death. 4. Children—Counseling of. 5. Children—Counseling of—
Case studies. I. Webb, Nancy Boyd.
 [DNLM: 1. Bereavement—in infancy & childhood. 2. Psychotherapy—
in infancy & childhood. WS 105.5.E5 H483 1993]
BF723.G75H34 1993
155.9'37'083—dc20
DNLM/DLC
for Library of Congress   93-3506
                                                                 CIP

Contributors

Teresa Bevin, M.A.   Formerly, School Based Mental Health Program, Children's Hospital, National Medical Center, Washington, DC; Presently, Montgomery County Government Crisis Stabilization Services, Bethesda, Maryland; Assistant Professor, Montgomery College, Takoma, Maryland

Jo-Lynn Depta, B.S.W.   Bereavement Outreach Worker, Lethbridge Family Services, Lethbridge, Alberta, Canada

Gail Doster, M.S.W., L.I.C.S.W.   School Counselor, Greater Boston Area, Boston, Massachusetts

Lucy Oppenheimer Hickey, M.A.   Group Social Worker, The Bereavement Support Program, Caledonia Home Health Care, St. Johnsbury, Vermont; Award recipient from National Hospice Organization in 1990, for coauthored program, "Learning About Grief"

Hannah Joslin, Ph.D.   Clinical Psychologist, Child and Adolescent Services, Rockland County Community Mental Health Center, Pomona, New York

Carol P. Kaplan, Ph.D., B.C.D.   Assistant Professor, Fordham University Graduate School of Social Service, New York, New York; Former Director, Adolescent Treatment Unit, Rockland County Community Mental Health Center, Pomona, New York

Jane Le Vieux, M.S., M.Ed., R.N.   Director, The Caring Corner, Dallas, Texas; Formerly, Staff Nurse and Child Life Specialist, Children's Medical Center of Dallas, Dallas, Texas

Caroline Q. McElroy, M.S.W., A.C.S.W., L.I.C.S.W.   School Counselor, Greater Boston Area, Boston, Massachusetts

Mary Munsch, R.D.C., M.S., M.S.W.   Sister of Divine Compassion; School Counselor, Bronx, New York

Donna Casey Tait, M.C.   Chartered Psychologist, Alberta, Canada; Formerly, Clinician, Family and Community Development Program, Lethbridge, Alberta, Canada

Nancy Boyd Webb, D.S.W., B.C.D.   Professor, Fordham University Graduate School of Social Service, Tarrytown, New York; Founder and Director, Postmaster's Certificate Program in Child and Adolescent Therapy, Fordham University Graduate School of Social Service, Tarrytown, New York

Acknowledgments

I knew that this book needed to be written when a former student, now a colleague with many years' post-M.S.W. experience in hospice, told me that as a father with young children, he could not bear the pain of working with bereaved *children*. I hope that he and others who counsel bereaved adults will now be more knowledgeable and comfortable when circumstances bring them in contact with a bereaved child.

The evolution of the book depended heavily on the ten contributing authors who carefully followed my detailed outline and completed the necessary revisions in keeping with my deadline. My circle of personal and professional contacts has widened in the course of seeking out and working with the skilled practitioners who have written about their direct interventions with bereaved children. We are all grateful to them and to their child clients, some of whom proudly and eagerly agreed to share their counseling/therapy experiences for the benefit of others.

Jill Krementz was especially open and generous about permitting me to quote excerpts from her wonderful book *How It Feels When a Parent Dies,* and for putting me in contact with Amira Thoran who enthusiastically agreed to provide an update of her early childhood bereavement.

My own child clients and their families have been equally open in granting me permission to write about our work together. I value the trust they have accorded me, and hope they will take deserved pride in knowing that their experiences of loss can train therapists/counselors to help other bereaved children. Except for the examples noted otherwise, all the clinical cases have been disguised to protect the confidentiality of the children and their families. The situations and the dynamics are based on reality, but the identities of the individuals have been altered. Christopher Lukas and Signe Hammer deserve my special thanks for permitting me to refer to their autobiographical accounts.

Time is a serious pressure in producing a book such as this. I especially appreciate the help and support of my husband who has witnessed first-hand the full range of both the irritants and the satisfactions. He has helped in numerous ways, both substantive and menial, always managing to buoy me up and move me ahead.

Once again, my Dean, Mary Ann Quaranta, has supported my efforts and understood my time pressures. She truly appreciates the importance of educating students and practitioners to serve children and families. I am grateful for her support.

It has been a pleasure to work with the editors of The Guilford Press. I would like to recognize both Sharon Panulla and Judith Grauman who have exhibited the highest professional standards. My personal typists, Ann Gannon and Angela Moray, have been patient, competent, and good-humored in dealing with my numerous revisions and deadline pressures.

I thank all the dozens of individuals who have been involved in the production of this book. I hope that they will take pride in participating in this effort to break through the taboo surrounding the topic of children and death. Bereaved children *can* be helped and this book is dedicated to that helping process.

NANCY BOYD WEBB

Preface

This book grew directly from *Play Therapy with Children in Crisis,* which, because of its comprehensiveness, could not present in-depth attention to the topic of bereaved children. As a child therapist, I have worked with many children who experienced a death during the time I was in contact with them, as well as with others who had been bereaved previously. Death, unlike many other crisis situations, is inevitable and universal. Therefore, anyone who works with children must be prepared to offer help to a child who can become bereaved suddenly, traumatically, or naturally.

Like other crisis situations, the bereaved child's reactions and need for professional intervention differ depending on the child's personal background, availability of supports, and the circumstances of the event. Although there is a growing body of children's psychoeducational literature dealing with fictionalized death situations, detailed guidance for counselors and therapists working with bereaved children is still scanty. My intention in this book is to present not only the theoretical principles that guide intervention with bereaved children, but also detailed case examples of the helping process.

As a professor of social work, I appreciate the needs of students who want specifics about what to say and what not to say. Although there are, of course, no formulas to plug in, I have tried to include as much dialogue as possible to make the work come alive through the actual interchanges between therapist/counselor and client. The Discussion Questions at the end of each chapter offer opportunities to evaluate the dynamic features of the case and to consider alternative interventions.

The book is divided into three major sections. The first presents the theoretical framework for understanding the child's views about death, the assessment, and the counseling/therapy of the bereaved child. Chapter 2, on assessment of the bereaved child, includes several forms that can be used to record significant information about the child's background as well as particulars about the death situation and the family, social, and religious supports. Each death occurs in a context that affects survivors uniquely. Therefore, it is essential to consider this context thoroughly to understand the nature of the child's bereavement and the appropriate helping role of the therapist / counselor.

The second section of the book focuses on deaths occurring in families, including a range of situations from the anticipated, timely death of a grandparent to the traumatic murder–suicide of both parents. Included, also, is a chapter on sibling death and on a death occurring at the same time as another loss, that of parental divorce. The treatment modalities reflect a range of interventions including family therapy, individual play therapy, and a play therapy group for bereaved children.

The third section of the book deals with death situations when these have occurred in the community and when groups of school children have been affected by the shared loss of a peer, a counselor, or a teacher. Several of these chapters demonstrate the need for multilevel interventions including individual, small group, and large group approaches to helping bereaved children. As always, the age of the children and their unique personal histories affect their responses to death. Often the school-based counselor must identify children who require individual follow-up and possible referral to mental health practitioners.

The Appendix of the book is a resource for those seeking further training and information about play therapy, grief counseling, and trauma/crisis counseling. It also provides a list of references to different religious/cultural and ethnic practices related to death.

This book serves two major groups of professionals who work and come in contact with bereaved children: those who are trained in the mental health fields of psychology, psychiatry, psychiatric nursing, and clinical social work, *and* those who are trained in counseling fields such as pastoral counseling and educational counseling. School-based personnel have extensive contact with children. They can provide bereavement counseling in the school, and refer "at-risk" children to mental health specialists when the grief is traumatic or complicated. As will be discussed, a timely referral permits initial focus on the trauma in order to permit subsequent grief work.

The preface of a book is always written after it is completed. As a contributing author and the editor I can use this opportunity to evaluate the book's strengths and shortcomings. I am pleased with the range of approaches presented here to help children bereaved in a variety of situations. We have presented bereavement counseling during and after the crisis of death. The important "unfinished business" at the completion of this book is to emphasize the advisability of helping children *before* a death occurs. I would be very happy if this book leads to inclusion of death education units routinely at the elementary school level. This would serve in a primary prevention model to educate and prepare children *before* they have to deal with the pain of a loss. Death touches children's lives in many ways, and we must do everything we can to help them before, during, and after their inevitable death experiences.

NANCY BOYD WEBB

Foreword

It has been almost 30 years since I wrote *Explaining Death to Children*. At that time the subject was considered taboo. Somehow it was believed that if death were not discussed it would magically disappear.

We have since learned that just as we cannot protect ourselves from life, so we cannot protect children from death. Traumatic experiences belong to both adulthood and childhood. Death is that universal and inevitable process that must be faced by people of all ages.

Helping Bereaved Children: A Handbook for Practitioners, edited by Nancy Boyd Webb, is a gem that must be in the library of all health care professionals, religious counselors, and school and recreational personnel who work with children. So much comprehensive and practical wisdom is superbly expressed in this single volume! Despite an array of diverse contributors, a unique cohesiveness guides the reader full circle in exploring every aspect of the feelings of the bereaved child, the family, the community, and the practitioner, offering penetrating insights and methods of sensitive intervention.

Thoroughly researched and lucidly written, Nancy Boyd Webb's book is an affirming gift that will touch us all in its compelling depth of emotional understanding and guidance.

EARL A. GROLLMAN, D.D.
Author of *Talking about Death:
A Dialogue between Parent and Child*
and *Straight Talk about
Death for Teenagers*

Contents

I. INTRODUCTION

II. DEATH IN THE FAMILY

PART ONE

INTRODUCTION

CHAPTER ONE

The Child and Death

NANCY BOYD WEBB

A simple child
That lightly draws its breath
And feels its life in every limb
What should it know of death?
— WORDSWORTH
(1798/1928, pp. 74–75)

What, indeed, should the child know about death and when should he/she know it, and by what means should he/she find out? The notion of childhood innocence as portrayed by the poet conveys the wish that children's knowledge about death could be avoided or postponed. Becker refers to adults' "ever-present fear of death," as well as to the adults' "utter obliviousness to this fear" (Becker, 1973, p. 17). If adults cannot confront and make peace with their own fears about the end of life, how can they possibly admit to the reality of death in the lives of children? Many adults refrain from discussing death with children because of their own anxiety about the subject. In addition, they may inadvertently want to avoid distressing the child; it is as if they believe that knowledge about the end of a story will spoil its unfolding. Inured in the 1990s to the necessity of informing young people about the risks of "unprotected" or anal intercourse, these same adults may choke and stammer when they need to give the news to a child about the sudden death of a teacher or peer. As in Wordsworth's era, discussion about death today still stimulates a powerful taboo.

The taboo contradicts the reality of the contemporary child's life, however, since most children, through television, view hundreds of deaths, both real and fictionalized, in the daily course of watching cartoons, news, and G/PG-rated dramatizations and movies. Images of all types of deaths

3

imprint on the minds and psyches of the watching children, but their understanding and feelings about what they see remain unknown. Does familiarity bring desensitization and/or easy acceptance about death? Obviously, children must make a huge step from knowing that death occurs to strangers or fantasy creatures on television to awareness that it occurs to everyone, and that in real life, unlike on television, the dead person does not return.

CHILDREN'S PROGRESSION TOWARD MATURE UNDERSTANDING ABOUT DEATH

The necessary truth about death that all humans eventually come to know is that it is irreversible, inevitable, and universal. Most children achieve this knowledge by approximately 9 or 10 years of age due to their normal cognitive development and life experience. Some may achieve a mature conception at younger ages (Wass & Stillion, 1988), especially if they have had experience with the death of an animal (Yalom, 1980) or if they have early experience with the death of a family member (Kane, 1979). For most children, the natural evolution of their ability to think rationally leads gradually to a mature understanding about death.

Cognitive Development: From Immaturity to Conceptual Understanding

Although Piaget's work did not specifically address children's understanding about death, his theories about the development of children's thinking apply directly to the topic. I will focus on the three major developmental phases identified by Piaget and connect these with children's ideas about death in each phase.

The Young Child: Ages 2-7; Piaget's Preoperational Stage

According to Piaget, the preschooler tends toward magical thinking and egocentricity. He/she does not differentiate between thoughts and deeds, and therefore a young boy of this age may believe, when his sister dies suddenly in an accident, that his anger toward her caused her death (see Kaplan & Joslin, Chapter 7). The young child also cannot comprehend the irreversibility of death, and at this age may think that if he screams loudly enough he can awaken his deceased father, who he believes is sleeping (Saravay, 1991). Even when the young child has witnessed a burial he/she may not realize that the dead body in the casket will no longer feel anything, nor perform its usual activities. The child may wonder how a dead man can breathe with dirt on him, and how he will go to the bathroom (Fox, 1985). A child in the movie *My Girl* insisted on putting eye glasses on her deceased friend in the casket so that he could see!

These vignettes all relate to Piaget's preoperational stage (ages 2–7) during which the child's thinking is concrete (literal) and sometimes distorts reality to conform to his/her idiosyncratic understanding, despite logical contradictions. Piaget refers to this type of thinking as "egocentric" since the child believes that everyone else sees the world as he/she sees it.

The work of Maria Nagy (1948) continues to be widely quoted with regard to her study and identification of three stages in children's perceptions of death. Nagy's first stage (ages 3–5) corresponds roughly to Piaget's preoperational phase. Nagy found that children at this age deny that death is a final event; they consider the state of death as temporary and reversible. Therefore, they wonder and may ask about when their dead father is coming home, even though they viewed his body in the casket at the wake. I will discuss the implications of these immature beliefs later in the chapter with respect to children's grieving. Before proceeding, however, I must caution against taking these age references too literally. Development is an individual process that proceeds *generally* as outlined, but as with all matters human, individual variations occur frequently. Furthermore, the lack of synchrony between ages in Nagy's and Piaget's stages should not cause serious concern. The main point is that development progresses gradually from immature to mature understanding about death.

The Latency-Age Child:
Ages 7–11; Piaget's Concrete Operational Stage

Reduced egocentricity and improved capacity for reasoning contribute to the progressive realization among children of elementary school age that death is irreversible. Fox states that "latency youngsters begin to know that dead is dead and that at some time each of us will die. However, their own increasing sense of power and control make it difficult for them to believe such a thing could happen to *them*" (1985, p. 11). Solnit, referring to this realization, states that "the concept that inevitably each of us has to die becomes a threatening, unpleasant, ineffable quality of the *future*. Most children *are able to lay aside this oppressive sense of inevitability,* denying the feel of it because it is so far off . . . the juices of life and the joy of living help block out the fearful, painful conviction about death" (1983, p. 4; emphasis mine). The latency-age child's improved understanding of time permits this conceptualization about the "future" as a remote, distant expectation.

Piaget notes increased capacity for reasoning and the ability to organize sequentially and count backwards (subtract) during the period from 6 to 8 years (Piaget, 1955, 1972). The fact that children are learning to read and use language further signals their developing cognitive abilities.

This development not only facilitates mastery of reading, writing, and arithmetic, it also opens the child's thinking to more accurate comprehension of the mysteries of life and death. Whereas the concept of the body and the spirit confuses the preschool child who puzzles about how the deceased can simultaneously be in heaven and in a grave at the cemetery (Saravay, 1991), children of 9 or 10 can dramatize a puppet play that expresses the wish to visit their parents in heaven, despite knowing clearly that they are buried in a cemetery (Bluestone, 1991).

The latency-age child knows that death is final and that it will happen to everybody "sometime." However, children of this age believe that death happens mainly to the elderly and weak who cannot run fast enough to escape the pursuing "ghost, angel, or space creature" who will cause their death (Fox, 1985; Nagy, 1948). Six- to 8-year-olds, therefore, believe that young people their age usually do not die because they can run fast! According to Lonetto, "death for the child from six to eight years old is personified, externalized, and can be avoided if one sees death in time. Death is not yet finalized; rather, it assumes various external forms (skeletons, ghosts, the death-man)" (1980, p. 100). By 9 or 10 years of age children develop a more realistic perception.

The Prepubertal Child:
Ages 9-12; Bordering on Piaget's Formal Operational Stage

"The mental development of the child appears as a succession of three great periods. Each of these extends the preceding period, reconstructs it on a new level, and later surpasses it to an ever greater degree" (Piaget & Inhelder, 1969, p. 152). Thus, as we consider Piaget's third and "final" stage of cognitive development, that of formal operations, we note the building on preceding stages in addition to the ultimate spurt into the complex arena of mature thought and understanding.

Piaget's stage of formal operations usually begins around age 11 or 12 when the youngster's thinking becomes truly logical, able to handle many variables at once, and capable of dealing with abstractions and hypotheses. As previously stated, most authorities on the topic of children's understanding about death (Anthony, 1971; Grollman, 1967; Kastenbaum, 1967; Lonetto, 1980; Nagy, 1948; Wolfelt, 1983) believe that children acquire a realistic perception of the finality and irreversibility of death by age 9 or 10. This is somewhat earlier than Piaget's designation of the inception of formal thought "around the age of eleven or twelve" (1968, p. 63). Yet, perhaps it attests to the complexity of death itself—connecting both "concrete" elements—that is, a body that no longer functions (comprehensible to the 9- and 10-year-old)—and the "abstract"—that is, a notion of spirituality and life after death (understood by children older than 10). In Lonetto's (1980) study of children's drawings at different ages, an intriguing shift to the representation of death in abstract terms among 12-years-olds was found. They portrayed death with black crayon markings which they described as "darkness." Lonetto states that "children from nine to twelve years old seem capable not only of perceiving death as biological, universal, and inevitable, but of coming to an appreciation of the abstract nature of death, and of describing the feelings generated by this quality. This complex recognition pattern associated with death is joined by an emerging belief in the mortality of the self, but for these children death is far off in the future and remains in the domain of the aged" (1980, p. 157).

CHILDREN'S EMOTIONAL RESPONSES TO DEATH

What is the implication of children's cognitive development on their ability to mourn the death of a loved one? Can children grieve, and, if so, how do they grieve? Is children's grieving different from that of adults? What factors other than the child's age and level of cognitive development impact on the nature of the child's emotional response to death? This chapter and Chapter 2 will explore these questions in detail, after first defining and distinguishing between the concepts of grief, mourning, and bereavement. Obviously, these terms all relate to loss following death, but they are not synonyms, even though the general public and some professionals use them interchangeably.

Bereavement

Signifying the objective fact that a meaningful person has died, the term refers to the status of the individual who has suffered a loss and who may be experiencing psychological stress; the term does not, however, spell out the precise nature of that stress (Kastenbaum, 1991).

Grief

Bowlby describes grief as "the sequence of subjective states that follow loss and accompany mourning" (1960, p. 11). Wolfelt points out that grief is a process, rather than a specific emotion like fear or sadness; it can be expressed by a variety of thoughts, emotions, and behaviors (1983, p. 26).

Mourning

The psychoanalytic definition of mourning describes it as "the mental work following the loss of a love object through death" (Furman, 1974, p. 34, quoting S. Freud, 1915/1957). This "mental work," often called "grief work," involves the "painful, gradual process of detaching libido from an internal image" (A. Freud, 1965, p. 67) thereby freeing libidinal energy for new relationships. This definition of mourning encompasses not only the *initial* grief reaction to the loss, but also the *future* resolution of that grief (Grossberg & Crandall, 1978). In order for mourning to be resolved, according to Krueger, the bereaved person must comprehend the "significance, seriousness, permanence, and irreversibility" of his/her loss (1983, p. 590). In other words, in addition to feeling typical grief reactions such as sadness and anger, the individual must also come to understand that the deceased person will never return and that life *can* be meaningful nonetheless. This adaptation or acceptance to the irrevocable loss is referred to by Bowlby as "relinquishing the object" (1960, p. 11).

Can Children Mourn?

This question has been asked and debated in the literature, with responses depending on both the definition of mourning and on the specific theoretical framework of the respondent. If one's definition of mourning requires mature awareness regarding the finality of death, as stated above by Krueger (1983), a positive response would not be possible until prepuberty. This is the position of Nagera (1970). At the other extreme, Bowlby argues forcefully for the existence of grief and mourning in even very young children when separated from their mothers. Quoting Robertson's 10-year study of children ages 18–24 months who experienced maternal separation, Bowlby presents the following position:

> If a child is taken from his mother's care at this age, when he is so possessively and passionately attached to her, it is indeed as if his world

has been shattered. His intense need of her is unsatisfied, and the frustration and longing may send him frantic with grief. It takes an exercise of imagination to sense the intensity of this distress. *He is overwhelmed as any adult who has lost a beloved person by death.* To the child of two with his lack of understanding and complete inability to tolerate frustration, it is really as if his mother had died. *He does not know death, but only absence;* and if the only person who can satisfy his imperative need is absent, *she might as well be dead.* (1960, p. 15, quoting Robertson, 1953; emphasis mine)

Sigmund Freud, toward the end of his life, in discussing the responses of young children to their mothers' absences, referred to their crying and facial expressions as evidence of both anxiety and pain. Freud stated, with regard to the distressed child, "it cannot as yet distinguish between temporary absence and permanent loss. As soon as it loses sight of its mother, it behaves as if it were never going to see her again" (1926/1959, p. 169). These desperate reactions point to the child's total lack of understanding that the mother continue to exist when she goes away (object constancy). They also indicate the child's lack of a "mental representation" (memory) of the mother that can be evoked in her absence. The beginning stage of object constancy usually occurs in the second half of the first year of life, but the child's capacity to recall the mother's image in her absence is ephemeral until completion of Mahler's rapprochement stage at around 25 months of age (Furman, 1974; Masur, 1991).

It seems only logical that the child must have a clear idea about the separate, independent existence of a person before the child can grieve the loss of that person after his/her death. A. Freud (1960) maintains that the child can mourn only when he/she has developed reality testing and object constancy, and the Furmans (1974) agree with this position.

While it is indisputable that even very young children react strongly to the loss of a meaningful person, and show their reactions in conformity with Bowlby's (1960) stages of protest, despair, and detachment, it seems to me inaccurate to refer to these responses as "mourning" when the young child understands neither the finality of the loss not its significance in his/her life. Thus, feelings of sadness, rage, and longing following the loss of a significant person may qualify as *grief* reactions, but, without mature understanding of the finality and meaning of that loss, cannot accurately be termed as "mourning," in my view.

Although this may appear to be semantic hair-splitting, the implications for the grief counselor or therapist point to the necessity of respecting children's feelings, without expecting more of the child than developmentally appropriate. Thus, the question, Can children mourn?

should ask instead, Can children grieve?, to which an unqualified positive response can be given.

What about "Relinquishing the Object"?

The requirement that resolution of mourning involves "decathecting" or "relinquishing" emotional investment in the deceased creates something of a stalemate when applied to children's mourning. Some child therapists (Nagera, 1970; Wolfenstein, 1969) have pointed to children's ongoing psychological need to hold onto their relationship with their parents in order to successfully complete the tasks of development. Such a fantasied relationship with a deceased parent obviously precludes any "relinquishing" of libido from that fantasy until the adolescent stage has been completed. Nagera states that "the evidence seems to point to the fact that the latency child strongly cathects a fantasy life where the lost object may be seen as alive and at times as ideal" (1970, p. 381). This explains the position of Nagera and Wolfenstein that mourning is not possible until "detachment from parental figures has taken place in adolescence" (Nagera, 1970, p. 362).

A recent article on childhood grief (Baker, Sedney, & Gross, 1992) conceptualizes it as a series of psychological tasks that must be accomplished over time. In these authors' views, decathexis, or detachment, is not essential to the mourning process since they found that many children maintain an internal attachment to the mental image of the lost person that serves an important function in terms of the child's and, later, the adult's development. Therefore, in my opinion "decathexis"/detachment does not equal "relinquishing;" but, rather, a diminution in longing for the deceased so that development and life may proceed.

CASE VIGNETTES

The Grief of a 6-Year-Old

This example comes from Krementz's *How It Feels When a Parent Dies* (1981/1991, pp. 107–110). A 7-year-old girl describes the events and her feelings around the sudden death of her father in a car accident 7 months prior to the interview. The child, Gail, discusses what she and her 3-year-old brother were told about the accident and about the family's funeral and memorial service. I will comment on aspects of the child's report that demonstrate both her developmental stage and that of her younger brother, especially with regard to their expression of grief.

In describing the graveside service, Gail mentioned the number, color, type, and significance of flowers that the family put on the coffin. It was important to her that each family member place a rose on the coffin. Gail then spoke of "waving goodbye to Daddy," a concrete familiar activity that clearly symbolizes leave-taking. Later, when the family returned to their home and had another memorial service (since the funeral had occurred out-of-state) this confused Gail because she thought her father had "died again" and she did not like it. She also did not understand the explanation that crying would help people feel better. Crying made *her* feel very sad!

Gail reported that her brother still believes that their father is "away" and that he is going to come back. When they returned home after a vacation, Gail's brother thought their father would be in the house waiting for them. Gail herself thinks her father is an angel in heaven, watching her from overhead.

Gail has many happy memories of times she shared with her father. She does not like to talk about him to other people, however, because she is afraid of being treated differently; and she thinks her friends might tease her.

Gail likes to sit in her father's chair on Saturday mornings. At these times she feels her father is out working and that he may come back. She does not like to have other people sit in his chair.

Comment

This child's reactions and those of her younger brother demonstrate the inability of the younger child to comprehend the finality of his father's death, and some evidence of more mature understanding on the part of the 7-year-old. The fact that Gail thinks of her father as an angel in heaven and, yet, at other times when sitting in his chair expects him to come home, points to her as yet incomplete understanding about the irreversibility of his death. Also, she wants him to return. The fact that the interview occurred only 7 months after the death may account for some of Gail's denial. She is actively remembering her father and is very aware of missing him.

The Grief of a 9-Year-Old

Also from Krementz (1981/1991, pp. 29–35), this example involves another sudden death of a father in a car crash. Peggy, interviewed at age 11, was the eldest of three girls when her father died. She describes the physical sensations of her chest hurting as if someone had hit her when she learned of her father's death. She recalls screaming to "let all the anger out," and wanting to be left alone. Peggy went to the funeral, but not to the burial. She says now that she is older she likes to visit the cemetery. She states, "I don't think I can grasp the fact that my father is really lying there underneath the ground. I think of him more as a ghostlike person floating around everywhere. *And I do keep thinking that maybe one day he'll come back*" (emphasis mine).

Comment

Although 11 years of age when the interview was conducted, Peggy was still clinging to the possibility that her father's death was not final. This wish for reunion may be particularly strong among survivors of sudden death, who do not have the opportunities for anticipatory grieving as occurs in situations of terminal illness or disability preceding death. An element of this child's report that resembles the previous example and that may be especially vivid among latency-age children, is the dislike of discussing the parent's death with peers, because of the fear of being pitied.

The Grief of a 12-Year-Old

I selected another case example from Krementz (1981/1991, pp. 1–7) because it also involves a girl whose father died suddenly. Laurie, age 12, wrote about her father's death in a plane crash, and about her reactions with regard to her peers, her mother, and her younger brother. Like the children in the previous examples, Laurie finds it hard to believe her father really died, and she would like to know all the details about why the plane crash occurred. She is quite protective of her mother, however, and hesitates to ask questions because of her fear of causing her mother any pain. Laurie has rationalized her father's sudden death as better than if he had to endure pain and suffering. She does not like to have people talk to her about her father, because it "makes her feel worse." She thinks about what should be done with her father's ashes, and hopes that they will be scattered at her grandmother's farm, rather than in the church cemetery, because at the farm she would not have "to go visit him, so everything would be easier." Laurie is somewhat jealous of her younger brother, who has received special attention from his hockey coach since their father's death; however, she has been able to verbalize her feelings to her mother, who has been sensitive to her needs.

Comment

This example shares many similarities with the previous two, and does not, in the brief vignette, reveal distinct progression toward mature understanding about death in the older child. Laurie exhibits a protective attitude toward her mother and seems to want her companionship. This may reflect either her age-appropriate preteen development or her concern about her mother's safety. Often children who have lost one parent worry about the possibility of losing the other.

Even 3 years later, Peggy wants to avoid reminders about her father's death. Although convinced of its reality, she prefers that his ashes not be buried in the nearby cemetery, because she then would have to visit and, of necessity, think about her father's absence.

IS CHILDREN'S GRIEF DIFFERENT FROM ADULTS'?

The case vignettes, professional literature, and clinical experience with bereaved children all attest to some marked differences, as well as to some similarities, between the grief of children and the grief of adults. Wolfelt reminds us that "grief does not focus on one's ability to 'understand,' but instead upon one's ability to 'feel.' Therefore any child mature enough to love is mature enough to grieve" (1983, p. 20).

Denial, anger, guilt, sadness, and longing are felt by young and old alike in response to the loss of a loved person. Adults, who expect children to have many of the same feelings they, themselves, experience at a time of bereavement, may be able to help the children realize that these feelings are justified. It is even more important, however, for adults to recognize that most children have limited ability to *verbalize* their feelings, as well as very limited capacity to tolerate the pain generated by open recognition of their loss. Thus, in the vignettes, we note the children's various attempts to avoid talking about their losses.

We also note in the vignettes the children's fear of being "different" from their peers with regard to having a deceased parent. Unlike adults, who may obtain solace and comfort from the condolences of their friends, children *dread* this process, and frequently their peers feel equally uncomfortable at the prospect of having to speak to a bereaved friend. Children in latency and adolescence are trying to gain control over their feelings, so they resist and feel uncomfortable with an invitation to openly express their emotions. Furman (1974) comments that children consider crying babyish, so they may do their crying in private. The child's "short sadness span" (Wolfenstein, 1966) reflects the low capacity to tolerate acute pain for long periods, characteristic of childhood. Rando (1988/

1991) explains that a child may manifest grief on an intermittent basis for many years in an approach–avoidance cycle with regard to painful feelings. Children often use play as an escape from their pain and as a way to gain mastery over their complex and confused feelings about the death. Insofar as play is the language of childhood, children can deal with their feelings through play in a displaced, disguised manner. The trained play therapist understands and knows how to communicate in this symbolic language and, through the use of play therapy, can help the child work through his/her painful feelings. The purpose of this book is to demonstrate many techniques of play therapy that can help bereaved children with their grief.

In summary, the following considerations serve to differentiate the grief of children from that of adults':

1. Children's immature cognitive development interferes with understanding about the irreversibility, universality, and inevitability of death.
2. Children's limited capacity to tolerate emotional pain.
3. Children's limited ability to verbalize their feelings.
4. Children's sensitivity about "being different" from their peers.

RELIGIOUS/CULTURAL INFLUENCES ON CHILDREN'S CONCEPTIONS OF DEATH

Any analysis of a child's understanding about death must include not only the individual factors related to the child's cognitive and emotional development, but also the influences impacting on the child that emanate from the cultural and religious beliefs in the child's home environment. A psychosocial assessment of the child examines both internal and external elements contributing to the child's understanding about death. McGoldrick et al. warn that "clinicians should be careful about definitions of 'normality' in assessing families' responses to death, [since] the manner of, as well as the length of time assumed normal for mourning differs greatly from culture to culture" (1991, pp. 176–177). They further point out that "cultures differ in major ways about public versus private expressions of grief" (1991, p. 178). Because of these differences, it behooves therapists to try to find out from a family member "what its members believe about the nature of death, the rituals that should surround it, and the expectations of afterlife." The child absorbs and interprets these beliefs and customs, questioning what is not clear, and supplying his/her own answers when the responses to his/her questions are vague and incomprehensible.

The Appendix to this book lists resources for information about the different religious practices and about mourning observances in different cultures. It is not practical to attempt a comprehensive overview of various religions and cultures here. However, grief counselors and therapists working with bereaved children must take responsibility to learn about the typical practices in the cultural and religious group of the bereaved child's family. It is especially important to know about whether the children are expected to participate in the formal and informal rituals of grieving, or whether the children are excluded from these due to the belief that involving the children would be upsetting to them. Most thanatologists believe that it assists the child's grieving when he/she is included in the funeral and other rituals associated with the death of a loved one (Rando, 1988/1991; Wolfelt, 1983; Kastenbaum, 1991). When children are told in advance about what to expect and are given the opportunity to decide whether or not to participate, many elect to do so. Rando points out that rituals are well suited to children, since they are fascinated by these types of behaviors (1988/1991, p. 216). Of course, if there is an open casket at the funeral, the child must be prepared in advance for this, and assured that the family will have some private time to say their farewells to the deceased. James Agee's Pulitzer Prize-winning novel *A Death in the Family* contains a moving, detailed account of a 5-year-old's viewing of his dead father at the wake, during which time the child came to synthesize his observations about his father's appearance in the casket with his first true understanding of the meaning of the word "dead" (Agee, 1938/1969, pp. 288–298).

Children's accounts about attending wakes and funerals often project their ambivalence about the death. They prefer to remember their loved one when alive, but also want to be included in the services. A 15-year-old boy in Krementz's book, whose mother died when he was 9, reflects as follows:

> The night before the funeral we all went to the funeral parlor, and I spent a lot of time right next to her coffin. She was wearing a white dress, but that's all I remember. I remember her more when she was alive because *I think my mind wants to remember her alive rather then dead.* I'm glad, though, that I got a chance to get a last look at her. I drew a picture for her and wrote a little note on it, asking her to wait in heaven for all of us. I gave it to daddy to put in her coffin with her, and even though she was dead, I like to think that she got that last message from me. (Krementz, 1981/1991, p. 54; emphasis mine)

Children differ in their feelings about how they want to remember their deceased relative, but the idea of avoidance of the cemetery is a theme that repeats in several children's accounts in Krementz's book. A 16-year-old Puerto Rican girl, whose mother died when she was 11, states:

> I'm not sold on going to the cemetery. That's the worst place to remember her because I associate it with putting her into the ground. Why would I want to remember that part? My aunt is very religious and she's really into going to the cemetery and lighting candles in church and all that stuff. I don't think anybody should have to go the cemetery. I can't see it. I think the most vivid thing in a person's mind should be the happy moments, and when you visit the grave, you're left with the sad parts . . . I *cannot* relate to my mother by looking at her tombstone. It's hard to imagine there's a body underneath the ground even if I know it's there. The body's not that important to me. It's the soul that counts, and once that's gone, forget it. I wish my mother had been cremated. (Krementz, 1981/1991, pp. 48–49)

This child clearly has attained a mature understanding of death, and she appears to have accepted the finality of her loss, while able to appreciate and remember "the happy moments" of her mother's life.

REFERENCES

Agee, J. (1969). *A death in the family.* New York: Bantam. (Original work published 1938)

Anthony, S. (1971). *The discovery of death in childhood and after.* London: Penguin.

Baker, J. E., Sedney, M. A., & Gross, E. (1992). Psychological tasks for bereaved children. *American Journal of Orthopsychiatry, 62*(1), 105–116.

Becker, E. (1973). *The denial of death.* New York: Free Press.

Bluestone, J. (1991). School-based peer therapy to facilitate mourning in latency-age children following sudden parental death. In N. B. Webb (Ed.), *Play therapy with children in crisis: A casebook for practitioners* (pp. 254–275). New York: Guilford Press.

Bowlby, J. (1960). Grief and mourning in infancy and early childhood. *Psychoanalytic Study of the Child, 15,* 9–52.

Fox, S. (1985). *Good grief: Helping groups of children when a friend dies.* Boston: New England Association for the Education of Young Children.

Freud, A. (1960). Discussion of Dr. John Bowlby's paper. *Psychoanalytic Study of the Child, 15,* 53–62.

Freud, A. (1965). *Normality and pathology in childhood.* New York: International Universities Press.

Freud, S. (1954). Mourning and melancholia. In *Standard Edition* (Vol. 14, pp. 237–258). London: Hogarth Press. (Original work published 1915)

Freud, S. (1959). Inhibitions, symptoms and anxiety. In *Standard Edition* (Vol. 20, pp. 77–175). London: Hogarth Press. (Original work publishd 1926)

Furman, E. (1974). *A child's parent dies.* New Haven: Yale University Press.

Grollman, E. (Ed.). (1967). *Explaining death to children.* Boston: Beacon Press.

Grossberg, S. H., & Crandall, L. (1978). Father loss and father absence in preschool children. *Clinical Social Work Journal, 6*(2), 123–134.

Kane, B. (1979). Children's concepts of death. *Journal of Genetic Psychology, 134,* 141–153.

Kastenbaum, R. (1967). The child's understanding of death: How does it develop? In E. Grollman (Ed.), *Explaining death to children* (pp. 89–109). Boston: Beacon Press.

Kastenbaum, R. J. (1991). *Death, society, and human experience* (4th ed.). New York: Merrill.

Krementz, J. (1991). *How it feels when a parent dies.* New York: Knopf. (Original work published 1981)

Krueger, D. W. (1983). Childhood parent loss: Developmental impact and adult psychopathology. *American Journal of Psychotherapy, 37*(4), 582–592.

Lonetto, R. (1980). *Children's conceptions of death.* New York: Springer.

Masur, C. (1991). The crisis of early maternal loss: Unresolved grief of 6-year-old Chris in foster care. In N. B. Webb (Ed.), *Play therapy with children in crisis: A casebook for practitioners* (pp. 164–176). New York: Guilford Press.

McGoldrick, M., Almeida, R., Hines, P. M., Garcia-Preto, N., Rosen, E., & Lee, E. (1991). Mourning in different cultures. In F. Walsh & M. McGoldrick (Eds.), *Living beyond loss: Death in the family* (pp. 176–206). New York: Norton.

Nagera, H. (1970). Children's reactions to the death of important objects: A developmental approach. *Psychoanalytic Study of the Child, 25,* 360–400.

Nagy, M. (1948). The child's theories concerning death. *Journal of Genetic Psychology, 73,* 3–27.

Piaget, J. (1955). *The child's construction of reality.* New York: Basic Books.

Piaget, J. (1968). *Six psychological studies.* New York: Vintage Books.

Piaget, J. (1972). Intellectual evolution from adolescent to childhood. *Human Development, 15,* 1–12.

Piaget, J., & Inhelder, B. (1969). *The psychology of the child.* New York: Basic Books.

Rando, T. A. (1991). *How to go on living when someone you love dies.* New York: Bantam. (Original work published 1988)

Robertson, J. (1953). Some responses of young children to the loss of maternal care. *Nursing Times, 49,* 382–389.

Saravay, B. (1991). Short-term play therapy with two preschool brothers following sudden paternal death. In N. B. Webb (Ed.), *Play therapy with children in crisis: A casebook for practitioners* (pp. 177–201). New York: Guilford Press.

Solnit, A. J. (1983). Changing perspectives: Preparing for life or death. In J. E. Schowalter, P. R. Patterson, M. Tallmer, A. H. Kutscher, S. V. Gullo, & D. Peretz (Eds.), *The child and death* (pp. 4–18). New York: Columbia University Press.

Wass, H., & Stillion, J. (1988). Dying in the lives of children. In H. Wass, F. Berardo, & R. Neimeyer (Eds.), *Dying: Facing the facts* (pp. 201–228). Washington, DC: Hemisphere.

Wolfelt, A. (1983). *Helping children cope with grief.* Muncie, IN: Accelerated Development.

Wolfenstein, M. (1966). How is mourning possible? *Psychoanalytic Study of the Child, 21,* 93–126.

Wolfenstein, M. (1969). Loss, rage and repetition. *Psychoanalytic Study of the Child, 24,* 432–460.

Wordsworth, W. (1928). Now we are seven. In *The complete poetical works of William Wordsworth.* London: Macmillan. (Original work published 1798)

Yalom, I. D. (1980). *Existential psychotherapy.* New York: Basic Books.

CHAPTER TWO

Assessment of the Bereaved Child

NANCY BOYD WEBB

Thanatologists agree that expressions of grief take many forms, and that its duration varies (Wolfelt, 1983; Fox, 1985; Rando, 1988/1991) depending on individual, cultural/religious, and circumstantial factors. How, then, do we determine when a bereaved child's grief response is progressing on a "normal" course, and when does the child's reaction suggest the need for referral and assessment by a trained mental health professional? This question begs for a precise formula, yet, its answer depends on the complex interplay among factors related to the child, the circumstances of the death, and the ability of the concerned adult to weigh these variables and arrive at a decision.

This chapter tackles the thorny question about "normal" and "pathological," or "disabling" grief as it applies to children, and offers some guidelines about when a professional assessment would be appropriate. Various therapeutic approaches helpful for bereaved children will be outlined in Chapter 3, as will the qualifications of the therapist or grief counselor who works with bereaved children.

DISTINGUISHING BETWEEN "NORMAL" AND "DISABLING" GRIEF

Granted the generous leeway for individual variability in both the nature and duration of grieving, how can we determine when the bounds of "normal" grief have trespassed into the dangerous territory of "disabling" grief? Furthermore, given the distinctions between adult and children's grief, as outlined in Chapter 1, how relevant is the literature on adult grieving to the normal and pathological assessment of children's grief? Is it helpful or pejorative to use the term "disabling" when referring to responses to a death that appear to greatly exceed the range, duration, or intensity of expression considered appropriate in a given situation? I will begin with the latter question.

Terminology

Lindemann's landmark article on the symptomatology and management of acute grief spelled out in great detail the "normal" grief reactions following traumatic experiences such as war or disastrous fire, and contrasted these with delayed or distorted responses, considered "morbid" (1944, in Parad, 1965, pp. 8–16). In studying 101 relatives and survivors of the Coconut Grove fire in Boston, and members of the armed forces, Lindemann concluded:

1. Acute grief is a definite syndrome with psychological and somatic symptomatology.
2. This syndrome may appear immediately after a crisis; it may be delayed; it may be exaggerated or apparently absent.
3. In place of the typical syndrome, there may appear distorted pictures, each of which represents one special aspect of the grief syndrome.
4. By use of appropriate techniques, these distorted pictures can be successfully transformed into a normal grief reaction with resolution. (1944, in Parad, 1965, p. 7)

I will not review Lindemann's work in detail here since it did not focus specifically on children's grief nor did it distinguish between various forms of "acute" grief. However, Lindemann's designation of delayed or distorted grief reactions does seem applicable to children's grief despite his unfortunate labeling of these responses as "morbid." Lindemann emphasized that "not only over-reactions, but under-reactions of the bereaved, must be given attention because delayed responses may occur at unpredictable moments and the dangerous distortions of the grief reaction, not conspicuous at first, may be quite destructive later" (1944, in Parad, 1965, p. 18). Rando refers to a category of grief she terms "unresolved grief," and within this group of responses, she includes absent grief, inhibited grief, delayed grief, distorted grief, chronic grief, and unanticipated grief (Rando, 1988/1991, pp. 81–84). Several cases in this book describe children who manifest various forms of unresolved grief. Indeed, one might propose that "absent," "inhibited," and "delayed" grief may be the norm for children because of their age-appropriate inability to bear the pain of extended grief.

Bowlby, in contrast to both Lindemann and Rando, focuses on the impact of loss in *childhood*. He believes that separation or death of a parent during the years of early childhood may predispose the individual to "unfavorable personality development" that leads to future psychiatric illness (1963, p. 500). Bowlby's views about the impact of loss on subsequent grief present a rationale about terminology that may be applicable here.

> If the experience of loss is likened to the experience of being wounded or being burned, the processes of mourning that follow loss can be likened to the processes of healing that follow a wound or burn. Such healing processes, we know, may take a course which in time leads to full, or nearly full, function being restored; or they may on the contrary, take one of many courses each of which has as its outcome an impairment of function of greater or less degree. In the same way, processes of mourning may take a favorable course that leads in time to restoration of function, namely to a renewal of the capacity to make and maintain love relationships, or they may take a course that leaves this function impaired in greater or less degree. *Just as the terms healthy and pathological are applicable to the different course taken by healing processes, so may they be applied to the different courses run by mourning processes.* (1963, p. 501; emphasis mine)

With due respect to Bowlby's concern about the possible devastating effects of separation and loss in early childhood, it is reassuring to note his opinion that "not every child who experiences either permanent or temporary loss grows up to be a disturbed person" (1963, p. 527).

What, then, is the accurate label to describe grief gone awry when referring to a child? And judgment about the appropriateness of a grief response always considers temporal factors related to the relative recency of the death. Since many, if not most, children avoid facing their upsetting feelings, and can tolerate discomfort in only small doses, the terms "unresolved," "absent," or "delayed" grief do not seem apt for describing children's grief. One must *expect* children's grief to require the passage of time before expression and eventual resolution. Therefore, timeliness is not a useful consideration in evaluating children's grief.

Rather than timeliness, it is the degree of intrusiveness into the child's life created by the grieving that must be evaluated. Specifically, we must determine the extent to which a child can carry out his/her usual activities and proceed with his/her developmental tasks despite the grief. When the child's social, emotional, or physical development shows signs of interference, the grief process can justifiably be considered "disabling," and the deliberate use of the term indicates that something is wrong. The grief has become all-encompassing and detrimental, instead of helping free the child to proceed with his/her life. The child is "stuck" and needs help which family members may be unable to provide. It is important to recognize and help such a struggling and blocked child so that, in Lindemann's words, "these distorted pictures *can be successfully transformed into a normal grief reaction with resolution"* (1944, in Parad, 1965, p. 7; emphasis mine).

Although identifying a cluster of grief reactions as "disabling" may seem extreme, and even pejorative, the result provides the avenue for professional intervention, and avoids the unfortunate stance of joining the child's helplessness and hopelessness. Waiting for the child to "work it out" according to his/her individual timetable sounds respectful and logical, but also may fail the child who is floundering and even drowning in emotional crosscurrents. Because of the preventative possibilities that flow from recognition that some grief reactions are "disabling," I prefer this term to others such as "unresolved" or "delayed," which may inadvertently result in neglect of someone who truly needs and would benefit from timely professional intervention and assistance. What, then, are the indicators that a child should be referred for an evaluation by a mental health professional, and what components will such an assessment include?

Indications for Professional Assessment

Grollman points out that the

> line of demarcation between "normal psychological aspects of bereavement" and "distorted mourning reactions" is thin indeed. The difference is not in symptom but in intensity. It is a *continued* denial of reality even many months after the funeral, or a *prolonged* bodily distress, or a *persistent* panic, or an *extended* guilt, or an *unceasing* idealization, or an *enduring* apathy and anxiety, or an *unceasing* hostile reaction to the deceased and to others. Each manifestation does not in itself determine a distorted grief reaction; it is only as it is viewed *by the professional* in the composition of the *total* formulation. (1967, p. 21; emphasis mine)

Fox believes that "professional mental health services are indicated if there are questions about suicidal risk or if a child has been involved in some way in the death of another person" (1985, p. 17). Fox elaborates further regarding children who may require special assistance with the grieving. Referring to these as "vulnerable or troubled children," Fox identifies the following groups:

1. Children who themselves have a life-threatening or terminal illness.
2. Children who have already been identified as emotionally disturbed.

3. Children who are developmentally disabled and who may have difficulty understanding what has happened.
4. Children who remain "frozen" and in shock long after most grievers have returned to their usual daily activities. (1985, pp. 39–40)

In addition to identifying these groups of potentially vulnerable children, Fox enumerates some symptoms which she considers "red flags" suggesting the need for careful assessment of the grieving child. These "red flag" symptoms include:

- Suicidal hints
- Psychosomatic problems
- Difficulties with schoolwork
- Nightmares or sleep disorders
- Changes in eating patterns
- Temporary regressions

Fox clarifies that "none of these presentations suggests a formal; diagnosis of emotional problems, but each is a possible indicator that the child's grief work may not be proceeding smoothly. Therefore, *each deserves the attention of someone who has been trained in the broad field of mental health so if intervention is indicated, it can begin promptly*" (1985, p. 42; emphasis mine). Rando (1988/1991) wisely admonishes that when there is a question, it is better to err on the side of going for professional help.

Symptoms of Depression

Many of the "red flag" behaviors noted by Fox and the distorted reactions listed by Grollman duplicate the clinical syndrome of depression as listed in the revised third edition of the *Diagnostic and Statistical Manual of Mental Disorders* (DSM-III-R; American Psychiatric Association, 1987). See Table 2.1 for the precise diagnostic criteria for Major Depressive Episode, which Rapoport and Ismond (1990) state has been underdiagnosed in children until recently. As indicated in the DSM-III-R criteria, there must be at least five of the symptoms present during the same 2-week period and this must represent a change from previous functioning. An important and possibly confusing consideration in identifying a child with "disabling" grief is the requirement in DSM-III-R that "the disturbance is not a normal reaction to the death of a loved one (Uncomplicated Bereavement)" (American Psychiatric Association, 1987, p. 223). The caveat implies that although some bereavement responses might duplicate many of the same symptoms as for Major Depressive Episode, if a loss has occurred, the symptoms are considered "secondary" to that; Rapoport

TABLE 2.1. DSM-III-R Diagnostic Criteria for Major Depressive Episode

Note: A "Major Depressive Syndrome" is defined as criterion A below.

A. At least five of the following symptoms have been present during the same two-week period and represent a change from previous functioning; at least one of the symptoms is either (1) depressed mood, or (2) loss of interest or pleasure. (Do not include symptoms that are clearly due to a physical condition, mood-incongruent delusions or hallucinations, incoherence, or marked loosening of associations.)

   (1) depressed mood (or can be irritable mood in children and adolescents) most of the day, nearly every day, as indicated either by subjective account or observation by others

   (2) markedly diminished interest or pleasure in all, or almost all, activities most of the day, nearly every day (as indicated either by subjective account or observation by others of apathy most of the time)

   (3) significant weight loss or weight gain when not dieting (e.g., more than 5% of body weight in a month), or decrease or increase in appetite nearly every day (in children, consider failure to make expected weight gains)

   (4) insomnia or hypersomnia nearly every day

   (5) psychomotor agitation or retardation nearly every day (observable by others, not merely subjective feelings of restlessness or being slowed down)

   (6) fatigue or loss of energy nearly every day

   (7) feelings of worthlessness or excessive or inappropriate guilt (which may be delusional) nearly every day (not merely self-reproach or guilt about being sick)

   (8) diminished ability to think or concentrate, or indecisiveness, nearly every day (either by subjective account or as observed by others)

   (9) recurrent thoughts of death (not just fear of dying), recurrent suicidal ideation without a specific plan, or a suicide attempt or a specific plan for committing suicide

B. (1) It cannot be established that an organic factor initiated and maintained the disturbance

   (2) The disturbance is not a normal reaction to the death of a loved one (Uncomplicated Bereavement)

   Note: Morbid preoccupation with worthlessness, suicidal ideation, marked functional impairment or psychomotor retardation, or prolonged duration suggest bereavement complicated by Major Depression.

C. At no time during the disturbance have there been delusions or hallucinations for as long as two weeks in the absence of prominent mood symptoms (i.e., before the mood symptoms developed or after they have remitted).

D. Not superimposed on Schizophrenia, Schizophreniform Disorder, Delusional Disorder, or Psychotic Disorders NOS.

Note. From *Diagnostic and Statistical Manual of Mental Disorders* (3rd ed., rev., pp. 222–223) by the American Psychiatric Association, 1987, Washington, DC: Author. Copyright 1987 by the American Psychiatric Association. Reprinted by permission.

and Ismond state that "it is crucial for the diagnosis, that the mood disturbance be primary and not secondary to some other disorder" (1990, p. 101). Although there is no diagnostic category for "Complicated" or "Disabling/Pathological" Grief in DSM-III-R, extensive overlapping clearly exists between depressed states and my use of the term "disabling/pathological" grief. The designation of Uncomplicated Bereavement in DSM-

III-R clarifies that "morbid preoccupation with worthlessness, prolonged and marked functional impairment, and marked psychomotor retardation are uncommon and suggest that the bereavement is complicated by the development of a Major Depression" (American Psychiatric Association, 1987, p. 361).

As a child and family therapist, I am familiar with DSM-III-R and use it regularly in the assessment of clients who consult me with a variety of problems, some of which include bereavement. Several of my child clients have become bereaved unexpectedly during the course of my contact with them (see Chapters 4 and 6). I believe that *all* counselors who work with bereaved children would find it helpful to become knowledgeable about the DSM-III-R criteria for depression since they describe in detail many of the behaviors and responses that occur in grieving children, especially those whose grief has become "disabling." In my own practice, I have treated several children whose life experience combined depression and bereavement in different ways.

Pre-Existing Depression

Sometimes a child exhibits signs of depression prior to and independent of any experience with loss. Many of these children are "undiagnosed," since their form of depression permits minimal or passing school performance, without extreme behaviors that draw attention to them. This category includes the quiet child, who seems "withdrawn," but who "gets by." The child may have few or no friends, and sometimes he/she may be scapegoated because peers consider him/her "different."

These children are at extreme risk when they become bereaved, since their survival was precarious even before the loss. An example of such a child (Chapter 4) involves a boy with poor self-esteem, related to learning disabilities, who suffered the loss of two grandparents in 1 year. Without the loving familial support and the pre-existing supportive relationship with his therapist, this child's grief might have become disabling.

Depressive Symptoms following Loss

Sometimes symptoms of depression occur in a child with no previous psychiatric diagnosis. This speaks to the importance of obtaining a careful history to arrive at the correct diagnosis. Susan, in Chapter 11, illustrates an example of a child who was functioning normally until the sudden violent death of her friend precipitated a grief reaction with some accompanying symptoms of depression. When Susan's grief reaction was treated through play therapy, her depressive symptoms abated.

Suicidal Risk

Fox emphatically states that "each bereaved child must be considered potentially at risk for suicide" (1985, p. 16). While this advice may appear to be extreme, practice wisdom dictates caution. We know that young children do not comprehend the irreversibility of death. Therefore, their wish to "go to heaven" to be with their deceased mother and father represents their literal interpretation of their experience and their remedy for their loss.

Even latency-age children, who understand the finality of death, may express suicidal thoughts with reference to wanting a reunion with a deceased parent. Bluestone describes her skillful use of puppet play to assist two bereaved latency-age children who therapeutically "play out" their painful losses and longing for reunion with their deceased parents (1991, pp. 254–275). It is noteworthy that the therapist not only helped these children with their grief through play therapy, but she also conducted a suicide evaluation to determine the degree of suicidal risk of the girl who had been most upset during the play. When this case was presented at the Annual Meeting of the Association of Death Education and Counseling (March 1992), one member of the audience was surprised that the therapist had taken the child's suicidal ideation "so seriously," since "it is common for bereaved children to fantasize about reunions with their parents." I agree with Bluestone that we must take all such fantasies seriously, especially when they include the desire to escape the pain of the loss. Evaluation of degree of risk for suicide provides information about the individual's degree of intent and, in addition, provides the therapist the opportunity to permit the child's wish and the longing for reunion while simultaneously emphasizing the vast difference between the wish and the irrevocable action that would implement it.

Counselors who are not familiar with the assessment of degree of suicide risk may consult Table 2.2 and the references at the end of the chapter (Pfeffer, 1986; Peck, Farberow, & Litman, 1985). In situations where the counselor or therapist has any lingering doubts about the child's intent, it is wise to seek another opinion, and to tell the child and family that you are doing so because you are so concerned about him/her that you want to be certain that he/she will not do anything to harm him/herself. It is better to overreact than to underreact in these circumstances.

When the Child's Bereavement Is Due to Suicide of a Family Member

Hurley (1991) points out that these children require urgent intervention, since there is evidence that children who lose a parent to suicide are at

TABLE 2.2. Questions to Ask in the Evaluation of Suicidal Risk in Children

1. *Suicidal fantasies or actions:*
   Have you ever thought of hurting yourself?
   Have you ever threatened or attempted to hurt yourself?
   Have you ever wished or tried to kill yourself?
   Have you ever wanted to or threatened to commit suicide?

2. *Concepts of what would happen:*
   What did you think would happen if you tried to hurt or kill yourself?
   What did you want to have happen?
   Did you think you would die?
   Did you think you would have severe injuries?

3. *Circumstances at the time of the child's suicidal behavior:*
   What was happening at the time you thought about killing yourself or tried to kill
      yourself?
   What yas happening before you thought about killing yourself?
   Was anyone else with you or near you when you thought about suicide or tried to
      kill yourself?

4. *Previous experiences with suicidal behavior:*
   Have you ever thought about killing yourself or tried to kill yourself before?
   Do you know of anyone who either thought about, attempted, or committed suicide?
   How did this person carry out his suicide ideas or action?
   When did this occur?
   Why do you think that this person wanted to kill himself?
   What was happening at the time this person thought about suicide or tried to kill himself?

5. *Motivations for suicidal behaviors:*
   Why do you want to kill yourself?
   Why did you try to kill yourself?
   Did you want to frighten someone?
   Did you want to get even with someone?
   Did you wish someone would rescue you before you tried to hurt yourself?
   Did you feel rejected by someone?
   Were you feeling hopeless?
   Did you hear voices telling you to kill yourself?
   Did you have very frightening thoughts?
   What else was a reason for your wish to kill yourself?

6. *Experiences and concepts of death:*
   What happens when people die?
   Can they come back again?
   Do they go to a better place?
   Do they go to a pleasant place?
   Do you often think about people dying?
   Do you often think about your own death?
   Do you often dream about people or yourself dying?
   Do you know anyone who has died?

(continued)

TABLE 2.2. (Continued)

What was the cause of this person's death?
When did this person die?
When do you think you will die?
What will happen when you die?

7. *Depression and other affects:*
Do you ever feel sad, upset, angry, bad?
Do you ever feel that no one cares about you?
Do you ever feel that you are not a worthwhile person?
Do you cry a lot?
Do you get angry often?
Do you often fight with other people?
Do you have difficulty sleeping, eating, concentrating on school work?
Do you have trouble getting along with friends?
Do you prefer to stay by yourself?
Do you often feel tired?
Do you blame yourself for things that happen?
Do you often feel guilty?

8. *Family and environmental situations:*
Do you have difficulty in school?
Do you worry about doing well in school?
Do you wory that your parents will punish you for doing poorly in school?
Do you get teased by other children?
Have you started a new school?
Did you move to a new home?
Did anyone leave home?
Did anyone die?
Was anyone sick in your family?
Have you been separated from your parents?
Are your parents separated or divorced?
Do you think that your parents treat you harshly?
Do your parents fight a lot?
Does anyone get hurt?
Is anyone in your family sad, depressed, very upset? Who?
Did anyone in your family talk about suicide or try to kill himself?

Note. From *The Suicidal Child* (pp. 187–188) by C. R. Pfeffer, 1986, New York: The Guilford Press. Copyright 1986 by The Guilford Press. Reprinted by permission of the publisher and author.

greater risk for suicide and depression than are children in the general population. Response to the grief of children bereaved by suicide requires great professional skill and sensitivity, since the meaning of such a death "often becomes distorted in the mind of the child, who usually cannot face the 'voluntary' nature of the suicidal death" (Hurley, 1991, p. 238). Also, the family is usually emotionally devastated in this situation and may be incapable of offering the child essential information and support. When the family feels shame associated with the suicide, they may want to disguise or distort the truth about the death. This further confuses the child, who needs and wants accurate information about how his/her loved one died. The shame associated with stigmatized death, such as suicide, complicates the grief process for all involved and leaves the child bereft and angry. These children should be referred to a mental health professional for evaluation and treatment. (See Hurley, 1991, for an example of play therapy with a 4-year-old whose father committed suicide, and Webb, Chapter 8, for further discussion of maternal suicide.)

THE TRIPARTITE ASSESSMENT OF THE BEREAVED CHILD

Mental health practitioners, teachers, religious leaders, nurses, school-bus drivers, and scout leaders all may have had occasions to counsel a bereaved child. They may or may not have had training in grief counseling or in child development but, nonetheless, most respond effectively out of their own compassion and instinctive respect for the child's feelings. Many bereaved children are not referred to mental health professionals, and many can go through their grieving without assistance from specialists.

Since the 1970s, however, there has been growing awareness in the general public about issues related to death and dying, sparked by the work of Kübler-Ross (1969) and reflected in the growth of the interdisciplinary field of death education. Interest in knowing more about how to help children has increased enormously.

Because of my firm belief in the necessity and value of a thorough assessment prior to counseling or treatment, I will now focus on the elements of such an assessment. I developed the tripartite assessment of the bereaved child as an adaptation of the tripartite crisis assessment that was designed to facilitate evaluation of the child in a variety of crisis situations (Webb, 1991).

Assessment of a bereaved child involves consideration of three groups of factors:

1. Individual factors
2. Factors related to the death
3. Family, social, religious/cultural factors

All of these interact and must be evaluated in order to fully appreciate the bereavement experience of a given individual. Figure 2.1 illustrates the components and interaction among the three sets of variables.

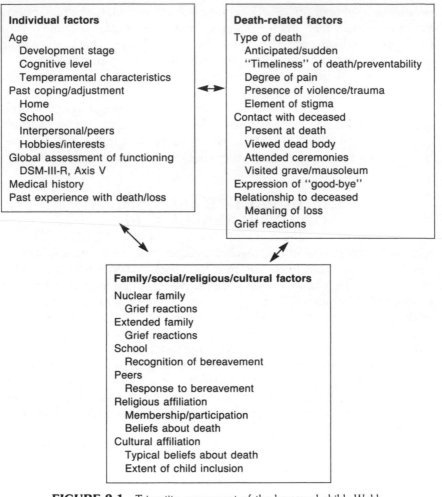

Individual factors

Age
  Development stage
  Cognitive level
  Temperamental characteristics
Past coping/adjustment
  Home
  School
  Interpersonal/peers
  Hobbies/interests
Global assessment of functioning
  DSM-III-R, Axis V
Medical history
Past experience with death/loss

Death-related factors

Type of death
  Anticipated/sudden
  "Timeliness" of death/preventability
  Degree of pain
  Presence of violence/trauma
  Element of stigma
Contact with deceased
  Present at death
  Viewed dead body
  Attended ceremonies
  Visited grave/mausoleum
Expression of "good-bye"
Relationship to deceased
  Meaning of loss
Grief reactions

Family/social/religious/cultural factors

Nuclear family
  Grief reactions
Extended family
  Grief reactions
School
  Recognition of bereavement
Peers
  Response to bereavement
Religious affiliation
  Membership/participation
  Beliefs about death
Cultural affiliation
  Typical beliefs about death
  Extent of child inclusion

FIGURE 2.1. Tripartite assessment of the bereaved child: Webb.

Individual Factors in Childhood Bereavement

The assessment of a bereaved child begins with the individual who has been bereaved. Many of the elements in the assessment of the individual focus on the reality of the child's life prior to the death, for example, his/her level of cognitive understanding and overall adjustment. I have developed a form (see Table 2.3) on which this information can be record-ed to assist the bereavement counselor in organizing and summarizing

TABLE 2.3. Individual Factors in Childhood Bereavement: Webb

1. Age _____ years _____ months   Date of birth _____
                                                    Date of assessment _____

    a. Developmental stage   b. Cognitive level
       Freud _____   Piaget_____
       Erickson _____   c. Tempermental characteristics
                                                 Thomas and Chess _____

2. Past coping/adjustment
    a. Home (as reported by parents) Good _____ Fair _____ Poor _____
    b. School (as reported by parents and teachers) Good _____ Fair _____ Poor _____
    c. Interpersonal/peers Good _____ Fair _____ Poor _____
    d. Hobbies/interests (list) _____

3. Global assessment of functioning: DSM-III-R, Axis V
    Current _____   Past year _____

4. Medical history (as reported by parents and pediatrician)—describe serious illnesses, operations, and injuries since birth, with dates and outcome _____
    _____
    _____
    _____

5. Past experience with death/loss—give details with dates and outcome *or* complete Wolfelt's Loss Inventory _____
    _____
    _____
    _____

Note. This form is one of the three-part assessment of the bereaved child, which also includes an assessment of death-related factors (Table 2.4) and family/social/religious/cultural factors (Table 2.6).

the relevant personal information about the child. The five subcategories in this assessment consist of the following:

- Age/development/cognitive/temperamental factors
- Past coping/adjustment
- Global assessment of functioning: DSM-III-R, Axis V
- Medical history
- Past experience with death/loss

Age/Developmental/Cognitive/Temperamental Factors

Chapter 1 contains a detailed review of age/development/cognitive factors with reference to how these impact upon the child's understanding about death. The temperamental components refer to Chess and Thomas's (1986) profiles of general temperamental style which reflect a child's typical approach to routine and to stressful life experiences. Chess and Thomas identify three distinct profiles describing children's level of responsiveness; these are the difficult child, the easy child, and the slow-to-warm child. Although these categories might seem overly simplistic, they are potentially useful to the bereavement counselor. It is valid to expect that a child who has always approached new situations with difficulty would have a more difficult time when faced with a death than would a youngster whose usual adaptation to new and stressful experiences was generally adaptive.

Past Coping/Adjustment

While it may not be entirely true that the past determines the future (and most of us resist this idea strongly), nonetheless, it is only logical that someone who has been successful managing life stresses in the past will benefit from this track record and confront new challenges with a sense of confidence and resolve. Conversely, an individual who has barely managed to "get by" will probably have a more difficult time when he/she is confronted with a death experience. A somewhat unjust Biblical teaching maintains that the person who has much will be given more, whereas the person with less becomes further deprived. The concept of ego strength explains why a child who is well adjusted will be more capable of dealing with the stress of a death than will a child who already is exhibiting difficulties in coping with routine daily stresses.

Global Assessment of Functioning: DSM-III-R, Axis V

This scale will be of use to mental health practitioners who wish to rate the child's overall psychological, social, and school functioning at the time of the evaluation and during the previous year. (See DSM-III-R [American Psychiatric Association, 1987, pp. 12, 20] for a description of the scale and how to use it.) A useful function of the scale is that it provides ratings for two time periods—current and past year—so that the comparison may point to the need for treatment and the prognosis for future functioning, based on the scoring of the previous level of adjustment. The Global Assessment of Functioning constitutes a formalized, validated method of assessing past coping/adjustment.

Medical History

Sickness, injury, and hospitalization all constitute loss experiences in which the child has had to assume an altered sense of identity as an ill or injured person. None of us likes to be sick or hospitalized, least of all a child, who wants more than anything to view himself/herself as functioning on a high level. The child who has had extensive past experience in which he/she has felt medically vulnerable or disabled may feel less than confident when confronting a death experience. Children who, themselves, are terminally or seriously ill may have very diminished reserves with which to undergo grieving for someone who has died.

Past Experience with Death/Loss

In addition to personal experiences of *physical* vulnerability, it is essential to obtain a history of the child's past experiences with death and loss, no matter how insignificant these may seem. Wolfelt (1983) has devised a detailed Loss Inventory which documents a whole range of losses from death of a parent to a change in living situation as minor as having to share a room; Wolfelt scores each loss in terms of degree of impact and also with regard to elapsed time since the loss, ranging from 0–6 months to 1–4 years. The Loss Inventory appears to be a very useful instrument to use with the grieving child to help him/her understand that one experiences loss and attendant grief not only from death experiences, but also from the myriad of seemingly petty problems of everyday life (Wolfelt, 1983, pp. 83–85). It also provides a literal overview of loss that contributes to documenting an individual's cumulative losses.

Death-Related Factors in Childhood Bereavement

Death is simple, and it is complex. A person stops breathing and that single event can produce a sense of relief or of horror in the survivors. Family members who knew that their loved one was in a coma with no hope for recovery may have anticipated the death and feel relief when it occurs. In contrast, the cessation of breathing can create feelings of horror in a child who views his/her brother lying by the side of the road following a fatal two-car collision.

In evaluating the impact of a death on a child, we must consider the interaction of factors related to his/her personal background and experience, plus factors related to the death itself, and, in addition, how the influences of family/religion/culture and community mediate the expression of grief. Death related factors include the following:

- Type of death
- Contact with deceased
- Expression of "good-bye"
- Relationship to deceased
- Grief reactions

Table 2.4 provides a form for recording these factors.

Type of Death

Children listen and try to understand the many comments made by family and friends about the circumstances associated with a death. Rando refers to "the death surround" to describe all the details of a death; these include the location, type of death, reason for the death, and the degree of preparation of the survivors (1988/1991, p. 52). Factors that I consider especially important with regard to children's understanding include whether the death was anticipated or sudden; whether family members consider it was "timely"; to what extent it might have been prevented; whether pain, violence, and trauma accompanied the death; and whether the death occurred due to circumstances associated with a sense of "stigma."

A sudden death contributes to a tendency toward denial among survivors. If a classmate who was not sick yesterday drowns today in his family pool, anxious feelings of personal vulnerability are stimulated among all his peers, who probably would not experience the same level of anxiety if the death had occurred to a different classmate who was known to be very sick with cancer. The degree of perceived preventability of the death is important both to adults and to children. Bugen (1983) discusses the interaction between the perception of preventability and the closeness of the relationship with the bereaved as predictors of the grief response. This will be discussed more fully in Chapter 6 with reference to the death of a godfather who was terminally ill.

Children are very sensitive about pain. They fear it with reference to themselves, and if they hear details about a very painful death, this may arouse their anxiety, depending on the extent to which they can empathize. Elements of violence and trauma associated with a death also raise anxiety levels and may interfere with the grief process. Eth and Pynoos warn that "children are particularly vulnerable to the additive demands of trauma mastery and grief work. The obligatory efforts at relieving traumatic anxiety *can complicate the mourning process, and*

TABLE 2.4. Death-Related Factors in Childhood Bereavement: Webb

1. Type of death
   Anticipated _____ If yes, how long? _____ or sudden _____

   "Timeliness" of death   Age of the deceased _____
   Perception of preventability
      Definitely preventable _____ Maybe _____ Not _____
   Degree of pain associated with death
      None _____ Some _____ Much _____
   Presence of violence/trauma   Yes _____ No _____
      If yes, describe, indicating whether the child witnessed, heard about, or was present
      and experienced the trauma personally. _____
      _____
      _____

   Element of stigma   Yes _____ No _____
      If yes, describe, indicating nature of death, and degree of openness of family in
      discussing. _____
      _____
      _____

2. Contact with deceased
   Present at moment of death?   Yes _____ No _____
      If yes, describe circumstances, including who else was present and whether the
      deceased said anything specifically to the child. _____
      _____
      _____

   Did the child view the dead body?   Yes _____ No _____
      If yes, describe circumstances, including reactions of the child and others
      who were present. _____
      _____
      _____

   Did the child attend funeral/memorial service/graveside service?   Yes _____
   No _____ Which? _____
   Child's reactions _____
      _____
      _____

   Has the child visited grave/mausoleum since the death?   Yes_____ No_____
      If yes, describe circumstances. _____
      _____
      _____

3. Did the child make any expression of "good-bye" to the deceased, either spontaneous
   or suggested?   Yes _____ No _____
      If yes, describe. _____
      _____
      _____

Note. This form is one of the three-part assessment of the bereaved child, which also includes an assessment of individual factors (Table 2.3) and family/social/religious/cultural factors (Table 2.6).

greatly increase the likelihood of a pathological grief response" (1985, p. 179; emphasis mine). (Cases involving treatment of traumatic grief are presented in Chapters 7 [Kaplan & Joslin], 8 [Webb], 9 [Bevin], and 14 [Munsch].)

Another important consideration with regard to the type of death is the degree to which the death may be associated with stigma. Some examples of stigmatized deaths are those occurring because of suicide, AIDS, drug overdose, or murder/homicides. Doka (1989) uses the term "disenfranchised grief" to refer to losses that cannot be openly acknowledged, socially sanctioned, or publically mourned. The concomitant feelings of shame complicate the grief process and compound reactions of guilt and anger in all of the survivors.

Contact with Deceased

As I have previously indicated, children are very literal and they are also curious. Family members may argue about the degree to which they believe that children should be included with the family in their various rituals associated with a death. I will consider four pivotal points in time at which the child may be permitted to have personal contact with the deceased. These include the following:

- Present at the death
- Viewing the body
- Attending ceremonies
- Visiting grave or mausoleum

Rando (1988/1991) is adamant about the appropriateness of including children with the family in all rituals and observances surrounding a death. According to Rando, when children are separated from the family and not given accurate information, they will have more difficulty resolving their loss (1988/1991, p. 215). However, some children may prefer not to attend a funeral when they understand that many people will be crying. Most mental health professionals and thanatologists believe that the child should be given the choice, after having been told about the circumstances that will occur at each event.

Expression of "Good-Bye"

Although death is not the usual form of leave-taking, nonetheless, some form of farewell can be meaningful to the child. The wake and/or funeral ritual may serve this purpose for adults, who "pay their last respects" as a final good-bye. A sudden death, in which the body may be lost (as in a drowning at sea), or the situation of a death in families that do not engage in any formalized funeral or memorial, deprives all family members of the opportunity to come in contact with their loved one's body and to achieve definitive confirmation of the person's death.

Children, who may be unable to comprehend the abstraction "death," may benefit from doing something tangible for the dead person. Some of the children described by Krementz (1981/1991) felt good about putting a rose on the casket, or in putting a note with a poem inside the casket. Bowen (1976) relates a moving example of his work with a family in which a young mother died very suddenly of a heart attack, leaving her husband and three young children. Each of the children took satisfaction in the private viewing of his/her mother's body, during which time each child spontaneously said or did something special or meaningful in the spirit of good-bye. Perhaps the value of these gestures is that they give some measure of personal control in a situation that is beyond everyone's control.

Relationship to Deceased

The closer the relationship, the more profound will be the impact on the survivor. Wolfelt's Loss Inventory (1983) ranks the death of a parent or sibling as having the highest impact, the death of a close relative next, and the death of a friend several points lower in terms of impact on the child. Unfortunately, there is no ranking for the death of a pet, which can be quite devastating to a child and which constitutes the first experience of death for many children.

It is very important to consider the personal meaning of each loss in terms of the unique aspects of that relationship to the surviving child. The grief counselor can obtain details about this by asking the child to talk about the dead person, and especially, about what they used to enjoy doing together.

Grief Reactions

In the assessment of the bereaved child, the therapist will note the grief reactions that the child currently demonstrates, including in this review both the child's feelings and behaviors as self-reported and as observed by the family and by the counselor. Table 2.5 provides a means of recording the details about the nature of the child's grief.

TABLE 2.5. Recording Form for Childhood Grief Reactions: Webb

Age of child _____ years _____ months   Date of birth _____

                                                 Date of assessment _____

See the form "Individual Factors in Childhood Bereavement" [Table 2.3] for recording of personal history factors.

Date of death _____

Relationship to deceased _____

   Favorite activities shared with deceased _____

   What the child will miss the most _____

   If the child could see the deceased again for 1 hour, what would he/she like to do or say?

_____

_____

Nature of grief reactions (describe) _____

_____

Signs of the following feelings? Y = Yes; N = No

Sadness _____ Anger _____ Confusion _____ Guilt _____ Relief _____

Other _____

Source of information on which this form has been completed

_____ Parent _____ Observation _____ Other

Note. This form is an extension of "Death-Related Factors in Childhood Bereavement" (Table 2.4), focusing specifically on the nature of the child's grief.

Family/Social/Religious/Cultural Factors in Childhood Bereavement

The growing child becomes socialized into the belief systems of the adults in his/her family, school, and community. Those adults, in turn, maintain beliefs about life and death based in large part on their own childhood experiences. A book about childhood bereavement would have to be enormous in size to include the practices and beliefs of all cultures and religions. This is not my intent here, as I indicated in Chapter 1. I believe, however, that the therapist or counselor must take into account the particular belief system of any bereaved child with whom he/she is working.

    The significance of the following general spheres of influence on the bereaved child are included as part of the assessment, and may be recorded on Table 2.6:

- Family influences (nuclear and extended)
- School/peer influences
- Religious/cultural influences

TABLE 2.6. Family/Social/Religious/Cultural Factors in Childhood Bereavement: Webb

1. Family influences

   Nuclear family: How responding to death? Describe in terms of relative degree of openness of response.

   Very expressive _____ Moderately expressive _____ Very guarded _____

   To what extent is child included in family discussions/rituals related to the deceased?

   Some _____ A great deal _____ Not at all _____

   Extended family: How responding to death? Describe, as above, in terms of relative degree of openness of response.

   Very expressive _____ Moderately expressive _____ Very guarded _____

   To what extent do the views of the extended family differ or agree with those of the nuclear family with regard to the planning of rituals and inclusions of child?
   Very different _____ Very similar _____
   If different, describe the nature of the disagreement _____

2. School/peer influences

   Child's grade in school _____
   Did any of the child's friends/peers attend the funeral/memoral services?
   Yes _____ No _____
   Was teacher informed of death? Yes _____ No _____
   Did child receive condolence messages from friends/peers? Yes _____
   No _____
   Does child know anyone his/her age who has been bereaved? Yes _____
   No _____
   If yes, has child spoken to this person since the death? Yes _____ No _____
   Does child express feelings about wanting or not wanting peers/friends to know about the death? Yes _____ No _____
   If yes, what has the child said? _____

3. Religious/cultural influences

   What is the child's religion? _____
   Has he/she been observant? Yes _____ No _____
   What are the beliefs of the child's religion regarding death? _____

   What about life after death? _____
   Has child expressed any thoughts/feelings about this? _____

Note. This form is one of a three-part assessment of the bereaved child which also includes an assessment of individual factors (Table 2.3) and death-related factors (Table 2.4).

Family Influences

Bowen points out that "family systems theory provides a broader perspective of death than is possible with conventional psychiatric theory, which focuses on death as a process within the individual" (1976, in Walsh & McGoldrick, 1991, p. 92). My position is that *both* individual and family systems factors must be assessed. Certainly it is essential to know how the family perceives the death and to what extent the child is included in the mourning rituals of the family. A family that believes it is appropriately shielding a young child from pain by arranging an outing with a favorite baby sitter at the time of a grandmother's funeral cannot be criticized for being cruel. Families differ greatly in their degree of comfort about open expression of feelings, and the child might indeed become upset upon witnessing adults in the throes of grief.

Family members may hold differing views about the rightful role of children as participants in significant life passages such as death. Some parents, at a time of diminished emotional reserves, do not have the resolve to argue their position with a member of the older generation who may appear weak and vulnerable, but who may hold more "traditional" views about "protecting innocent children" from exposure to the pain of death. In the ideal situation, young and old family members cry together and obtain strength and comfort from the unity of their mutual support. Hopefully, in the years to come, there will be increasing inclusion of children in all of the family's rituals and personal expressions following death.

School/Peer Influences

The preschool child, who attends day care may have growing awareness of the wider world outside the family. Nonetheless, young children continue to be influenced mainly my the attachment figures in their close family network. Once a child enters school, however, he/she is much more alert to the opinions of teachers and classmates. When a child experiences a death of a loved one, the reactions of friends and school personnel are important to him/her. As I have already discussed, children have a strong need to "fit in" and feel accepted by their peers. Frequently they interpret this to mean conformity. When someone close to them dies, this event makes them "different" from their peers, and many children feel uncomfortable about the difference. They may need reassurance that they will still be respected and admired for their own qualities, even though they may no longer have a father. Similar to the need to reassure the young child that he/she will still be taken care of after a death, the friends and teachers of the school-age child may need to remind him/her of their ongoing esteem and friendship. A child grieving the loss of a family member or friend is in a very vulnerable state, and will appreciate genuine communications that recognize his/her value and importance as a person.

Religious/Cultural Influences

In counseling a bereaved child, it is helpful to know not only what the child has been taught, but also what he/she has "caught" with regard to the religious/cultural practices of the child's family. When children are confused, they combat their confusion with their own idiosyncratic logic. Thus, the child in the movie *My Girl,* whose friend died of an allergic reaction to numerous bee stings, began to feel better when she reasoned that her own mother, who had died in childbirth and who now "resided" in heaven, could take care of her recently deceased young friend.

We will learn more about the views of children following parental death from the work of Silverman and Worden (1992) whose early findings suggest that many bereaved children retain an image of their parents that incorporates the view of the deceased parent "watching over" the child from the parent's heavenly position. This view incorporates not only the concept of the parent as "superego," but also the feeling of parent as protector.

SUMMARY

The complete assessment of the bereaved child weighs the interactions between the various components of the individual factors in childhood bereavement, the death-related factors, and the family social/religious/cultural factors. While few therapists or counselors have all this information at their fingertips, nonetheless, they must appreciate the power of both what they know and what they do not know as potentially influential on children's grief.

REFERENCES

American Psychiatric Association. (1987). *Diagnostic and statistical manual of mental disorders* (3rd ed., rev.). Washington, DC: Author.

Bluestone, J. (1991). School-based peer therapy to facilitate mourning in latency-age children following sudden parental death. In N. B. Webb (Ed.), *Play therapy with children in crisis: A casebook for practitioners* (pp. 254–275). New York: Guilford Press.

Bowen, M. (1976). Family reaction to death. In P. Guerin (Ed.), *Family therapy* (pp. 335–348). New York: Gardner Press.

Bowlby, J. (1963). Pathological mourning and childhood mourning. *Journal of the American Psychoanalytic Association, 11,* 500–541.

Bugen, L. A. (1983). Childhood bereavement: Preventability and the coping process. In J. E. Schowalter, P. R. Patterson, M. Tallmer, A. H. Kutscher, S. V. Gullo, & D. Peretz (Eds.), *The child and death* (pp. 358–365). New York: Columbia University Press.

Chess, S., & Thomas, A. (1986). *Temperament in clinical practice.* New York: Guilford Press.

Doka, K. (Ed.). (1989). *Disenfranchised grief.* New York: Free Press.

Eth, S., & Pynoos, R. (1985). Interaction of trauma and grief in childhood. In S. Eth & R. S. Pynoos (Eds.), *Post-traumatic stress disorder in children* (pp. 171–183). Washington, DC: American Psychiatric Press.

Fox, S. (1985). *Good grief. Helping groups of children when a friend dies.* Boston: New England Association for the Education of Young Children.

Grollman, E. A. (Ed.). (1967). *Explaining death to children* (pp. 3–27). Boston: Beacon Press.

Hurley, D. J. (1991). The crisis of paternal suicide: Case of Cathy, age 4½. In N. B. Webb (Ed.), *Play therapy with children in crisis: A casebook for practitioners* (pp. 237–253). New York: Guilford Press.

Kastenbaum, R. J. (1991). *Death, society, and human experience* (4th ed.). New York: Merrill.

Krementz, J. (1991). *How it feels when a parent dies.* New York: Knopf. (Original work published 1981).

Kübler-Ross, E. (1969). *On death and dying.* New York: Macmillan.

Lindemann, E. (1944). Symptomatology and management of acute grief. *American Journal of Psychiatry, 101,* 141–148. [Reprinted in Parad, H. J. (Ed.). (1965). *Crisis intervention: Selected readings* (pp. 7–21). New York: Family Service America.]

Parad, H. (Ed.). (1965). *Crisis intervention: Selected readings.* New York: Family Service America.

Peck, M. L., Farberow, N. L., & Litman, R. E. (1985). *Youth suicide.* New York: Springer.

Pfeffer, C. R. (1986). *The suicidal child.* New York: Guilford Press.

Rando, T. A. (1991). *How to go on living when someone you love dies.* New York: Bantam. (Original work published 1988)

Rapoport, J. L., & Ismond, D. R. (1990). *DSM-III-R training guide for diagnosis of childhood disorders.* New York: Brunner/Mazel.

Silverman, P., & Worden, J. W. (1992). Children's reactions in the early months after the death of a parent. *American Journal of Orthopsychiatry, 62*(1), 93–104.

Walsh, F., & McGoldrick, M. (Eds.). (1991). *Living beyond loss: Death in the family.* New York: Norton.

Webb, N. B. (1991). Assessment of the child in crisis. In N. B. Webb (Ed.), *Play therapy with children in crisis: A casebook for practitioners* (pp. 3–25). New York: Guilford Press.

Wolfelt, A. (1983). *Helping children cope with grief.* Muncie, IN: Accelerated Development.

CHAPTER THREE

Counseling and Therapy for the Bereaved Child

NANCY BOYD WEBB

As we will see in the cases presented in this book, children experience death at home, at school, and in the community at large. Death may occur in their own backyard, in a hospital, on the highway, and in their classroom. The children may witness death, hear about it from a relative or school counselor, or may not be told until years later because of the family's sense of shame and inability to discuss the death openly. Sometimes the child may be advised that a death is imminent, so that he/she can say a last "good-bye" to the loved one; the child may also accompany the family to the funeral and graveside service. On the other hand, some families give the child no information at all, and may send the child away to avoid his/her knowledge about or involvement with the death.

Obviously, these "death-related factors" and "family factors" will interact with unique "individual factors," and result in different grief responses for each bereaved child. In the "best possible scenario," for example, a late latency-age boy is informed by his parents that his elderly grandmother is very sick and may not get better, and that it might be a good idea for him to give Grammy a special kiss and tell her that he loves her and will always remember her (Chapter 4 describes a situation more or less like this). Many children in these circumstances feel some anxiety and sadness, and may benefit from brief, supportive counseling from the family's religious leader or funeral director.

By contrast, an example of the "worst possible scenario" might involve the violent deaths of both parents of a preschool child who is too young to comprehend the finality of death and who, in all likelihood, will require intensive, long-term psychotherapy to help him overcome and live with the knowledge that his father shot his mother before killing himself (Chapter 9 describes the initial therapeutic intervention in a traumatic situation like this).

There are countless variations between these two types of death situations: one "timely," anticipated, and of natural causes; and the other, "untimely," sudden, and violent. Because of this wide variability in the circumstances of deaths and in the responses of the child survivors, mental health professionals and community leaders should be prepared to offer a range of counseling and therapy options according to different individual needs. These will be described in detail later in this chapter. However, before presenting these options I will discuss the rationale for professional intervention with bereaved children and the appropriate training for performing this work.

PROFESSIONAL INTERVENTION: RATIONALE AND TRAINING

Is professional assistance necessary and beneficial when children are bereaved? Death is a part of life that every person sooner or later will experience. These characteristics of inevitability and universality could lead to the conclusion that professional help should not be necessary to assist individuals through an essentially normal life passage. Indeed, the support of family, friends, and community does provide sufficient assistance for many bereaved individuals.

However, the situation of the bereaved *child* is different. Many adults feel uncomfortable talking with children about death. Reflecting the attitude implicit in the Wordsworth quote at the beginning of Chapter 1, these adults prefer that the child remain innocent of knowledge about this terrible fact of life. The well-meaning adults want to "protect" children from exposure to death, and therefore they refrain from discussion about death with children.

Another contributing factor in adult reluctance to talk with children about death can be the mutuality of the loss experience. Frequently, when children are bereaved, the adults in their family also are grieving the same loss. Quite understandably, this means that the adults are less available to comfort the child since they are immersed in their *own* grieving process. Furthermore, the child may not display his/her feelings openly, which may suggest (erroneously) to family members that "the child is doing fine."

With the family members, thus, not open or available to the bereaved child, who can offer assistance? We know that bereaved children do not welcome the support of their friends, because being bereaved sets them apart and makes them feel "different." Unlike adults who appreciate and respond positively to condolences from friends, many bereaved children do not like to have their friends speak to them about their loss. In addition, the child's peers are, themselves, uncomfortable in this situation and do not know what to say. This, then, eliminates another source of potential support for bereaved children. In many instances, the bereaved child has neither family nor friends to console him/her. Even when someone might be available and able to reach out, comforting a bereaved child is not easy because the child is so confused and uncomfortable about his/her feelings. The bereaved child may be unable to tolerate the pain of talking about the deceased.

All of these reasons argue for the assistance of a trained professional to help bereaved children. Even an experienced child therapist may find it challenging to attend fully to the bereaved child's varying moods. The therapy must move at the child's pace, using play therapy methods of symbolic communication, in addition to verbal interaction.

Grief Counseling and Grief Therapy

What kind of counseling or therapy is appropriate for bereaved children? Worden, with primary focus on *adult* bereavement, distinguishes between grief "counseling" and grief "therapy" based on whether the client's grief is viewed as uncomplicated (i.e., "normal") or pathological (i.e., complicated). Worden specifies the goal of grief *counseling* (for uncomplicated grief) as "helping the survivor complete any unfinished business with the deceased and say a final good-bye" (1991, p. 38). The goal in grief *therapy* (for complicated grief) is "to identify and resolve the conflicts of separation which preclude the completion of mourning tasks in persons whose grief is absent, delayed, excessive, or prolonged" (1991, p. 79).

Do these distinctions apply to *children's* bereavement? I think they do not, and that we must conceptualize the tasks of children's grief differently because of the child's immature development and ongoing developmental changes. As I discussed in Chapter 1, the child may not understand the finality and irreversibility of death until age 9 or 10, so the goal of saying a *final* good-bye may not be realistic until the child is older. Similarly, when a child has lost a parent, he/she may need to *retain* a relationship with that deceased parent, in fantasy, as a source of comfort and ego integrity. Baker, Sedney, and Gross (1992) state that the "ability to maintain an internal attachment to the lost person may be a sign of healthy recovery, not of pathology" (p. 109). These authors propose that the psychological tasks of bereaved children take a considerable span of time for completion, even in the best circumstances extending for many years following the death. So the notion that delayed or prolonged grief constitutes "pathology" is not applicable to children, as previously discussed in Chapter 1.

Rather than following Worden's terminology that refers to intervention goals and procedures that do not seem applicable to helping bereaved *children,* I propose to use the terms "therapy" and "counseling" according to their more conventional usage: namely, by *therapy* referring to a process of help conducted by a mental health professional, and by *counseling* referring to the process of help as provided by religious leaders and educational personnel. The goals and procedures in each method will differ according to the needs of the specific child and according to the training of the helper. There are probably more similarities than differences between the bereavement work of counselors and therapists. However, the training of therapists in psychopathology and psychodynamics facilitates their ability to work with the *traumatically* bereaved and to understand and help when the bereavement process is grossly atypical or dysfunctional. In situations of traumatic, violent, or multiple losses, the services of a therapist will be essential because the aftermath of the trauma must be addressed before the grief work can proceed (see Eth & Pynoos, 1985; and Chapter 8, section on traumatic components of suicide bereavement).

Qualifications of Counselors/Therapists

Because of the importance of developmental issues in working with children, it is necessary for the grief counselor/therapist to have a firm grounding in child development. In addition, counselors and therapists who work with children need to utilize play therapy in order to engage and interact effectively with their child clients. Some verbalization, of course, always occurs depending on the child's age and ability to communicate directly about the painful topic of death. However, it would be foolhardy to attempt therapy or counseling with a child using *only* verbal communication. Therefore, the grief counselor/therapist who intends to work with children must either already possess or arrange to obtain specialized training in child development and play therapy. In addition, the therapist who works with *traumatized* children must have a thorough knowledge of psychodynamics and of normal regressive as well as dysfunctional reactions of children in situations of extreme stress.

Training of Grief Counselors/Therapists for Work with Bereaved Children

The task of helping bereaved children is demanding and requires specialized knowledge and experience. Although it certainly is possible for a scout leader or school nurse to offer very appropriate supportive help to a grieving child based on intuitive empathy for the child's grief, it could be equally possible for these helpers to fail to identify a child suffering from traumatic grief who would benefit from timely referral to a mental health professional.

Ideally, community caregivers such as school, hospital, and recreational personnel should receive in-service training to recognize the situations that suggest the advisability of referral to a therapist who specializes in work with bereaved children. The referral must be made, however, in a manner that "normalizes" the need for it. The last thing a traumatically bereaved child needs is the covert message that there is "something wrong" with him/her! Worden comments that "there is always the risk of making grief seem pathological because of the formal intervention of a mental health worker, but with skilled counseling this need not be the case" (1991, p. 38). "Normalizing" the need for referral involves making a statement to the child and family that they have suffered a very serious loss and that there are people who are specifically trained to help in situations like theirs.

A list of training programs in play therapy, in grief counseling, and in trauma counseling appears in the Appendix. The professional associations of each group publish newsletters in which workshops and training seminars are listed.

COUNSELING/THERAPY OPTIONS

Depending on the age of the bereaved child, the nature of the death, and the availability of different intervention alternatives, the following options may be appropriate for helping a bereaved child: family therapy, bereavement groups, and individual therapy. Regardless of the counseling/therapy method it is important for the therapist/counselor to respect the unique needs of the child and to be mindful about the timing implications of the child's bereavement process.

Pychological Tasks at Early, Middle, and Late Stages of Bereavement

Baker et al. (1992) conceptualize the grief process in bereaved children as a series of psychological tasks that must be accomplished over time. The tasks of the *early phase* involve "gaining an understanding of what has happened, while employing self-protective mechanisms to guard against the full emotional impact of the loss. *Middle phase tasks* include accepting and reworking the loss, and bearing the intense psychological pain involved. *Late tasks* include the consolidation of the child's identity and a resumption of developmental progress on age-appropriate developmental issues" (Baker et al., 1992, p. 105). Whether the intervention method is primarily group, family, or individual therapy/counseling, the therapist/counselor should be aware of the tasks with which the child is dealing in order to provide help at the level that will be most appropriate for him/her.

The following discussion presents the three major forms of professional intervention with bereaved children, with some consideration given to the advantages/disadvantages of each approach and to the specific indicators for selecting one approach over another.

Family Counseling/Therapy

As emphasized in Chapter 2, an understanding of the family context is essential to appreciate the unique significance of a particular child's bereavement. A family systems perspective maintains that the response of one family member will reverberate among all family members; in an interlocking system one person's pain becomes everyone's pain. Therefore, to help a bereaved child effectively, the family will need to be involved to some extent. If the death has occurred to a member of the family, *all* will be grieving. In this situation, the therapist/counselor may come to represent the only adult who listens fully to the *child's* questions and concerns because the other family members are so focused on their own grieving they cannot attend fully to the child.

It is very helpful to see the family together after a death. Seven to 14 days allows time for the initial shock of the death to have passed, and yet the family will still be very preoccupied with bereavement issues. The purpose of the family meeting differs, depending on the circumstances of the death and the age of the child. The therapist/counselor working with a bereaved child can utilize the information and observations of the family session to understand the significance of the loss to the family as a whole, while obtaining some perspective on how they are managing in the face of this experience.

Walsh and McGoldrick identify two *family* tasks that benefit the immediate and long-term adaption of both individual family members and the family as a functional unit. The tasks are (1) shared acknowledgment of the reality of death and shared experience of loss, and (2) reorganization of the family system and reinvestment in other relationships and life pursuits (1991, pp. 8–13). Obviously, the time table for achievement of these tasks varies greatly, but the authors believe that if these tasks are not achieved eventually, the family members will be vulnerable to dysfunction. Walsh and McGoldrick's task of acknowledgment and sharing dovetails nicely with that of Baker et al. (1992) whose first-stage task focuses on understanding. The family task of system reorganization, on the other hand, subsumes the child's role into functions of the system as a whole. For example, after a mother's untimely death from cancer, a 9-year-old girl might be expected to fulfill some of the mother's previous caretaking of her 3-year-old brother. In a family session with a counselor/therapist the father might be helped to realize that this arrangement is not fair or appropriate for the 9-year-old even though the girl had agreed to perform the duties. With the help of the child/family therapist some compromise could be achieved congruent with both child's and family's needs. The provision of psychoeducational guidance, such as this, is an important purpose of a family session following a death. Examples of family interventions with bereaved children following a death can be found in Chapters 4 and 6.

Table 3.1 summarizes the advantages/disadvantages and special indications for family, group, and individual counseling/therapy options.

Bereavement Groups for Children

We know that children dislike being different from their peers and that when a death occurs in their family they do not like to be singled out, even for the purpose of receiving condolences. Many of the children in Krementz's book (1981/1991) as quoted in Chapter 1 referred to their fear of being pitied because of the death.

These sentiments make the rationale for bereavement groups very clear: Everyone in the group has suffered the loss of a loved one, therefore the group members can offer support to one another, based on the commonality of their shared experience. A typical format is a time-limited (8–10 weeks) group that utilizes a variety of drawing, writing, and other group exercises to enable the children to express their feelings about death. Chapters 10 and 13 each describe the content and process of two such groups, both of which are based on the "mutual aid" model of group work (Schwartz & Zalba, 1971).

A distinct advantage of these groups is the opportunity that they provide to counteract the sense of isolation of the bereaved child through the experience of peer support. In addition, the group is a place where questions can be aired, either verbally or anonymously, through the use of a question box.

Insofar as bereavement groups often include the recently bereaved with members who are in middle or later stages of bereavement, the groups

TABLE 3.1. Comparison of Counseling/Therapy Options: Webb

	Advantages	Disadvantages	Special indications
Family	Observation of child's role in family Assessment of "availability" of family members to the child Members share reality of death "Education" of family members re: different pace and form of children's grieving	Child's "voice" may not be heard by adults Family so involved in own grieving, they cannot empathize with child	Early in grief process *Purposes/goals* To establish alliance To assist in engaging child To offer psycho-educational guidance
Group	Relieves isolation of child "Normalizes" death experience Child sees others in later stage of grief who have "survived"	Child may hear "horror" stories from others in group Child may be over-whelmed by intense feelings of other group members Shy child may not participate	Most appropriate for child dealing with tasks of *middle stage* of bereavement
Individual	Child's needs receive one-to-one attention Therapy/counseling can be paced according to the child's individual needs Permits in-depth exploration of idiosyncratic feelings	Sense of stigma/blame for being "singled out" Engagement of the bereaved child is often difficult	For traumatic bereavement For suicide bereavement For complicated bereavement

offer the child a first-hand experience with children who have withstood the pain of bereavement and survived. It also can be very therapeutic for the children who are further along with their own grieving to be able to offer support to more recently bereaved children (Yalom, 1985; Schiffer, 1984). Sometimes, however, a recently bereaved child may feel overwhelmed when exposed to the feelings of others. The therapist needs to be attuned to this possibility and consider delaying entry into the groups for the recently bereaved child.

For reasons that will be discussed fully in Chapter 8, bereavement groups are not usually recommended for the child who is bereaved by a suicide. Also, a child who has been exposed to a traumatic death experience will need individual help dealing with the trauma, and would not be an appropriate referral for a bereavement group.

Individual Therapy/Counseling: Play Therapy

In situations of suicide and traumatic bereavement and in situations of complicated bereavement, the treatment of choice is individual therapy with a therapist who can help the child cope with some of the intrusive memories and fears associated with the trauma. Often this occurs through the method of play therapy, utilizing drawing, doll play, and other techniques to help the child express his/her feelings and gain some support. Chapter 7 (Kaplan & Joslin) illustrates helpful play therapy interventions using clay and a dollhouse with a 7-year-old boy whose sister died after falling into their backyard well.

The rationale on which the practice of play therapy rests is that the child identifies with and projects his/her own conflicts and concerns onto play materials. As Enzer (1988) points out, the play therapy interaction with the therapist encourages the child to experience catharsis, reduction of troublesome affects, redirection of impulses, and a corrective emotional experience.

As I explain in *Play Therapy with Children in Crisis*, "in crisis situations, the child has felt helpless and afraid. Through replay of the crisis experience the child transforms the passivity and impotence he or she experienced into activity and power. . . . Just as the mourning adult needs to review over and over the details surrounding the death of a loved one, a traumatized child may repeatedly seek to reconstruct a crisis experience symbolically through play" (Webb, 1991, p. 30). A range of play therapy methods, such as art techniques, doll play, puppet play, storytelling, and board games are all described and illustrated through detailed case examples in *Play Therapy with Children in Crisis* (Webb, 1991). Since death is clearly a crisis, many of the techniques are also applicable to work with bereaved children.

Some of the distinct advantages of individual therapy over group or family therapy are that it permits maximum attention to the particular needs of the child, and allows the therapist to move at the child's pace in a careful, in-depth exploration of the child's underlying feelings about the death. As previously indicated, and as will be demonstrated in various examples in this book, the play therapist uses verbalization judiciously, and only tentatively ventures to make connecting statements between the child's play themes and the child's life experience. This matter of "interpretation" or of "clarification" is one of the trickiest tasks of the play therapist, and one that requires many years of supervised experience to master (Webb, 1989). Terr states that "overinterpretation may be more confusing and wasteful than is play without much direct interpretation. An entire treatment through play may be engineered without stepping far beyond the metaphor of the 'game' " (1989, p. 14).

Combined Approaches: Treatment Planning

Often it is desirable to employ a combination of individual, family, and group therapy/counseling in helping a bereaved child. One approach does not negate the other, and, in fact, different purposes are served through each modality.

As already mentioned, a family session is often very useful initially, just as it is helpful to see the child individually soon after the death. In the initial stages of work with a bereaved child, the counselor makes an assessment of the nature of the child's bereavement, even as he/she is also begins to develop rapport and offer supportive help to the child. Depending on the therapist/counselor's evaluation, the decision may be to recommend a limited number of individual sessions, with a follow-up family session after 6–8 weeks. Referral of the child to a bereavement group might occur following this initial period of individual and family therapy/counseling.

There are no hard and fast rules about treatment planning. If the counselor/therapist found, in the family session, that the family as a unit seemed to be involved in dysfunctional behaviors such as scapegoating, withdrawal, or failing to function adequately to meet their own needs, then the treatment recommendation might more appropriately focus primarily on family therapy. Or individual family members might be referred for individual bereavement counseling. On the other hand, if the family appeared to be functioning adequately despite its bereavement, the treatment plan might be to see the child individually, with parent counseling, or family sessions on an "as needed" basis. Terr states, with reference to working with traumatized children, "Most likely the treatment of childhood trauma will remain a multifaceted one, relying upon *several different approaches used simultaneously or in tandem*" (1989, p. 18; emphasis mine). This statement is equally applicable to work with bereaved children.

School-Based Group Approaches for Children Exposed to Violent Death

Because of the serious increase of violence in our society, children may be exposed to violent deaths on the street corner, the playground, and even in the school building. For example, the psychiatric literature of the past few years reports research investigations and interventions following a sniper attack on a school playground (Pynoos et al., 1987), the murder of a teacher in her classroom (Danto, 1983), and a massacre of 21 persons in a McDonald's restaurant (Hough et al., 1990). Whether or not the traumatic death occurred on the school premises, the children come together in the school following the occurrences of violent deaths, making this setting the ideal locale for implementing a preventive mental health intervention in a group format.

Pynoos and Nader (1988) describe a clinical intervention program that can be implemented in schools for children exposed to violence, trauma, or sudden bereavement. Implicit in this approach is the principle of *timely* "first aid" intervention because of the possible negative impact of violent crime on children's ego-oriented thought. "After a violent death, especially one witnessed by a school age child, attempts at trauma mastery can complicate the bereavement process and greatly increase the likelihood of pathological grief (Pynoos & Nader, 1988, pp. 452–543). They view the classroom as an appropriate site for dealing with fears of recurrence of the trauma, and for publicly addressing issues related to dying and loss. Terr elaborates further that "teachers can be trained to use art, musical expression, poetry, or storytelling as expressive therapeutic techniques after traumatic events" (1989, p. 6). In this book, Chapters 13 and 14 describe a variety of interventive approaches in schools following students' exposure to death; Chapter 14 deals especially with intervention after a violent death.

WHEN NO THERAPY/COUNSELING IS AVAILABLE: HOW DO CHILDREN COPE?

Although awareness is growing about the value and role of bereavement counseling and therapy for children, this need has not yet received sufficient recognition to merit *routine* attention in the schools. Death is ubiquitous, yet the response to it of most educational institutions occurs on a case-by-case basis. The notion of "psychological immunization" (Kliman, 1968) argues for "small doses" of information about stressful topics, such as death, for the purpose of preparing children in advance for the certain reality of future exposure. Whereas the *"Good Touches/Bad Touches"* curriculum (Turkel & Fink, 1986) appropriately informs and guides young children in New York State about the danger of sexual abuse, there is no similar preparation about the far greater certainty that they will encounter death experiences. Children *can* cope without such assistance, but how much better equipped would they be if a standard curriculum in the schools helped prepare them in the elementary grades for the real-

ity that death exists and that it is a topic that can be discussed. There
are some excellent children's books that could be used at different grade
levels to stimulate such discussion.

Case Example: Amira Thoron—Bereaved, Age 3; "Recovered," Age 23

One of the children portrayed in _How It Feels When a Parent Dies_
(Krementz, 1981/1991), Amira, was 3 years old when her father died
of cancer. Krementz interviewed her when she was 9. Amira holds a picture of her father and reminisces about the few memories of him she can
recall. In her account, the 9-year-old acknowledges that she has been fearful about the possibility of both her own and her mother's death. She
had nightmares about something happening to her mother and she would
wake up crying because she was so frightened. At that time Amira prayed
as her method of consoling herself. She also was beginning to demonstrate some ability to think about her life, apart from death issues. She
commented as follows:

> I used to be a real worrywart and worry that I was going to die. But
> now I realize that the most important thing is to have fun. There are
> so many things in my life I'd like to do that I just want to try and do
> them and not worry about dying . . . when somebody dies, it's just
> like taking away a part of me, but I try to replace them with someone
> else I know. Now I realize that no one can last forever and I think
> it's made me a stronger person. (Krementz, 1981/1991, pp. 98–99)

Eleven Years Later

Amira, then a college student, wrote the following letter to Jill Krementz,
in which she speaks eloquently about her gratitude about having been
asked in the interview about how she felt about her father's death:

> Jill,
>   I just wanted to tell you that you were one of the first people to
> ask me how I _felt_ about my father's death. I am so grateful to you
> and your gentle and caring questions. I really felt you cared.
>   And _it is only now that I am truly grieving and processing my loss_
> [emphasis mine]. I want to thank you though, because I do feel _you
> planted a seed that what I felt and said was worthy of being heard
> and listened to_ [emphasis mine].
>   You gave me the beginning of a gift that I'm really learning and prac-

ticing now—that it's only in talking about my thoughts and feelings that I can heal the past and embrace my present with love, energy and courage. Thank you.

I love you.

Amira

This letter is published with the permission of both writer and recipient. When I contacted Amira to ask her permission to reproduce it in this book, she shared additional information with me relevant to the topic of how children cope with the death of a parent.

Amira asked me to include the fact that she had attended the same boarding school as her father, and she realizes now that she was "looking for him there." She was a high achiever and won several awards at graduation. She recalls feeling very strongly that her father would be present to see her graduate from "his" school, especially since she had done so well.

This realization did not come spontaneously to Amira, but, rather, in the course of a grief-recovery workshop she attended one summer when she was in college. Amira sought out this workshop, traveled some distance to attend it, and credits it with making a tremendous difference in her life. The "step-by-step" program (James & Cherry, 1988/1989) emphasizes moving beyond the memories and pain of bereavement so that the individual can live more fully in his/her present life. Amira believes that since the 3-day workshop she has been more "free" to pursue her *own* interests, rather than following upon the path of her deceased father. Amira movingly described the finale of the workshop during which she was instructed to imagine her father's face as she spoke the words: "I love you, I miss you, and good-bye."

Timing Questions

Impressed as I was with the sincerity and importance of Amira's grief work, I wondered if she might have achieved this state of acceptance about her father's death at a younger age. Those who believe mourning can be complete only after adolescence would see Amira's progression as normative. I asked Amira if she thought that she might have been helped sooner to talk about her father with a school counselor, nurse, clergyman, or teacher. She says now, at age 23, that she thinks she could have been helped sooner. She remembers no one reaching out to ask about her feelings before Jill Krementz interviewed her when she was 9 years old—5 years after her father's death. She is very supportive of my attempt, through this book, to recognize the needs of bereaved children.

Amira wrote to me as follows: "I'm so grateful that I can give back some of what was given so freely to me . . . I am so *relieved* that you, too, believe that children's voices and feelings should be heard. Thank you!"

EFFECTS ON COUNSELORS/THERAPISTS: VICARIOUS TRAUMATIZATION

The rewards of receiving appreciation and thanks from bereaved and traumatized children rarely take the form of warm and spontaneous letters such as those Jill Krementz and I received from Amira Thoron. More often the therapist/counselor is left with varying degrees of uncertainty about whether or not an intervention with a child was useful. Whereas the evaluation of the "success" of psychotherapy is almost always somewhat subjective, in work with the bereaved, the therapist/counselor faces an irreconcilable barrier: We can *never* really achieve what the client wants—the return of the deceased. Therefore, the therapist/counselor must have very clear goals about what he/she *can* achieve: not taking away the pain of the loss but, rather, helping the client gradually learn to live despite that loss. We must be able to tolerate tears and pain without becoming engulfed in it, and we must be able to withstand "horror stories" when we know that the child has witnessed traumatic scenes and needs to obtain whatever relief may come with the verbal or pictorial description of that horror.

There has been growing awareness in the field of traumatology about the possible negative side effects of this work. The term "vicarious traumatization" refers to the profound psychological effects that therapists may experience in response to exposure to the graphic and painful material presented by their clients. McCann and Pearlman state that "exposure to the traumatic experiences of the victim may be hazardous to the mental health of people close to the victim, including therapists involved in the victim's healing process" (1990, p. 135). According to these authors, the therapist's reactions may even replicate posttraumatic stress disorder, evidenced by intrusive thoughts and painful emotional reactions (p. 144). I will discuss some of the strategies therapists can use to protect themselves against serious and harmful aftereffects of working with victims later in this chapter.

When the client is a *child,* the therapist may even be more prone to strong reactions. These can include feelings of protectiveness, sorrow, grief, as well as feelings of "existential insecurity." Dyregrov and Mitchell state that "more than any situation, pediatric trauma and death triggers thoughts about life's meaninglessness and unfairness. . . . Since children are unable to protect themselves, their suffering is seen as unjust and unfair" (1992, p. 11). Dealing with a grieving adult is hard enough; when the bereaved is a young *child*, the therapist may feel a sense of outrage that, if unchecked, can interfere with the therapist's ability to help.

Coping Strategies for the Therapist/Counselor

There are methods that can help the therapist/counselor. These include the following suggestions culled from the literature (McCann & Pearlman, 1990; Dyregrov & Mitchell, 1992; Johnson, 1989; Worden, 1991):

1. Avoid professional isolation through contact with other colleagues who work with victims and/or bereaved. "Debriefing" through talking to others soon after a stressful experience is helpful.

2. Normalize and avoid pathologizing the emotional responses of helpers. McCann and Pearlman (1990) view vicarious traumatization as a normal reaction to the stressful and sometimes traumatizing work with victims. Worden (1991) recommends "active grieving" for the counselor as a way to avoid burnout.

3. Understand one's personal limitations and avoid undertaking work that goes beyond one's ability to be effective. These limits will differ for different people, and refer both to types of bereavement and to the quantity of bereavement work. Johnson states that "too much drain for too long can make any well dry up" (1989, p. 172).

4. Explore one's own personal history of losses, to identify "any ir-resolution still present from prior losses" (Worden, 1991). Because of the advisability of counselors to have "worked through" their own grief, someone who has been *recently* bereaved should not undertake this type of work.

5. Recognize the positive consequences that can result from working with traumatized and bereaved children. In addition to identifying the stress of this work, we must admit the satisfactions. It can bring many personal rewards, flowing from the knowledge that we are contributing to a child's ability to proceed with his/her life.

REFERENCES

Baker, J. E., Sedney, M. A., & Gross, E. (1992). Psychological tasks for bereaved children. *American Journal of Orthopsychiatry, 62*(1), 105–116.

Danto, B. I. (1983). A man came and killed our teacher. In J. E. Schowalter, P. R. Patterson, M. Tallmer, A. H. Kutscher, S. V. Gullo, & D. Perctz (Eds.), *The child and death* (pp. 49–74). New York: Columbia University Press.

Dyregrov, A., & Mitchell, J. T. (1992). Work with traumatized children—Psychological effects and coping strategies. *Journal of Traumatic Stress, 5*(1), 5–17.

Enzer, N. B. (1988). *Overview of play therapy.* Paper presented at the annual meeting of the American Academy of Child and Adolescent Psychiatry, Seattle, WA.

Eth, S., & Pynoos, R.S. (Eds.). (1985). *Post-traumatic stress disorder in children.* Washington, DC: American Psychiatric Press.

Hough, R. L., Vega, W., Valle, R., Kolody, B., del Castillo, R. G., & Tarke, H. (1990). Mental health consequences of the San Ysidro McDonald's massacre: A community study. *Journal of Traumatic Stress, 3*(1), 71–102.

James, J. W., & Cherry, F. (1989). *The grief recovery handbook: A step-by-step program for moving beyond loss.* New York: Harper & Row. (Original work published 1988)

Johnson, K. (1989). *Trauma in the lives of children.* Alameda, CA: Hunter House.

Kliman, G. (1968). *Psychological emergencies of childhood.* New York: Grune & Stratton.

Krementz, J. (1991). *How it feels when a parent dies.* New York: Knopf. (Original work published 1981)

McCann, I. L., & Pearlman, L. A. (1990). Vicarious traumatization: A framework for understanding the psychological effects of working with victims. *Journal of Traumatic Stress, 3*(1), 131–149.

Pynoos, R. S., Frederick, C., Nader, K., Arroyo, W., Steinberg, A., Eth, S., Nunez, F., & Fairbanks, L. (1987). Life threat and posttraumatic stress in school-age children. *Archives of General Psychiatry, 44,* 1057–1063.

Pynoos, R. S., & Nader, K. (1988). Psychological first aid and treatment approach to children exposed to community violence: Research implications. *Journal of Traumatic Stress, 1*(4), 445–472.

Schiffer, M. (1984). *Children's group therapy: Methods and case histories.* New York: Free Press.

Schwartz, W., & Zalba, S. (1971). *The practice of group work.* New York: Columbia University Press.

Terr, L. C. (1989). Treating psychic trauma in children: A preliminary discussion. *Journal of Traumatic Stress, 2*(1), 3–20.

Turkel, D. & Fink, M. (1986). *Good touches/bad touches: A child sexual abuse prevention program.* White Plains, NY: Mental Health Association.

Walsh, F., & McGoldrick, M. (Eds.). (1991). *Living beyond loss: Death in the family.* New York: Norton.

Webb, N. B. (1989) Supervision of child therapy: Analyzing therapeutic impasses and monitoring counter-transference. *The Clinical Supervisor, 7*(4), 61–76.

Webb, N. B. (Ed.). (1991). *Play therapy with children in crisis: A casebook for practitioners.* New York: Guilford Press.

Worden, J. W. (1991). *Grief counseling and grief therapy* (2nd ed.). New York: Springer.

Yalom, I. (1985). *The theory and practice of group psychotherapy.* New York: Basic Books.

PART TWO

DEATH IN
THE FAMILY

CHAPTER FOUR

Death of Grandparent— Family Therapy to Assist Bereavement
Case of the Silver Family— Siblings, Ages 11, 9, and 5

NANCY BOYD WEBB

Children who were blessed with grandparents have gained much to sustain and enrich their lives. They have learned that death can be regarded as a peaceful completion of life, rather than something to be feared. . . . Children of any age in grieving are unconsciously expressing gratitude for the gifts from the past given to them.
—PATTERSON (1983, p. 77)

A child's first experience with death may be the death of a grandparent. Certainly a grandparent's death occurs more frequently in the life of a child than does the death or a parent. Raphael (1983) and Crenshaw (1991) point out that the reaction of the child to a grandparent's death varies with the quality of the attachment. The response depends on the closeness of the relationship, and on the warmth and frequency of the interaction. Rando comments that "for some children, the death of their grandparents is a nonevent. They know that the death has occurred but cannot really feel much about it because of the lack of relationship with their grandparent. While they may be quite affected by their own parent's distress at the loss, they may have little to grieve for themselves" (1988/1991, p. 150). The child, therefore, responds to the grandparent's death in both *personal terms,* based on the quality of the lost relationship, and in *family systems terms,* based on the reactions of other family members to the death. Walsh and McGoldrick point out that in

61

cases where the grandparent has suffered a prolonged illness, the parent will be "stressed by pulls in two directions: toward the heavy responsibilities of caring for young children and toward filial obligations for the dying and surviving parent" (1991, p. 40).

This chapter deals with the death of two grandparents in 1 year's time, and the meaning of this experience to a 9-year-old boy who was in therapy for difficulties related to school and family relationships. His elderly grandmother died from cancer and 4 months later his grandfather, who was placed in a nursing home following her death, also died. Because I had previously worked with the boy's 11-year-old sister and had occasionally seen the family together, I decided to include the whole family in a bereavement counseling session following the grandmother's death.

FAMILY LIFE CYCLE CONSIDERATIONS

It is understandable that the serious illness and death of any family member will "lead to disruption in the family equilibrium" (Brown, 1989, p. 458). In determining the degree of disruption Brown weighs a number of factors including:

1. The social and ethnic context of death
2. The history of previous losses
3. The timing of the death in the life cycle
4. The nature of the death or serious illness
5. The position and function of the person in the family system, and
6. The openness of the family system. (1989, p. 458)

The Silver family is Jewish, white, and middle-class, with no experience of deaths among their immediate or next generation of relatives in either the mother's or father's family. The diagnosis of terminal cancer in Mr. Silver's mother was an implicit warning of her imminent death in "several months' time." In her late 70s, "Grammy" lived a few blocks from the Silvers in a home she shared with her husband, 81, who was almost blind and suffered from a variety of physical ailments. The severity of Grammy's condition meant that she would no longer be able to cook and perform routine chores, including, especially, the physical care of her husband. Fortunately, the elderly couple had resources to pay for home nursing and housekeeping care. Grammy's illness thus precipitated psychological anticipation of her death, while the family provided emotional support to her and to "Grampa." Although there is no intent here to minimize the significance of this family's stress over their impending loss, they and I were in agreement that her death was "timely." She had lived a long, healthy life, and their concerns were to make her last months as comfortable as possible. Brown states that "generally the farther along in the life cycle, the less is the degree of family stress associated with death and serious illness. *Death at an older age is viewed as a natural process"* (1989, p. 463; emphasis mine).

The death in this family actually proved to be of less significance than were the unresolved old sibling conflicts that the anticipatory bereavement stirred up among Mr. Silver's siblings. Matters of necessary decision-making such as arranging health care, planning for Grampa's care after Grammy's death, and selling their home and disposing of its contents, all provoked discord between Mr. Silver and his middle-aged brother and sister. The deaths of the first generation provided me with a view of second-generation sibling battles that I might otherwise never have seen. It gave me an intergenerational perspective of the sibling rivalry I had been witnessing first-hand between Victoria, age 11, and Todd, age 9. Mr. and Mrs. Silver were very open with me regarding their difficulties with Mr. Silver's siblings and this information deepened my diagnostic understanding and led to interventive strategies intended to release Mr. Silver from his unconscious need to replay his own sibling battles through his children.

Of Brown's (1989) six factors affecting the impact of death and serious illness on the family system, the fifth, "the position and function of the person in the family system," seemed to be the most relevant in this case. The prospective deaths of the family patriarchs led to great instability and jockeying for control among the adult-child second-generation survivors. Awareness of this process helped me understand more fully the intensity of Todd's antagonistic relationship with Victoria. On a different level, the work with this case in a family systems context increased my appreciation of intergenerational family issues as precipitated by the anticipated and subsequent deaths of the first-generation "heads of the family."

Scapegoating following a Death

Although increased solidarity in a family is a frequent reaction to death, according to Goldberg, "scapegoating may also occur in a family as a way of reachieving homeostasis when the previous family balance included a scapegoat" (1973, p. 402). This proved to be an operative factor in this case situation with regard to criticism and disdain expressed by Mr. Silver's siblings toward him which seemed exaggerated and unwarranted in view of his essential and valuable role in supporting his parents. In time, I came to learn that Mr. Silver's father, Grampa, was considered by the family as a demanding tyrant who was very inconsiderate of his wife's feelings. This, evidently, was one of the few areas of agreement between Mr. Silver and his siblings; they had all relied on Mr. and Mrs. Silver to hire and orient health aides and intervene in their mother's behalf. Grammy was to be "protected" from the insensitivity and lack of consideration of her scapegoat husband. Once Grammy died, the family rallied to institutionalize Grampa, and, in the process, they began to criticize Mr. Silver's role as "on the spot" son, support, and financial manager over the past few years. In a family accustomed to a scapegoat as the brunt of their own hostilities, the death of the beloved matriarch led to the "punishment" of her consort through nursing home placement; the resultant vacuum sucked Mr. Silver into the scapegoat role. This is also the position of Todd within his nuclear family, a matter I understand better at the time of this writing than I did 3 years ago when I began working with the family.

ETHNIC/RELIGIOUS CONSIDERATIONS

According to Brown, "Jews are well prepared to deal with life's tragedies and life's suffering. . . . They are a very expressive ethnic group with a tradition of shared suffering. . . . These values and characteristics assist the Jews in dealing with death openly and directly. If they need assistance in this regard, it is to get in touch with the personal aspect of the death" (1989, pp. 460–461). Helping this family with the "personal aspects of the death" was very much the way in which I conceptualized my role. I knew that this family was accustomed to open expression of their feelings, and that the parents were appropriately preparing the children for the probability of Grammy's death. The reason they had contacted me originally was for help in dealing with Victoria's obstinate personality, not about Grammy's impending death. After several months of parent counseling and individual play therapy sessions with Victoria, the parents asked me to evaluate Todd. Victoria's attitude toward them and their parenting skills had improved significantly. Todd, however, presented unique problems which subsequently proved to be due to Attention-Deficit Disorder. He had many fears and was highly anxious.

At the time of Grammy's death I was seeing Todd individually, alternating every other week with parent counseling sessions. His problems, although certainly magnified by the family stress regarding his grandmother's impending death, were separate and idiosyncratic.

A question for me was how to recognize the death when it occurred and whether or not to attend the services or visit the home. I expected that Todd would be quite upset about his grandmother's death, and I wanted to be available to offer support to him and other family members. I knew that this family would follow traditional practices following the death, including immediate burial and subsequent observation of the mourning period (shiva). Mr. Silver had described the practices to me, indicating that there would be elderly relatives from out of town spending time with them, talking about his mother's life. I decided that it would not be appropriate for me to intrude on this family gathering. I asked Mr. Silver to notify me when the death occurred, and I suggested that it might be helpful to all of them to meet together with me in my office after all the relatives had returned home. I also made it clear that I would be available by telephone if any of the family wanted to talk with me before our meeting. The details of the family bereavement session will follow later.

Barth comments that "therapists must realize that no one method of treating problems related to death is the best one. . . . There is no 'correct' therapy for use with families. . . . The only correct approach seem to be to provide as few sessions as possible and leave the work of mourning to the family" (1989, p. 318). This approach proved beneficial in this case.

THE CASE: THE SILVER FAMILY— SIBLINGS, AGES 11, 9, and 5

Family Information

> Father, Edward, age 42, insurance business
> Mother, Joan, age 39, high school teacher/substitute
> Children: Victoria, age 11, sixth grade
> Todd, age 9, fourth grade
> Flora, age 5, kindergarten

> *Extended family*
> Mr. Silver, Sr., "Grampa," age 81, retired lawyer; blind; diabetic
> Mrs. Silver, "Grammy," age 79, cancer—2 years; recent terminal diagnosis

Edward has two older siblings: an unmarried sister, 9 years his senior, and a married brother, 4 years older; both live out of state.

Joan's parents are in their late 60s; they are retired and live nearby. Joan has one married sister, 9 years her junior, who lives out of state.

Background on Referral

The family was referred by the hospital social worker who had been in-volved with Grammy's medical treatment. The parents had expressed their concerns to her about Victoria's "impossible" behavior which was "driving them up a wall" to the point that Mother and Victoria were involved in daily screaming fights with one another. The hospital social worker, who had met all family members, characterized them as "a family of screamers." The parents had welcomed her suggestion that they seek therapy to try to reduce the tension and stress.

First Session with Victoria and Parents: Summary

Many of the issues presented by the parents as disturbing to them reflected rather typical preadolescent behaviors, such as Victoria's messy room, the timing of her homework completion, her refusal to wear her night brace, her desire to take Italian rather than Spanish, and her frequent arguments with her brother. Mother claimed that "everything is a fight and that Victoria won't give up until she gets her way." Vicky follows Mother around the house, persisting and persisting, and Mother cannot stop her or get any peace unless she gives in to her daughter's requests. Mother admitted that she screams in return, and sometimes even hits Victoria. Father, who seems calmer than Mother on the surface, eventually also feels pushed to the limit by Victoria's "defiance and provocativeness." Victoria is very bright, very verbal, and, ultimately, very intimidating toward her parents.

I saw all three together, Victoria alone, the parents alone, and concluded with all three together. In my summary remarks to the family I referred to Grammy's serious illness, and indicated that it had to be adding a certain amount of stress to everyone right now. They all nodded solemnly as I predicted that the months ahead might be even *more* stressful, and that especially during this difficult time they needed to be supportive rather than hostile toward one another. I offered to work with them around the agreed-upon goal of "fight-reduction," not blaming any one person for the arguments that were rampant but making it clear that *each* of them had an important role and the power to refuse to fight, so that the tension in their family could be reduced.

Preliminary Assessment and Treatment Plan

An overview of the presenting problem suggested two sources of strain for this family: first, Victoria's preadolescent development, especially her push toward autonomy and challenge to parental authority; second, the serious illness and impending death of Mr. Silver's mother. Both of these family life cycle transitions are expectable and "normal" developmental passages, either one requiring adjustment and capable of arousing anxiety. This family, which had been functioning reasonably well up to the time of referral, seemed to lack the psychological reserves to cope with the combined stress of the double losses of the prospective death of a member of the older generation, and the symbolic loss of the entry into adolescence of its eldest daughter.

My initial assessment, thus, was that this was a family struggling to cope with the stresses of normal developmental transitions, characterized by losses associated with growth and with death. I believed that a short-term behaviorally focused intervention would help them in relieving the tension generated by the parent–child conflict. Meanwhile, I hoped that my work with them around this would help build a relationship that would improve my ability to assist them with bereavement issues at the time of Mr. Silver's mother's death.

The Treatment Plan

Intending to remove Victoria from the position of being the "identified patient," I suggested that we plan alternating weeks of therapy so that every third week I would see Mr. and Mrs. Silver, with intervening weeks consisting of either sessions alone with Victoria, or with Victoria together with her parents.

Treatment Summary

Using a psychoeducational approach I helped the family implement the contract to which they all had agreed: namely, that all would consciously try to avoid fighting with one another. Some techniques they learned to use successfully were "time-out" hand signals, refraining from arguing when a disagreement was evident, leaving the scene of an argument, saving the disagreement for discussion in family sessions with the therapist, and planning special enjoyment times together. In many ways, my role was that of a mediator, accepting Victoria's push for autonomy while also supporting the parents' appropriate need for her respect and love. I encouraged mutual expressions of praise and genuine positive regard, which had been very much lost in the negative spiral of anger and recrimination.

After several months the relationship between Victoria and her parents improved substantially. Mr. Silver's mother continued to weaken, and the parents and Victoria spoke of her "gradually fading away." I had become more aware of the intense sibling conflict between Victoria and Todd and suggested that it would be appropriate to involve him also in some of our sessions. The parents were open to this, and, in fact, said that they hoped I would see Todd separately as well, since at times he seemed to them as "totally out of it," in a world of his own.

The next phase of treatment, therefore, included some sessions with parents, with Victoria and Todd, some with Victoria alone, and some with Todd alone. After a few months, the focus shifted more to Todd, since he appeared to be a very needy 9-year-old boy whose frustration tolerance and ego development seemed very immature.

Preliminary Assessment of Todd

Todd presented as a tall, lanky youngster with a variety of somatic complaints and many anxieties and fears. He was not doing well in school, and required intensive parental involvement to complete his assignments. He resented being reminded to do his homework, and would frequently whine, complain, and provoke very negative responses from his parents.

These difficulties did not, however, seriously interfere with Todd's social adjustment: He was perceived as a "nice kid" who had friends, and who was quite proficient in gymnastics and baseball.

The parents wanted Todd to be tested for possible learning disabilities since he seemed frequently to "forget" his school assignments and appeared unable to follow directions or to prioritize. The subsequent psychological evaluation confirmed their impressions. The evaluator described Todd as "a very smart boy who is not convinced of this."

My own assessment of Todd was that he was struggling to find his acceptance in this family as the only boy and middle child, between a very bright older sister and a younger sister who was "spoiled rotten," according to the mother. Todd was not comfortable with the idea of growing up. Because of his height people often mistook him as being older, yet his response to my question about what age he would like to be was: "In my Mommy. Then I'd be safe from everything except a nuclear bomb!"

Because Father more typically brought Todd to sessions with me, whereas Mother had brought Victoria, I tuned in to the issues of male identification. Father evidently also had been learning-disabled, although undiagnosed; he had also gone through several years of psychotherapy when he was Todd's age. Father's affect in conveying this to me was that of "history repeating itself," in rather a resigned way.

The Grandmother's Death

In the midst of Todd's evaluation, Mr. Silver's mother died. Mr. Silver telephoned me stating that her death had been peaceful, and that although he had not been with her at the exact moment of death, he had been with her for several hours earlier that same day.

I asked about the children's reactions and Mr. Silver said that Victoria had cried, that Flora was very excited about going to the funeral, and that Todd had been "distraught." He moaned and became very clingy, to the point that Mr. Silver asked the rabbi to speak to him. On the evening after the death (the night before the funeral) Todd had gone to his best friend's house to sleep. The family evidently felt that they could not console him and that his agitation would subside in the company of his friend.

Mr. Silver mentioned that Todd's class was anticipating a special holiday outing to see "The Nutcracker" on the following day, which was the day of the funeral. Mr. Silver said that his instinct was to permit Todd to remain with his class, since Todd indicated that he wanted to go. Mr. Silver did not really ask my advice about this and appeared comfortable with the decision to let Todd go to the performance. Mrs. Silver's sister was coming to be available to the children after the service. Mr. Silver felt that it might not be appropriate for the children to witness the burial service during which, as part of the tradition, the mourning family shovel dirt onto the lowered casket.

I expressed my condolences, and Mr. Silver said that "even when you expect it, the feeling of loss is very real." I indicated my concern for his feelings and also expressed my interest in speaking to Victoria and Todd. Each of them came to the phone and we spoke briefly. I set the appointment with Mrs. Silver for a family bereavement session 5 days later. The family planned to sit shiva for 3 days following the funeral and burial. I suggested that Mrs. Silver bring to the session pictures of the children with their grandparents. Mrs. Silver said that she would do this, and asked if she could also bring Flora to this meeting.

The Bereavement Counseling Session

My goal in suggesting this session was to provide a setting and a method (the photos) whereby the children could tune in to their memories about their grandparents and recognize that the grandparents had a life with their parents even before their own births. Todd and Flora were at the age in which "concrete thinking" still prevailed to some extent. I reasoned, therefore, that seeing pictures of their grandparents with their parents (when their parents were young) might convey to them the message of their family's history in a way that merely talking about memories would not. Even though I realized that the appreciation of a sense of "family history" might represent an unreasonable goal for Flora, due to her young age, I believed that it was possible for both Todd and Victoria and that it would help them grieve the loss of their grandmother.

I had received some recent training in phototherapy and was eager to use "people's personal photos and their interactions with these images as powerful adjunctive tools to move beyond the constraints of traditional verbal-only therapy" (Weiser, 1988, p. 339).

My own feelings in anticipating this session were a mixture of apprehension about whether it would accomplish a meaningful purpose and whether Flora would be able to participate significantly.

Content of Session	Analysis and Feelings
All come into the room together. Flora sits on her mother's lap. Todd and Victoria sit on the couch on either side of Mrs. Silver, and Mr. Silver sits by himself in a separate chair.	I sense Mr. Silver's separation from family, yet realize that my office furniture may have led to this family seating arrangement.
THERAPIST: I'm glad you all came. Flora, I never met you before. Hi. (*Flora looks at me warily.*) I know you've all lost a very important person: your grandmother. We're meeting together to talk about your feelings.	Wondering how it feels to Victoria and Todd to be here for this purpose.
MRS. SILVER: I brought the pictures (*taking an enormous group of loose snapshots out of her purse*).	
TODD: Let me see.	
MRS. S: Just give me a chance. I want *everyone* to see these.	Some annoyance in her voice.
TH: (*to Mr. Silver*) How are you doing? I'd like to hear a bit about the funeral and the service before we look at the pictures.	Aware that he has not said anything and that he is sitting apart. I want to include him.
MR. SILVER: Everything went fine. My Dad went to the grave, but sat in the car with one of the aides; we weren't sure he could hold up but he did.	Mr. Silver had been worried about his father's reaction. I am glad to hear that they worked out a compromise so he could be included.
T: Who is going to take care of Grampa now?	Expresses very concrete concerns.

MRS. S: The aides will continue. Just like before Grammy died. She wasn't taking care of anyone for a long time.

T: Yeah. But he will miss her.

TH: I'm sure Grampa will miss her. Even though she was very sick, she was *there*, and now she will not be in her bed anymore.

Validating his feeling and realizing that he is speaking both for himself and others as well.

VICTORIA: I can't believe she is dead.

I know it is hard to believe.

FLORA: Look at these pictures. Who *is* this?

MRS. S: That is Daddy and Grammy and Grampa when Daddy was about 12 years old. I didn't even know him then.

How wonderful to see Mr. Silver as a boy with his parents! He looks a lot like Todd looks now. I am impressed that Mrs. Silver brought some old pictures.

MR. S: (*Looking very interested.*) Todd, that was right before my Bar Mitzvah.

T: (*to Mr. Silver*) You look funny.

TH: It is strange to think that your father was once a boy like you.

MRS. S: Here is a picture of Victoria as a baby, and here's another one when she began to walk. See how pretty Grammy was then.

F: Where was I?

MRS. S: You weren't even born yet!

T: And I wasn't either. I want to see a picture of *me* with Grammy.

This is beginning to feel a bit competitive.

MRS. S: (*Shuffling through the photos.*) Here's one of you (*to Todd*) with Grampa when you learned to ride your bike.

V: And here's one of my birthday party.

T: (*to Victoria*) There are lots *more* of you than me (*he begins to whine and pout*).

MR. S: (*Trying to appeal to logic.*) Victoria is older. Of course there will be more pictures of her because she spent more time with Grammy and Grampa.

T: (*In a loud whine.*) It's not fair!

He manages to turn everything into proof that he has been gypped.

TH: I was hoping that looking at the pictures would bring back some happy memories of times with Grammy and Grampa.

T: These pictures are stupid!

He is irritated with me, and with the session. He does much better in one- on-one sessions.

TH: It's hard enough to think that Grammy has died. Now you have to see pictures of her with Victoria and your father, without you included.

MRS. S: Victoria really *was* lucky. She knew Ed's parents when they were healthy. Flora and Todd didn't have all those years.

The truth. But it is not going to make Todd feel better.

TH: That might be true, but it certainly doesn't mean that Grammy and Grampa loved Victoria more.

Hoping that Mrs. Silver will pick up my drift and come forth with some reassurance.

MR. S: (*to therapist*) My parents were *thrilled* when Todd was born.

MRS. S: (*Nodding in agreement.*) Todd, they loved *all* their grandchildren, and they were *very* proud of you when you got three home runs in that ball game last summer.

Thankful for concrete examples.

F: Can we play a game now?

Comment on Session

This session was a rude remainder that the death of a grandparent does not change family relationships. I did not expect that it would, but I must admit that I was somewhat startled by the resurgence of sibling rivalry stimulated by my suggestion for viewing of the old photos. Weiser comments that when we look at photos we interact with them and project onto them the meanings we need unconsciously at that time (1988, p. 353). I had intended the photos to help the mourning for the grandparents, but Todd was not ready for that process and needed to project onto them his own feelings of rivalry and disappointments. Nonetheless, I believe that the family session served a purpose that the photos facilitated, albeit not in the exact manner I had expected. The parents clearly experienced the review of the photos as meaningful to them. The photos, in addition, helped the parents affirm the grandparents' love for their grandchildren, despite the variation in the children's birth order. This was an important message for the children to hear.

Session with Parents

The family session had occurred immediately prior to my between-semesters 3-week vacation break. When I returned I met for several parent counseling sessions with Mr. and Mrs. Silver. I had been feeling that it might be most helpful to the family if we could focus on strengthening the parental subsystem. The family session following Grammy's death furthered my impression that the children, rather than the parents, in this family were "in control." Hearing more about Mr. Silver's conflicts with is *own* siblings in the aftermath of Mr. Silver's mother's death made me sensitive to the feelings of helplessness and hopelessness he conveyed about the prospect of putting some limit on Victoria and Todd's battles.

My goal in seeing the parents together was to introduce the idea that intense ongoing sibling battles were *not* inevitable in any family, and that it would be helpful to their family if Mr. and Mrs. Silver would work together to reduce the frequency and intensity of the arguments between Todd and Victoria. I was aware that Mrs. Silver often joined in these battles, almost as another sibling, while Mr. Silver's stance was to "let them fight it out." On an unconscious level, both parents were adding fuel to the conflict.

The marriage seemed solid, with a great deal of mutual respect, humor, and affection between the partners. My intent was to move them toward a united front, empowered to set appropriate limits when their children started fighting. I wanted to remove them from the "family of screamers" characterization to one of "family of talkers and actors." The segment that follows presents some details of this process.

Content of Session	Analysis and Feelings
THERAPIST: It's been a while since our last family session. How have things been going in the family?	Interval of a month.
MR. SILVER: Which family? Ours (*looking at his wife*) or mine?	He has had a lot to cope with.
TH: The fact that you mention both suggests that there are issues both places.	

MRS. SILVER: Where to start? (*She looks apprehensive.*)

TH: (*to Mr. Silver*) What is most pressing to *you?*

MR. S: You wouldn't believe what I've been through with my brother and sister! | He is stuck with family-of-origin issues.

MRS. S: They're treating him like dirt, after all he's done.

TH: We all would like some appreciation and recognition. (*to Mr. Silver*) What is the hardest?

MR. S: My sister just made the decision my father had to go to a nursing home. She never discussed it with me. She got into arguments with the aides and just out of the blue decided: "This is not going to work. He needs a nursing home." She made the arrangements and then left town. | I have gone through a similar experience in my own familly. I make a mental note to keep my own issues separate.

How abrupt and oblivious to the concept of a family making this decision together.

TH: It sounds as if she is "taking over" after all these months when you have had the responsibility.

MRS. S: That's the way she is. Now we won't hear from her until we have another crisis.

TH: How are Victoria and Todd reacting to all of this? | Deliberately making a rather general statement, but wanting to shift the focus.

MRS. S: They're not really aware of Ed's problems with their aunt and uncle. Todd is worried about how Grampa can live anyplace else besides his home. | Concrete, literal concerns.

MR. S: I usually take Todd with me to the nursing home when I visit my father. I want him to see that he is being well cared for. | Appropriate.

TH: I remember that Todd expressed concern about who would take care of Grampa after Grammy died.

MR. S: Sometimes in the car going home after a visit, Todd says that he doesn't like one of the nurses.

TH: This is a *big* change for him and you to get used to. What about Victoria?

MRS. S: She's okay. But they're still fighting all the time.

TH: "All the time???" What about?

MRS. S: It doesn't matter. Everything. Anything.

MR. S: It really gets on my nerves. They have no consideration.

TH: Have you thought about telling them you won't stand for it anymore?

MR. S: (*Looking surprised.*) They won't listen.

TH: Sounds like you've given up and they know it.

MRS. S: Yeah. They know how to beat a dead horse when it's down.

On some level Mrs. Silver knows that the kids are "out of bounds."

TH: (*to Mrs. Silver*) Maybe you could help. It's not right, and it [the fighting] does *not* have to continue. The beginning is for you and Ed to decide that it is *not* destiny. The daily battles are *not* inevitable. You can jump in and stop them before things get out of hand. If you work together on this you can do it.

Sounds like a pep talk. I wonder if my support can help break this intergenerational hostility.

MR. S: You don't know how vehement Victoria gets. She knows how to push my buttons.

He (and, implicitly Mrs. Silver) really feel dominated by their 11-year-old daughter.

TH: The buttons she is pushing are the same ones Sophie [sister] pushes. You are attributing to your daughter Sophie's strength and experience in riding herd over other people's experience. I doubt if this has made Sophie a happy person, and it certainly won't help Victoria to feel that she is making everyone in her family miserable.

I am risking an interpretation here. I want to extricate Mr. Silver from his trap.

MRS. S: Todd plays into this also.

As I say this, I feel the great challenge to the child and family therapist: to help "break the cycle," whatever form it may take.

TH: I see it as a *family* drama; You *all* have a role. Victoria and Todd are not here but when we have a family session

again we will talk about it together. For
now, I believe that *it is of prime im-*
portance for the two of you to be in
agreement. My experience tells me that
when parents agree that their kids should
not fight, and when they back each other
up on this principle, the fighting will
stop. It is now up to the two of you to
agree.

Can I convince them that they
do not have to repeat history?
Will the theory carry over into
real life?

MR. S: Sounds good to me. But what do
we do when they start on each other
again?

He really does feel helpless.

TH: The most important thing is to believe firmly that they do *not* have to fight,
and that you, as their father, can tell
them, "enough is enough." If you believe
this, they will get the message.

Repeat the principle. This will
require many repetitions, and
a *lot* of support.

MRS. S: Wow! That sounds great to
me. I'll give it a go, if you will (*to Mr.*
Silver).

Her enthusiasm is wonderful!

TH: This is not going to be magic. First
of all, the kids will not believe you when
you try to stop them. It will take many
repetitions. In the end, it will be better
for all of you, but you will need conviction, patience, and mutual support to
carry on.

I must prepare them for the
struggle of trying to change
behavior.

Comment on Session

This session was very exciting for me (and, I hope, for Mr. and Mrs.
Silver). I believed that I understood the dynamics at work flowing from
the second generation to the third generation (grandchildren), fueled by
the circumstances of Mr. Silver's mother's death. I saw this as a unique
opportunity to break a cycle of arguments and scapegoating that had persisted for at least two generations. In many ways I did feel like a
preacher/crusader trying to convey that "another way *was* a very real
possibility." I knew it would take time for change to occur, but this was
a beginning.

I sensed that Mr. and Mrs. Silver received my message. I knew that
the fulfillment would require ongoing support, encouragement, and patience.

Session with Todd and Father

A few months after the parent session just described, Todd came for an individual session. His psychological evaluation had been completed and he was taking Ritalin on a daily basis to counteract the effects of Attention-Deficit Disorder. The parents had commented on the calming effect of the medication and on the concomitant improvement in Todd's ability to concentrate. Todd came for this session accompanied by his father.

I noticed a positive change in Todd's ability to carry on a conversation without fidgeting. There was also a dramatic decrease in his whining and regressive squirming. Typically, Mr. Silver came into the session at the beginning with Todd, and then Todd and I would spend the remainder of the time together. This time, Todd asked his father to remain while we played a game together.

I mentioned that I had a new game they were welcome to play with me for the first time. It was Gardner's Storytelling Card Game, a therapeutic board game based on the creation of stories, using cardboard cutout figures and an array of story card settings, including different household rooms (such as the kitchen, bathroom, bedroom), community scenes

FIGURE 4.1. Card 7, the cemetery scene, from Gardner's (1988) *The Storytelling Card Game* (Creskill, NJ: Creative Therapeutics). Reprinted by permission of the author.

(such as the supermarket parking lot, the doctor's office, school, a cemetery), and several blank cards about which the child can create his/her own scene and story (Gardner, 1988). The players have a considerable amount of leeway about the story-settings they use for the creation of their stories, since the spinner gives a choice of four card pictures at any given time.

Because of this range of choices, I was very surprised when in the middle of the game, Todd's spinner instructions directed him to select card 5, 6, 7, or 8 and, after examining the various scenes, he selected card 7, the cemetery scene (see Figure 4.1). I knew at the time that Todd had not participated in his grandmother's burial ritual. Nonetheless, I was certain that he knew about it, and that he had probably overheard conversations about the circumstances. I was curious and somewhat apprehensive about what kind of a story Todd would create. His manner in the telling of this story was very matter of fact. Mr. Silver was playing the game with us, and I could sense his tension at Todd's selection. My best recollection of Todd's story follows:

> TODD: (*Placing a family group of the cardboard figures in the cemetery, around a monument in the center.*) Somebody has just died, and the family is here to throw dirt on the casket. The rabbi says prayers. The family all say things about the person. They feel very sad, and some of them are crying.
>
> THERAPIST: What happens next?
>
> T: They go home, because they are still a family.
>
> (*Mr. Silver and I exchange a meaningful glance, and I repeat Todd's last phrase, "They are still a family."*)

CONCLUDING COMMENTS

What originally was planned as a "short-term" contact with this family has extended for several years, involving different family members at various developmental stress points of their lives. In many ways I believe that I fill the role of the "mental health family doctor" available, as needed, for crises of deaths, new school entries, problems with peers and so forth. I continue to feel the presence of the first- and second-generation ghosts in the everyday lives of this nuclear family, but the parents are aware of the ghosts now, and they are far more able to respond to their own children in terms of current needs, rather than old scripts.

This is a family with both strengths and vulnerabilities. I have no doubt that they could have "made it" without professional intervention. However, I have frequently thought about the hospital social worker who referred them at the time of Mr. Silver's mother's terminal diagnosis. She gave the family the means to free themselves of the chains of the past. I am optimistic that Victoria's and Todd's children in years to come will not be locked in the same pattern of sibling hostility. The impending death of a family member is a crisis which, like all crises, offers both danger and opportunity.

DISCUSSION QUESTIONS

1. Comment on the family bereavement counseling session. Do you think that this was helpful to the family? If so, how? How could it have been more beneficial to them?

2. What is the appropriate role for the counselor/therapist at the time of the death of a family member? Do you agree with this therapist's decision *not* to make a condolence visit? On what basis should this decision be made?

3. Do you agree with the therapist's assessment about the sibling hostility re-enactment across generations? How else might the therapist have intervened with regard to this source of family conflict?

4. How do you think the family will react when Mr. Silver's father dies 4 months following his wife's death? What intervention would you suggest at that time?

REFERENCES

Barth, J. C. (1989). Families cope with the death of a parent: The family therapist's role. In L. Combrinck-Graham (Ed.), *Children in family contexts* (pp. 299–321). New York: Guilford Press.

Brown, F. (1989). The impact of death and serious illness on the family life cycle. In B. Carter & M. McGoldrick (Eds.), *The changing family life cycle: A framework for family therapy* (2nd ed., pp. 457–482). Boston: Allyn & Bacon.

Crenshaw, D. (1991). *Bereavement: Counseling the grieving throughout the life cycle.* New York: Continuum.

Gardner, R. A. (1988). *The Storytelling Card Game.* Creskill, NJ: Creative Therapeutics.

Goldberg, S. B. (1973). Family tasks and reactions in the crisis of death. *Social Casework, 54*(7), 398–405.

Patterson, P. R. (1983). The grandparent teaches the child about living and dying. In J. E. Schowalter, P. R. Patterson, M. Tallmer, A. H. Kutscher, S. V. Gullo, & D. Peretz (Eds.), *The child and death* (pp. 75–78). New York: Columbia University Press.

Rando, T. (1991). *How to go on living when someone you love dies.* New York: Bantam. (Original work published 1988)

Raphael, B. (1983). *The anatomy of bereavement.* New York: Basic Books.

Walsh, F., & McGoldrick, M. (Eds.). (1991). *Living beyond loss: Death in the family.* New York: Norton.

Weiser, J. (1988). Phototherapy: Using snapshot and photo-interactions in therapy with youth. In C. E. Shaefer (Ed.). *Innovative interventions in child and adolescent therapy* (pp. 339–376). New York: Wiley.

CHAPTER FIVE

Terminal Illness and Death of Father
Case of Celeste, Age 5½

JANE LE VIEUX

The death of a parent can have a significant effect on the psychosocial and developmental growth of the surviving children. Staudacher emphasizes that "the parental death is always a part of a child's life" (1987, p. 128). A child's emotional response to the death of a parent may not be obvious to those who know the child because children can disguise their grief in various ways depending on their age and stage of development (Anthony, 1973; E. Furman, 1974; R. Furman, 1970; Jewett, 1982; Nagy, 1948; Rando, 1984).

Children experience the loss of a parent profoundly. Many individuals believe that children do not have the capacity to grieve. Children do grieve, although they often express their grief in ways different from adults (Cook & Oltjenbruns, 1989; Furman, 1974). Bereaved children may experience not only emotional but also physical problems in response to the death of a parent (Koocher, 1983). The quality of the family relationship may affect the grief reactions of a child. This chapter deals with the grief reactions of a 5½-year-old girl following her father's terminal illness and subsequent death from cancer.

IMPACT OF TERMINAL ILLNESS OF PARENT

Children who have lost a parent as a result of a long-term illness are often the quiet observers of dying. The child knows that the parent is ill, in pain, and not the same individual he/she used to be. These children often experience intense reactions toward the infirmed parent. Their underly-

81

ing fears of abandonment and guilt may begin before the actual death occurs (Rutter, 1966). They know something is wrong from whispered conversations, concerned looks, relatives showing up at different times, and significant changes in their daily routine. In the case to be discussed, Celeste, age 5½, was told that her father had cancer when he was diagnosed 1 year before his death. He was hospitalized for the last 2 months of his life. He died in the hospital.

Developmental Considerations

Children from 3 to 6 understand their world in terms of day-to-day events that happen in their lives. As adults we conceive of time as an abstract system that exists apart from our own acts. Children consider time in terms of personally meaningful occurrences such as holidays, nap times, when "daddy" comes home, and "supper time." Time to a child is a culmination of personal activities and the accompanying emotional reactions to those events. This includes the secure feelings that his/her parents are taking care of him/her. "Future" is an abstraction that children only gradually comprehend as they move from the ability to remember past events of significance (i.e., their last birthday) to projection ahead to "next" Christmas (N. B. Webb, personal communication, November 19, 1992).

Anticipatory Grief

This term refers to "grief expressed in advance when the loss is perceived as inevitable" (Aldrich, 1974, p. 4). Therefore, information should be given based on the child's ability to comprehend the future and to anticipate future events. However, the preschool child does not understand the finality and irreversibility of death (see Chapter 1). The verbal information to the child that his/her parent is seriously ill and may die may not be sufficient. Children think literally and magically and their knowledge of anatomy and physiology is limited. When a child of Celeste's age is told her father has cancer she probably cannot comprehend the future implications for him or for her family (N. B. Webb, personal communication, December 9, 1992). It is often hard to convey to children that the illness caused the death. For the young child, seeing is believing (Piaget, 1962). In the case of Celeste, her father was seriously ill from December until his death in February. She witnessed the gradual changes in his physical appearance and certainly realized that he was very sick and weak.

What to Say

I am often asked, "What do you say to the child about a parent's impending death?" My first inclination is to answer only those questions which have been asked. I believe that the explanations given to children should be based on to the child's own ability to understand. *How* the information is conveyed to the child plays a part in his/her acceptance of death (Grollman, 1967, 1990). Children's questions should be answered immediately and honestly. Reassuring the child that he/she has a place in the family, continually showing affection, support, love, and talking to the child about the death is an ongoing process. Children may talk about the deceased at any time, when one least expects the topic to arise. Asking the same questions over and over is not uncommon.

Impact of Father's Death

Grossberg and Crandall (1978) believe that the father's role in the life of the young child flows from a combination of functions including being the protector, powerful, caring, and a giver and receiver of love and honor. Saravay (1991) in her chapter on sudden paternal death maintains that "the father's death represents far more than the loss of a person." When death takes a parent, the child sees the surviving parent as a being next in line to die. It is important for children to have the opportunity to talk about their grief and to have a safe place to work through in play what they cannot verbalize. In play, children's unconscious and conscious issues are played out.

CHILD-CENTERED PLAY THERAPY

The child-centered play therapist becomes an objective participant in the child's world by reflecting the inner world of the child with warmth, acceptance, and trust (Axline, 1950). Child-centered play therapy can be divided into two areas: responsive and facilitative. The responsive characteristics of the play therapist include attending, observing, and listening. The facilitative attributes involve initiating, personalizing, and responding to the child. Children blossom in an environment that encompasses empathy, respect, warmth, genuineness, and self-disclosure (Landreth, 1990).

Child-Centered Play Therapy with Bereaved Children

Grieving children have a need to be heard. The child-centered approach utilizes active listening, which allows the child to experience a world in which he/she is heard and understood. Children are sensitive to the real feelings and attitudes of those around them. Listening to children opens the doors that give the children the opportunity to release their feelings and thoughts without feeling threatened. Although children's verbal skills may be limited, nonverbal messages may be the most important clue to what the child is feeling and communicating. It is important for children to have the opportunity to talk about their grief and to have a safe place to work through in play what they cannot verbalize. In play, children's unconscious and conscious issues are played out. Play therapy offers the child the opportunity to share feelings that may be painful, frightening, and confusing. In addition, the child can engage in fantasy play which gives the child power over his/her fears. Children will use whatever toys are relevant to their situation. They can engage in burials of dolls, miniature toys, or even play out the illness. By establishing themselves as separate from the event, the young child reaffirms what he/she believes is reality.

THE CASE: CELESTE, AGE 5½

Celeste was a petite 5½-year-old white girl with two little pigtails and a bright smile, when she first came for therapy with her mother and two younger brothers. She was shy and stayed close to her mother initially.

Family Information

>   Celeste, age 5½, a kindergarten student
>   Mother, age 31, librarian, at home with the children since their births
>   Timothy, age 3
>   Brian, age 1½
>   Father, age 34, previously worked as an engineer, died 6 months
>   earlier following an illness of 1 year and 2 months
>
>   *Extended family*
>   Mother's parents and her sister were available to help. Additional
>   support and babysitting assistance were available from friends.

Religious/Cultural Affiliation

The family is Catholic. Following the father's death, memorial services were held which the children attended. Simple brief explanations were given to them and the children's questions were answered according to Celeste's ability to understand.

Presenting Problem

Celeste's mother phoned following the receipt of a brochure about the children's grief programs at the center. She explained that her husband had died of cancer 6 months earlier. Celeste's mother said that her husband's illness included several short hospitalizations and rounds of chemotherapy. From December until he died in February, 90% of the time was spent in the hospital. Mother reports that she and her husband "did as much as we could" (getting ready for Christmas) the first week in December because of the new rounds of chemotherapy. Celeste's mother had help from her parents and sister. In addition, she belonged to a "babysitting co-op" where the mothers took turns watching each other's children. In the final weeks before her husband's death, the children spent less and less time with him. Celeste's mother said that her husband did not want the children to see him in such pain. When he died, he was at the hospital. Celeste had known that her daddy was ill and that the medicine could not help him get better. Mother reported that her daughter was often moody and irritable since her husband's death. There were times when her daughter appeared to be uncooperative and refused to do things. This was not a behavior that had existed prior to Celeste's father's death. Celeste had recently spent the summer with her family and several relatives going to a theme park vacation. This was to have been a trip that would have included her father had he been alive. Mom had noticed prior to the trip that Celeste had become very distraught and up-set with those around her. Celeste appeared sad on occasions. Mom attributed this as a normal grief reaction for Celeste. Although they went on the vacation and had a good time, Mom reported that she noticed Celeste becoming impatient with her younger brothers since the vacation. In addition, there were times when Celeste would wonder "if the repair man or neighbor down the street would marry Mommy." Over the summer, Celeste's preschool teacher had given birth to a new baby. Celeste cried and was concerned about the new school year and a new teacher. Mom felt that some of these reactions were normal considering her daughter's age. However, she wanted to offer Celeste the opportunity to interact with other children who had lost a parent through death. Celeste's grandmother had received one of the brochures about our center for grieving children. Celeste's mother looked it over and felt it was just what Celeste needed.

Initial Meeting and First Session

Prior to coming to see me, Celeste's mother told her about coming to a very special place to play. It would be a time just for Celeste. During the intake session, I met with Mom and her three children; she spoke very softly and quietly about the months leading up to her husband's death. Celeste's father had been diagnosed with cancer and been treated with chemotherapy. The week of Thanksgiving was the last "normal holiday" for the family as described by the mother. The month of December was, the mother describes, a "very low point in our lives." Celeste's father was put on a new treatment regimen that consisted of frequent hospital stays as well as routine chemotherapy.

Whenever possible, the children were brought to the hospital to visit with their father. In the months of January and February, Celeste's father was reported to be somewhat distant from the children. This is a characteristic often seen in patients who have cancer. The children would visit on Dad's "good days." Because Celeste was in school she did not have the opportunity to go the hospital as often as she would have liked. She occasionally remarks now to her mother that her younger brothers got to see her father more than she did.

Celeste, her brothers, and mother came from the waiting room into my office. In my office I have a sand tray, books, and markers. As I spoke with her mother, I tried to include Celeste in the conversations. She was busy with the sandbox and exploring the office. I sensed from Celeste that she was glad to be here. Her shyness began to disappear. Following the intake interview, I told Celeste that I had a special room with toys where she could play in most any of the ways she would like. I told her that we would take her mother and brothers back to the waiting room. On our way, we would pass the playroom so everyone could know where she was. This would be our special time.

Content of Session	*Analysis and Feelings*
The first session consists of getting to know each other. I usually observe and track a child's movement in the playroom when the child is nonverbal (as is the case during the beginning of the session with Celeste).	I notice that Celeste seems unsure of me. I will let her take the lead, rather than direct the session.
THERAPIST: Celeste, this is the playroom. In here, you can play with the toys in most of the ways you would like.	I want to establish a feeling of permissiveness in our relationship so that Celeste will feel free to express her feelings.
CELESTE: (*Looking all around the room. Celeste walks around the room, not touching anything. Just looking.*)	I notice her looking around. I wonder how she reacts to strangers. There is a feeling of wanting to say more, but I sense that is *my* need.

T: In here, you can decide what you want to do, Celeste.

C: (*After a few minutes, she stands in front of the paints.*) I think I would like to paint. (*She turns and looks at me.*)

T: In here, Celeste, you can decide what to do.

This puts her in control.

C: Oh (*as she picks up the brush. She paints for several minutes.*) This is my mommy's sister.

As Celeste paints, I describe the colors.

T: Oh, your mommy has a sister.

I wonder what she will say about her. Mom had not mentioned her in the interview.

C: (*Immediately, she walks away from the paints and goes to the sandbox. Very intently and quietly she plays with the figures. She uses half of the sandbox. She chooses Mickey and Minnie Mouse, and several little Disney figures.*) This is Mickey's Birthday party.

Everyone is happy. I wonder if the Disney characters are chosen because of the recent trip. I also know that children her age enjoy these characters. In Disney Land everyone is happy.

T: Oh, it is a happy time for everyone. That looks like fun.

C: Oh, it is. I even went to Mickey's party at Disney. (*Before I speak, she reaches for a male figure and places him at the other end of the sandbox. She gets up, wipes her hands, and stands there looking at her creation.*)

Celeste's facial expression does not show happiness. But her voice is upbeat and cheerful. At this point, I notice a look of sadness on her face. I wonder if the male figure was a representation of her father.

T: You're looking at the picture in the sand.

I watch how Celeste looks at everything. Pausing briefly, carefully looking at the items in the room. I want her to decide for herself what to do.

C: Yes. (*This time I detect sadness in her voice.*)

T: Celeste, your voice sounds sad. I wonder if you feel sad.

I want her to know I hear her. I want her to know it is okay to talk about feelings.

C: (*Walking over to the table.*) You know, there used to be five of us. There still are, if you count my dog. My daddy died.

I can feel that pain in her voice as she speaks.

T: Your daddy died and you feel sad.

> I repeat what she said in hopes that she would continue to talk.

C: I get sad a lot. My little brothers even get sad. I have a birthday coming soon. Daddy won't be there.

> I take note that Celeste speaks of Daddy not coming back. This is a hard concept for a 5-year-old to understand.

T: You miss your daddy. You know that he died and can't come to your party.

> I want Celeste to know I hear her grief.

C: (*Looking at me, she turns and plays by the kitchen area quietly.*) I was at school when my daddy died. I came home to have lunch. They told me at lunch. You know, it was a Tuesday when he died.

> It is interesting that even young children can recall the day (and sometimes the date) that some one has died.

T: You remember what day it was when your daddy died. I wonder if you remember how you felt?

> I feel her sadness within me. I am in touch with my own feelings of sadness. Losing such a significant person in your life is painful.

C: Just like now, I am sad.

T: When your daddy died, you felt sad. That feeling is still with you. (*Celeste nods her head yes.*)

C: (*A little cheerfully.*) But you know what? I like it here. I want to come back. I didn't like Tuesdays, but now I do.

> We had our first session on a Tuesday afternoon.

Our time was over. Celeste left the playroom easily. Following our session she told her mother that she wanted to come back. An appointment for the same time next week was scheduled.

Preliminary Assessment and Treatment Plan

Celeste was reacting to the loss of her father and their relationship. Outwardly, she appeared to be cheerful and full of energy. In the playroom, her underlying feelings of sadness and loss were exhibited in her play and dialogue. I also sensed that Celeste was attempting to understand the fact that her father was never coming back. It usually takes several months for children to realize this. Not having the sense of time adults have, children often mark time in terms of holidays and special occasions. Celeste had already experienced Mother's Day, Father's Day, and the special vacation without her father. All were very vivid reminders that Daddy was not going to return.

The treatment plan was to provide Celeste opportunities for her to express feelings, either verbally or symbolically through her play. My hopes were that if allowed opportunities to grieve, Celeste would be able to integrate her father's death into her life. Children who have lost a parent often feel abandoned (Rando, 1988; Tatelbaum, 1980). Anger can surface in other areas of a child's life sometimes in the form of forgetfulness, daydreaming, losing things, and procrastinating (Cook & Oltjenbruns, 1989; Jewett, 1982). As Celeste works through her grief, the use of aggressive behavior with her brothers will diminish. Assessment will be ongoing. I planned to meet with Mom for 10 minutes every other week before sessions to get an update on how things are at home as well as to share with her a review of how Celeste was doing overall.

Session 2: Excerpt

Content of Session

Analysis and Feelings

THERAPIST: Now, you've decided to play in the sandbox.

CELESTE: I'm looking for the Beauty doll. Oh, here it is!

I notice she is happy that she found it. I see the delight on her face.

T: I can see you feel happy! You have a smile on your face.

I am deliberately commenting about her feelings.

C: Uh huh. (*Now she is working intently at burying Beauty under a rather large pile of sand.*)

T: You're working very hard. Look at how you pick up that bucket of sand. You feel strong.

A self-esteem-building comment.

C: I am strong! Now I need some other people. (*Gathers the figures and carefully places them on the pile.*) Oh, now everyone is looking for Beauty. They can't find her. She's buried.

T: Beauty is buried. No one knows where to find her.

I am curious to find out if Celeste would tell me where Beauty was.

C: They'll never see her again. (*This is said with a sad voice.*)

I wonder if she is referring to her father here.

T: You're feeling sad because they'll never see her again.

It is important to let her know it is okay to talk about her feelings. Naming the feeling helps to make them real. It also provides an emotional vocabulary.

C: Did you know that only one person has hazel eyes like my daddy?

Celeste focuses on concrete/specific memories

T: Hmm, you're daddy had hazel eyes. You remember that.

C: Uh huh. My little brother has eyes like my daddy used to.

T: Daddy used to have hazel eyes.

C: He died (*very matter of fact*).

T: Your daddy died. You still remember the color of his eyes.

C: (*Nods her head yes, then goes to play with a musical toy.*)

T: Celeste, our time is up for today.

In sessions 2–5, Celeste would come in and play with the Disney characters and bury things over and over. Occasionally she would talk about her mother and the changes in the family, school, and her brothers. In between sessions 6 and 7, Celeste missed an appointment. Before my session, I met Celeste's mother who reported that during the missed week Celeste seemed angry and noticed that her daughter was somewhat intolerant of her younger brothers. She went on to say that she felt Celeste had missed not coming the week before and she believed that Celeste needed the play sessions to help work through her grief. Mother commented that she was beginning to find it easier to talk with Celeste about her deceased father.

Session 8

I have a sand tray and toys that I use in my office when children appear to want to play solely in the sand. In addition, I keep colored pencils, markers, crayons, and paper in my room. These same items are in the play room which is adjacent to my office.

As I met Celeste for our session in the waiting room, she wanted to know if "we could spend half the time in the playroom and the other half in your office." I told her that it sounded like she had a plan in mind. She just smiled. Segments of Celeste's session in my office follow:

Content of Session	*Analysis and Feelings*

CELESTE: I'd like to draw a picture.

THERAPIST: Oh, so you do have a plan in mind.

C: Sit down near me.

T: You want me close by.

C: Uh huh. (*Celeste gets the paper and markers. As she draws she talks.*) This is a picture of me on my mommy's birthday [Figure 5.1]. This is how I felt shopping for my mommy.

Sometimes it is easier to visualize than to put feelings into words.

T: Hmm. These are all the feelings you had. Looks like several kinds.

This lets her know that you can feel more than one feeling at a time.

FIGURE 5.1. Celeste's drawing of herself on her mother's birthday.

C: Uh huh (*looking at me*).

T: I wonder if you've felt several things all at once before.

C: Uh huh. When my daddy died I felt sad and mad.

T: You felt two feelings at once. Mad and sad.

C: Now I want to draw another picture. (*She focuses on her drawing.*)

T: I see you putting color here and there.

C: This is a picture of my daddy [Figure 5.2]. Oh, let me draw big hands. My daddy had such big hands. I could put mine in and they were small.

She remembers how her hands felt. I have the feeling she felt safe with her father. This is very touching; a tender memory!

T: You remember how big your daddy's hands were.

FIGURE 5.2. Celeste's picture of her father.

C: (*She smiles.*) See, here he is all dressed up. Everyone gets dressed up for Thanksgiving. I wore a party dress.

Thanksgiving was the last good time. It is encouraging that she can bring up that image.

T: So everyone wears "party clothes." You feel happy when you think about that.

C: Uh huh. See, here's a bird in the sky. There was a bird in the sky when we took my daddy's picture.

T: Oh, so this looks like a photograph you have.

C: Of my daddy at Thanksgiving.

T: That must make you feel glad inside to remember that day.

Naming the feeling.

C: (*Laughing.*) This is a turkey flying before he gets cooked. That's in my imagination. (*She continues to laugh.*)

She has a sense of humor.

T: You are pleased with yourself.

Self-esteem remark. Reflecting feelings.

C: I am!

T: Our time is up for today.

Celeste left my office and we met her mother in the waiting room. Suddenly, Celeste said, "Excuse me." She left and came back with her pictures to show her mother who was looking intently and paying close attention to Celeste's remarks. There was an interchange between the two that I cannot seem to forget. I have tried to find feeling words that would best describe the moment. Perhaps, warmth and caring, mixed with an unspoken understanding between the two that "we can talk about Daddy and remember."

CONCLUDING COMMENTS

The death of a parent affects the child's development of a sense of trust and self-esteem. When a young child experiences the loss of that significant relationship, the core of his or her existence is shaken. Trust in the consistency and constant source of support and comfort is disrupted (Rando, 1984). In my practice, I make a point to schedule appointments with the child at the same time each week. This aids in establishing a routine that may be missing while the family is in transition.

I encouraged Celeste's mother to call whenever she feels the need. I believe that she is a key factor in the success of Celeste's treatment. Grossberg and Crandall (1978) contend that the mother's relationship to the child is important in the child's continued growth and development after a father's death. Celeste's mother is very open and concerned for her children. Her candor and willingness to share information with both me and Celeste is invaluable.

I am still seeing Celeste and will probably continue to see her through the first anniversary of her father's death. I plan to give Celeste a choice as to when she would like to terminate a week or two following the anniversary of her father's death. I usually allow the child four sessions before termination to help with the transition. I personally like to switch to every other week. I also believe it is important for the child to know that he/she can return should they ever feel the need. At the present time, she is eagerly looking forward to our sessions. It is important for me to remember that not every session will center around her father. Each session must be approached from where the child is at that particular moment in time. For Celeste, there are times when she comes in and plays with many different items in the playroom. She may not mention her father. In reviewing videotapes, I have noticed at those times (where she is playing), she is simply enjoying the opportunity to be a child. It is a time where she can be who she is. I have wondered if somewhere in her subconscious, if she remembers the times when she "simply played" with her dad. Perhaps during those moments of play where freedom is granted and creativity abounds, Celeste feels safe and comfortable. As she progresses through her grief, it is my belief that she will emerge with the renewed strength and self-esteem that will aid her throughout her life.

DISCUSSION QUESTIONS

1. Discuss the stress on therapists who work with children who have lost a parent. How can therapists deal with their own feelings about the loss of a parent?

2. Discuss the understanding of death of a typical kindergarten age student. How do you think Celeste's own understanding of death was being worked through in play therapy?

3. What other play therapy methods are especially appropriate in working with bereaved children?

4. Why is the client-centered approach beneficial with Celeste?

REFERENCES

Aldrich, C. K. (1974). Some dynamics of anticipatory grief. In B. Schoenberg, A. C. Carr, A. H. Kutscher, D. Peretz, & I. K. Goldberg (Eds.), *Anticipatory grief* (pp. 3–9). New York: Columbia University Press.

Anthony, E. J. (1973). Mourning and psychic loss of the parent. In E. J. Anthony & C. Koupernik (Eds.), *The child in his family: The impact of disease and death* (pp. 225–264). New York: Wiley.

Axline, V. (1950). Entering the child's world via play experiences. *Progressive Education, 27,* 68–75.

Cook, A. S., & Oltjenbruns, K. A. (1989). *Dying and grieving: Lifespan and family perspectives.* New York: Holt, Rinehart & Winston.

Furman, E. (1974). *A child's parent dies.* New Haven, CT: Yale University Press.

Furman, R. (1970). The child's reaction to death in the family. In B. Schoenberg, A. C. Carr, D. Peretz, & A. H. Kutscher (Eds.), *Loss and grief: Psychological management in medical practice* (pp. 70–86). New York: Columbia University Press.

Grollman, E. A. (Ed.). (1967). *Explaining death to children.* Boston: Beacon Press.

Grollman, E. A. (1990). *Talking about death: A dialogue between parent and child.* Boston: Beacon Press.

Grossberg, S. H., & Crandall, L. (1978). Father loss and father absence in preschool children. *Clinical Social Work Journal, 6*(2), 123–134.

Jewett, C. L. (1982). *Helping children cope with separation and loss.* Cambridge, MA: Harvard Common Press.

Koocher, G. P. (1983). Grief and loss in childhood. In C. E. Walker & M. C. Roberts (Eds.), *Handbook of clinical child psychology* (pp. 1273–1284). New York: Wiley.

Landreth, G. L. (1991). *Play therapy: The art of the relationship.* Muncie, IN: Accelerated Development.

Nagy, M. (1948). The child's theories concerning death. *Journal of Genetic Psychology, 73,* 3–27.

Piaget, J. (1962). *Play, dreams, and imitation in childhood.* New York: Norton.

Rando, T. A. (1988). *How to go on living when someone you love dies.* New York: Bantam.

Rando, T. A. (1984). *Grief, dying, and death.* Champaign, IL: Research Press.

Rutter, M. (1966). Bereaved children. In M. Rutter (Ed.), *Children of sick parents* (pp. 66–75). London: Oxford University Press.

Saravay, B. (1991). Short-term play therapy with two preschool brothers following sudden paternal death. In N. B. Webb (Ed.), *Play therapy with children in crisis: A casebook for practitioners* (pp. 177–201). New York: Guilford Press.

Staudacher, C. (1987). *Beyond grief: A guide for recovering from the death of a loved one.* Oakland, CA: New Harbinger Publications.

Tatelbaum, J. (1980). *The courage to grieve.* New York: Harper & Row.

CHAPTER SIX

Complicated Grief—
Dual Losses of Godfather's
Death and Parents' Separation
Case of the Martini Family—
Sisters, Ages 8 and 10

NANCY BOYD WEBB

Death occurs universally, but the responses to it vary greatly among family and friends of the deceased. Each survivor's life history and current situation influence the personal significance of the lost relationship, creating a distinctive grief reaction that is shaped by the individual's past and present losses and coping repertoire. Therefore, the terminal illness and death of a close friend/godfather impacts quite differently on various family members despite the fact they are all suffering the loss of the same person. The stress of that loss is superimposed upon each individual's own reality, which usually differs sharply from that of others even when all occupy the same home.

This chapter discusses the therapy with a family in which the parents were initiating a marital separation at the same time that a close family friend and the godfather of Linda, age 10, was terminally ill with cancer. Thus, the family was drawn together to support one another during the 3-month period of the godfather's illness and ultimate death at the very time they were facing the rupture of their intact family as they had known it.

The literature on grief reactions following death or divorce points out many similarities, as well as distinctions, between the two forms of loss. In the Martini family, because of the juxtaposition of the "loss" of the father (due to marital separation) and the anticipated and subsequent death of the godfather, the grief reactions of the girls were complicated.

GRIEF FOLLOWING DEATH

Furman (1974) refers to numerous clinical studies of normal mourning following death; these specify affects of pain, sadness, grief, anger, and guilt among mourners. Bowlby (1960, 1961, 1963) considers anger as a critical component of grief, related to yearning for the lost object. Bowlby (1980) believes that discharge of this anger serves a constructive role in the mourning process. Furman (1974) comments that "children, more easily than adults, acknowledge anger at the dead, both for having died and for their shortcomings when still alive" (p. 258). Anger is quite pronounced in the case of these bereaved girls who frequently express their feelings through sibling rivalry rather than by directing their anger toward either of their "lost" paternal objects.

Bowlby (1980) indentifies four phases of mourning, following the loss of a close relative:

1. Numbing (duration of a few hours to a week)
2. Yearning and searching (duration from months to years)
3. Disorganization and despair
4. Reorganization

While many of these reactions have been observed in child, as well as adult mourners, we do not know about the likelihood of their occurrence following the death of a nonblood relative, such as a godfather. Burgen (1983) offers a conceptualization of childhood bereavement that seems applicable to this situation. Burgen proposes that the intensity and duration of bereavement are related to two dimensions: *the closeness of relationship* and the mourner's *perception of preventability* of the death. In Burgen's model, "a griever who considered the deceased to be a central person in his life, and does not consider the death preventable in any way, is likely to experience an intense, but brief grief reaction" (1983, p. 359). This would seem to apply to the girls' reaction to the death of Linda's godfather from a fatal disease; he was a beloved person, helpless in the grip of a terminal illness.

GRIEF FOLLOWING DIVORCE

The professional literature indicates that the mourning of losses associated with divorce parallels in many ways that of grief following death. Viorst (1986) enumerates sorrow, pining, yearning, denial, despair, guilt, and feelings of abandonment as similar grief reactions in both types of losses. A major difference between the two is the intensity of the anger response

following divorce, which is often more pronounced because of the conflicts that precipitated the break-up and the underlying sense of blame
and guilt about the failed marriage. Raphael (1983) notes that in divorce
"the bereaved must mourn someone who has not died" (p. 228), and Weiss
(1975) refers to the necessity in families of divorce for the couple to relin-
quish their attachment to one another.

In the Martini family, the parents were at the very beginning stage
of initiating a marital separation. The girls did not have a clear idea of
how their future might change, and this was frightening to them. In fact,
both parents in this family were determined to retain their own special
relationship with their daughters. They each tried to clarify that the divorce
was between the adults, promising that it would not change their relationship with them. However, despite these reassurances, fear, anxiety,
and anger inevitably surfaced and required expression by the girls both
in therapy and to each of their parents.

Children must mourn the loss of their intact family, and their mourning is especially complicated because of the possible reversibility of the
decision and the omnipresent wish and fantasy about parental reunion
(Wallerstein & Kelly, 1980; Wallerstein & Blakeslee, 1989; Jewett, 1982).
According to Burgen's conceptualization of childhood bereavement, the
most intense and prolonged grief response occurs when the griever "considers the deceased to be a central person in his life and also believes that
the death was preventable" (1982 p. 357)

If we extend this concept to the loss and grief of *divorce* and apply
it to Linda, age 10, and Amanda, age 8, it is clear that the prospect of
having their parents separate and their father move out qualifies as a situation in which intense and prolonged grief might be expected. Certainly their father was very important to each of them and, although they
knew that their parents were in conflict, they probably believed that this
could have been resolved in the interest of preserving their family.

ROLE AND SIGNIFICANCE OF GODFATHER

In Catholic families the function of godparents includes the responsibilities of accompanying the godchild through important milestones, religious ceremonies such as baptism and confirmation, as well as providing
security for the godchild. Falicov comments that "godparents are equiva-
lent to an additional set of parents who act as guardians or sponsors of
the godchild and care for him or her in emergencies" (1982, p. 143). If
we consider Moitoza's (1982) statement that godparentage reflects the
belief that survival is insured with a second set of parents (p. 420), the
impact on Linda of her godfather's imminent death at the same time she

and Amanda learned of their father's plans to move out of their home certainly has deep significance. It must have seemed to these girls that they were losing two primary male sources of affection and protection at the same time.

IMPACT OF MULTIPLE STRESSORS

The revised third edition of the *Diagnostic and Statistical Manual of Mental Disorders* (DSM-III-R; American Psychiatric Association, 1987) ranks the severity of psychosocial stressors in children and adolescents on a scale of 0–6, with 6 being catastrophic. In this scale, the divorce of parents is ranked 4, and considered a *severe* stressor, whereas the death of a parent is ranked 5, and considered an *extreme* stressor. There is no ranking for the death of a godparent, but if we estimate that it would be scored as a 4, *severe,* or as a 3, *moderate,* the combination of the two stressors clearly places Linda and Amanda at the *severe* level of stress. The impact of multiple crises can lead to disorganization and fragmentation of coping abilities (Webb, 1991). Furthermore, Bowlby states that "persons subjected to multiple stressors are more likely to develop a disorder than are those not so subjected" (1980, p. 187). Certainly *either* the departure of the father from the home *or* the terminal illness of the godfather qualifies as a stressful event for Linda and Amanda, and their combined impact puts the girls at high risk.

INDIVIDUAL FACTORS IN ASSESSING THE IMPACT OF LOSS

I have identified six factors in making an assessment of the child in crises (Webb, 1991). Since terminal illness, death, and parental separation obviously are crises, it is appropriate to consider the interactive influences of these factors in the case under consideration. A form for recording the specific elements of these factors is available in a previous publication (Webb, 1991). The factors are as follows:

- Age/developmental factors
- Precrisis adjustment
- Coping style/ego assessment
- Global assessment of functioning: DSM-III-R, Axis V
- Specific meaning of crisis to the child

These factors will be considered with regard to Linda and Amanda following the presentation of family and referral information.

THE CASE: THE MARTINI FAMILY

Family Information

> Mother, Ann, age 34, buyer for department store
> Father, Jim, age 35, architect in building firm, recovering alcoholic
> (12 years)
> Linda, age 10, fifth grade, on gymnastics team
> Amanda age 8, third grade, very artistic
> Linda's godfather, Robert, age 35, former restaurant manager,
> recovering alcoholic (12 years)
> Linda's godmother, Terry, age 34, secretary
> *Note:* The godparents have two children, ages 6 and 4.

Amanda and Linda refer to Robert and Terry as "Aunt" and "Uncle."
Robert was Jim's Alcoholics Anonymous (AA) sponsor; they generally
attend meetings together three times per week. Ann has attended Ala-
non in the (past sometimes with Terry), and the girls attended a group
(Unicorn) for children of alcoholics several years ago. At the time of intake, Ann was engaged in her own therapy, as was Jim.

Religious/Cultural Heritage

This is a Catholic family that observes major milestones such as bap-
tisms and first communions according to the expected practice in their
religion. Their participation in church services tends to be sporadic; Ann
says, "We believe, but we are not really strict." The parents are of Euro-
pean cultural background; both are third-generation Americans. Ann is
Polish and Jim is Italian.

Past History

Linda

The initial referral occurred about 9 months prior to the events that constitute the focus of this chapter. The parents originally consulted their
pediatrician because of their concern about a sleep disturbance Linda had
been experiencing for approximately 2 months; she would wake in the
middle of the night, turn on many lights, enter the parents' bedroom,
and quietly stand by their bed until one of them awoke and took her back
to her own room.

A very frightening incident had initiated this sleep disturbance while the family had been vacationing with Linda's godparents and their children. Linda awakened in the middle of the night, convinced that a robber/kidnapper was in the vacation cabin. Actually in her disoriented state in a strange location, Linda had witnessed her godfather carrying his child, in the dark, to the bathroom. Her panic over this case of confused identity seemed excessive, but the parents were sympathetic initially, trying to comfort her, and convinced that the nightly waking would improve once the family returned home. When it continued unabated for a 2-month period, the parents appropriately sought a consultation from me, a child and family therapist.

Linda's therapy consisted of 11 sessions over the course of a 3-month period. Using a combination of art, behavior modification, and parent counseling, complete symptom alleviation occurred after approximately 6 weeks. Termination followed gradually lengthening intervals between sessions. In the course of work with this family I was impressed with their ability to follow through with the treatment plan we established together. Once or twice during this time I had met Amanda briefly, as she accompanied her sister and mother and waited in the room adjacent to the office.

Amanda

Approximately 6 weeks after terminating with Linda, Ann called with the request that I evaluate Amanda. The reason for the referral was not precise, but alluded to Amanda's not being happy about the way she looked and about her tendency to cry and overreact when things did not "go her way." I saw Amanda several times in a play therapy sessions where she became very involved in doll play, drawing, and using clay. I was still in the process of evaluating Amanda when Ann requested a family session to discuss with both girls the parents' decision to initiate a marital separation.

Presenting Problem

The parents had decided to separate, and realizing that this would have serious consequences for their daughters they sought support and help from the child and family therapist who knew them and with whom they already had had a positive therapeutic experience. I suggested that all family members attend the session, with the understanding that I might see the girls individually after first meeting with the family as a group.

In actuality, Jim did not come to the family session since Robert had been hospitalized on that day with pancreatic cancer and Jim felt obliged to remain with him in the hospital during visiting hours, which coincided with the appointment for the family session. Ann and the girls planned to go to the hospital after the session to see Jim briefly, since the hospital was located midway between their home and my office.

Although the family were not specifically identifying their concerns about Robert's illness at this time, it was evident to me that the impact of the *two* major stressors needed to be considered in evaluating the girls' responses to their parents imminent separation.

First Family Session

This meeting began with Ann, Linda, and Amanda together. They all sat together on the couch, with Ann in the middle. Linda sat closest to me, and appeared to be the most comfortable of the three, in that she showed no apparent anxiety. Linda, by contrast, sat very close to her mother, and appeared to lean on her. Mother had lost quite a bit of weight, and looked very pale, fragile, and somewhat anxious during this meeting. Excerpts from the session follow.

Content of Session

THERAPIST: Hello! It's unusual to see *all* of you together! Even though I know each of you and you each know me, we haven't all met together as a group before. I'm sorry your Dad couldn't be here also, but I know he must be *very* worried about Uncle Robert.

AMANDA: Do you know that he has *cancer?*

T: Yes. I knew he was being treated for cancer before he went to the hospital.

AM: We're going to see him after we leave here.

T: Have you ever visited anyone in the hospital before? What do you think it will be like?

AM: (*Eagerly.*) I *want* to see him. I want him to know that we love him!

Analysis and Feelings

Want to recognize that this session is different, while pointing out that they have some past experience with me and with therapy.

Wondering what this means to an 8-year-old.

How touching! I worry that the Oncology floor might frighten her.

T: I'm sure that will mean *a lot* to him. I know that your families are very close. You may be able to help in other ways also, as time goes on. (*to Ann and Linda, trying to include them while opening up the discussion for other possible topics*) There certainly is a lot going on right now in your family!

Responding in concrete terms that might help Amanda.

Also wondering how Ann and Linda are feeling.

ANN: The girls know about Jim and me. We talked about it on the way here.

T: That's really why you're here tonight. So we can talk about it all together. It's a *big* step! (*to Linda and Amanda*) How do you feel about your parents separating?

Want to clarify the purpose of session, and give everyone permission to express their feelings.

LINDA: (*Shrugging her shoulders and looking down.*) It's okay I guess. They fight a lot and maybe it'll be better for them.

Has beginning understanding, but looks upset.

T: But what about *you?* What do you think it will be like for *you?*

L: I don't know. I never lived with separated parents before. (*Ann laughs nervously.*)

Sounds sarcastic.

AM: Dad says we'll still see him every Wednesday and every other weekend, and we're *not* going to sell the house. I *love* my room and he put in bookshelves and my bed just where I wanted them.

Denying that things will be different.

T: Many kids *do* worry that their lives will be different after their parents split up.

Giving permission to express fears.

L: (*to Ann*) Are you and Dad going to get a *divorce?* (*Says the word with great distaste.*)

Groping with future possibilities.

ANN: We don't know yet. This is a trial separation. We're both in therapy and we're going to see how it goes. We may end up getting a divorce and we may not.

T: (*to Linda and Amanda, but also to sensitize Ann about the girls' feelings*) It's going to be hard not knowing what's going to happen, but you're just going to have to "hang in" and wait. It's really up

*Important for the girls to realize that this is an *adult* decision, and that they need to trust their parents.*

to your Mom and Dad to make this very
important decision, and because it is *so*
important, they need time to be sure. I'm
sure they'll tell you as soon as they
decide.

At this point I offered to see each girl separately, because I wanted
to explore their individual reactions. Since Linda is 2½ years older than
Amanda, the younger girl tends to blur her own feelings in deference to
her older sister. In the separate interviews, Linda expressed her thoughts
that maybe in the future she would choose to live with her father, but
she did not know how she could tell her Mom this without hurting her.
I offered to help, if and when the time came.

In the separate session with Amanda she admitted that she felt very
"scared." She could not identify what precisely frightened her the most,
but agreed that not knowing about what was going to happen was hard.
I reassured her of her parents' deep love for both her and Linda, and also
that I would try to be helpful to everyone in the family as time went on.

Preliminary Assessment and Treatment Plan

This is a family in crisis, with the prospect of the marital separation creating considerable anxiety in both children. In addition, the terminal illness of Jim's close friend, and Linda's godfather, posed the possibility
that the father's involvement with his friend might interfere with his ability
to support and reassure the girls at the time they truly needed reassurance that they would not be "losing" him when he moved out of the home.

On the positive side, I knew of both parents' genuine concern for
the well-being of their daughters. Because of my past positive relationship with them, I felt optimistic about their openness to parent counseling in matters relevant to the girls. I also felt relieved to know that each
parent was engaged in individual therapy and hoped that this might reduce
the acting out that sometimes occurs between couples in situations of marital conflict. I wanted to recommend marital counseling, but Ann made
it clear that they were "not ready yet."

The *treatment plan* was for biweekly play therapy sessions with Linda
and Amanda, and parent counseling with the parent who brought them
to sessions. The parents were to alternate bringing their daughters, so
that I could remain in contact with each of them on a monthly basis.

My *goals* with the girls were to provide support at a time of destabili-
zation and crisis in their lives. I wanted to give them a place where they
could safely express their fears and anxieties, and to offer clarification

and intervention with their parents, when appropriate. I also wanted to prepare the girls for their godfather/uncle's future death and help them get ready to say good-bye to him in a manner that would be meaningful to them, and developmentally appropriate.

With regard to the *individual assessment* of each girl, I noted that they both were doing well in school, and each was involved in an activity outside of school. Furthermore, each had friends in her own peer group, and appeared to be developing normally. At ages 8 and 10 they had a fairly realistic idea about the finality of death, and because of the nature of their godfather's terminal illness and the family's plan for frequent contact with him, I believed that they would naturally enter a phase of anticipatory grieving. The only area of concern about the girls was that each had some previous difficulty meriting therapeutic involvement. Given that this was a family in which therapy was the "norm," nonetheless, I made a mental note to watch for signs of excessive lability and possible depression in Amanda, and for indications of phobic fears and possible regression in Linda. On DSM-III-R, Axis V, Global Assessment of Functioning (American Psychiatric Association, 1987), I ranked the girls as follows: Linda—past year, 50; current, 90; Amanda—past year, 70; current, 80.

Play Therapy Sessions

The usual pattern of these meetings consisted of a 20-minute family session with the girls and whichever parent brought them. Sometimes, depending on issues raised in the individual session, I would see the parent alone for 10 minutes at the end (always related to something specific, and always with the child's permission to discuss the matter with their parent).

It was notable from the beginning that Linda and Amanda were involved in intense sibling rivalry. This often began in the car with a battle over which one would sit in the front seat with the parent, and it continued in therapy around which one would come in to see me first. I resolved this initially with a toss of a coin, but since we all tended to forget whose turn it was from session to session, the argument persisted. During the occasional times I consulted with a parent following the individual sessions, the girls would resume their battle in the waiting room, fighting about a desired magazine, or what station to listen to on the radio. The fighting sometimes was physical and included hair-pulling, screaming, and punching, often requiring my assumption of a very firm stance with them, since they seemed to ignore their parents' attempts to interfere. I believe that this fighting clearly represented a regression, and also served to show both me and their parents how angry and "out of control" they felt in view of their present life circumstances. Selected segments from the family therapy and individual play therapy sessions follow.

Two Weeks after Initial Family Session

Content of Session	*Analysis and Feelings*
This session begins with father and the girls together. Seating is similar to that of the initial session with Mother, except this time Amanda sits with her arm locked with Father's. Linda sits at the side appearing more autonomous.	

THERAPIST: Hello, Jim. It's been a while since I've seen you. I'm so *sorry* to hear about Robert!

JIM: He's in pretty bad shape. I'm sorry I couldn't get here for the family meeting last time. Robert doesn't have much time left and I'm trying to be with him as much as possible.

This man is really in the throes of grieving. How hard to have to watch a close friend die!

T: This must be incredibly *hard* for you!!

J: He's such a young guy, he's the same age as me—35. He was always so strong and healthy. Now he's just skin and bones. I can't believe it.

Vulnerability factor: "If it happened to him, it could happen to me." Wonder if the girls are thinking this also.

T: (*to Amanda and Linda*) Have you been visiting Uncle Robert?

AMANDA: Yeah. He's got all tubes and stuff connected to him. The first time he was sitting in a chair, but the next time he was lying in his bed, and I thought he was *dead*. I ran out of the room crying!!

Amanda expresses all the details and her fears while Linda watches and listens.

T: That must have been very scary? Were you with your Mom?

AM: Yeah, but I ran ahead into his room alone. He's so *skinny* now.

T: It's hard to see someone change like that. But he's still the same person inside that skinny body. Did you tell him that you love him like you wanted to?

AM: Yes, and I gave him a big kiss.

I am moved by her openness and affection.

T: What about you, Linda. What is it like for you, seeing your Uncle Robert now?

LINDA: We know he's going to die. I hate to see him suffer.

J: (*Strongly!*) We're not going to let him suffer. The doctor may start giving him very strong medication so he won't feel the pain.

Jim is trying to be reassuring.

T: That could mean that Uncle Robert won't be able to talk with you. (*to Jim*) Do you think it's important for the girls to keep on visiting?

Wanting Jim to consider that it is okay for the girls *not* to visit.

J: That's up to them.

T: (*to Linda and Amanda*) How *do* you feel about it?

L: There usually are a lot of people there—all his friends from AA and his family. Sometimes I take care of John and Susi [Robert's kids] so they won't make too much noise and bother the other patients.

She has found a way to be helpful, despite the sad situation.

T: That's really helpful. I'm sure Aunt Terry is pretty upset, and she must really appreciate your playing with John and Susi.

AM: Mom says she is going to sleep over at their house sometimes

There has been some advance planning for the last stages of Robert's illness.

T: You're *all* doing your part to help, and I'm impressed. (*to Linda and Amanda*) Is there anything else you want to tell or do for Uncle Robert while he can still hear you?

Crediting their caring, and helping them plan for his death.

L: Just that we're praying for him and we love him. (*Amanda nods.*)

T: That may sound like a little, but it really is a lot. And it's really all you *can* do for him.

Sad reality.

J: I want him to know that his kids will always have a father as long as I am alive.

How touching that he thinks to reassure Robert about his children.

T: I hope you each will spend a special moment with Robert and whisper in his ear just what you have said here. Then you can feel that you have done all you can for him. It's very sad, but there's nothing more anyone can do, except help his family and let him die in peace.

Does this sound preachy? I really feel moved, and saddened by what this family has to experience.

At this point I saw each of the girls separately. They made drawings, and played board games with me (Linda: Connect Four; Amanda: Candyland). I learned that Jim planned to move out this coming weekend, and that he had given each girl his new phone number, and they had set up a visitation plan in which they would spend weekends with him in the family's vacation home. This weekend visiting would not start right away, however, because of Robert's illness and Jim's decision to spend as much time as possible with him in the hospital.

Summary. Sessions took place, as planned, at biweekly intervals during the next month. Robert's condition continued its inevitable decline. Jim reported that Amanda was "all over me" (needing a lot of physical contact), and that Linda was "angry, but keeping it all in, like me." During the session before the Thanksgiving holiday Amanda asked her father why he would not be with them for Thanksgiving dinner at Gramma's house, as usual, this year. Jim tried to explain that it would not be "comfortable" for Ann and him to be together; he told the girls that they would have "their own" Thanksgiving together with him that weekend. This change in traditional plans around a major holiday seemed to mark the girls' first *true* realization that their parents had separated. In fact, all of the hospital visiting and collaboration to help Robert's family had, understandably, masked the reality of their *own* changed family situation.

Session following Death

The week after Thanksgiving Ann telephoned to say that Robert had died the night before and that a memorial service would be held at his home the coming Saturday. We scheduled a family session, to which Ann and the girls came. In retrospect, I cannot recall why Jim did not come with them. I am certain that I would have invited him. I suspect the reason was that because the couple was in conflict they avoided situations where they would have to talk with one another.

Content of Session

Analysis and Feelings

THERAPIST: Well, your uncle has died. Even though we all knew it was coming it must be hard to believe.

I wonder how the girls are feeling, and how much they will be able to verbalize their feelings. I want to be helpful, and wonder just how far words can go at a time like this in view of the girls' ages.

LINDA: We were all sleeping at Terry's so she could be at the hospital. Uncle Robert's friends and Dad were there with him. Someone called Mom in the middle of the night to tell her.

T: So it's all over now.

Stressing the finality.

AMANDA: There's going to be a memorial service at their house on Saturday.

T: Do you know what that will be like?

Wanting to anticipate the situation, and help prepare the girls.

L: The priest will be there to say prayers, and someone is going to play a guitar and sing.

ANN: And different people will get up and talk about Robert and his life. I asked Linda if she wanted to write something.

T: (*to Linda*) Is that something you want to do?

Wondering if Linda feels pressure to produce something.

L: I might. Last year in school when a teacher's wife died we all wrote notes, and he told us later that they helped him feel better.

The idea of doing something "concrete" is certainly age-appropriate.

T: (*to Amanda*) Are you wondering what you might be able to do?

AM: I could draw a picture for Terry and make her a card.

T: That's a good idea. We could all work here on a big, joint "card picture" like a collage. (*The girls seem interested and I proceed to get out the construction paper, scissors, glue, markers, and some magazines.*) Sometimes you can find pictures in

Are we moving away from expression of feelings here, or will the feelings come in conjuction with the activity.

magazines that remind you of something
about a person. You can either draw on
the paper, or cut something out and paste
it on.

I want to offer possibilities for
evoking memories that do not
depend on drawing abilities.

The girls and Ann became very involved in looking through magazines, cutting out pictures, and reminiscing about Robert. It proved to
be a meaningful activity that encouraged sharing of significant memories.
Each of them recalled different aspects of their relationship with Robert.
They planned to give the collage to Terry, and I learned that she not only
thanked them warmly for it but displayed it prominently at the memorial service. Linda later wrote a poem for her "uncle" which Ann read at
the service. It is printed here with her permission.

My Uncle Robert

My Uncle Robert was brave and strong
There was no test, I wasn't wrong
He loved us so very much
I know we will miss him much
And I couldn't help crying when my Uncle was dieing [sic]
But now he is dead and we bow our heads
So god up there take good care of my Uncle Robert

Two Weeks Later: Summary of Session with Father and Girls

We discussed Robert's death, the memorial service, and what "an ordeal"
(Jim's words) they had all been through. The upcoming Christmas holidays were a concern as related to Terry and her children, but Jim made
it clear that both he and Ann would see to it that they were not alone.
It seemed to me that the focus remained on Robert and his family, rather
than on their *own* situation. When I expressed this, Jim mentioned his
concern because the girls fought so fiercely at times when they stayed
overnight with him. He attributed this to their reaction, both to Robert's
death and to the separation. While I agreed with him, I emphasized the
necessity of his intervening firmly to keep them from hurting one another.
I told him that he must convey to them a sense that he will protect them
and that he will not allow them to hurt each other.

Two Months after Death:
Summary of Family Session with Mother and Girls

Conflict between Ann and Linda seemed to be escalating. Some of this
might have been preadolescent turmoil, but some also seemed related to

FIGURE 6.1. Linda's drawing of "Mr. Warewolf."

tension around the separation. Ann believed that Linda was similar to Jim insofar as she held things in, and then exploded. When this happened Ann overreacted, treating Linda as if she represented her father rather than as an anxious 10-year-old. Linda may have believed that the separation was Ann's fault since Jim told the girls that he still loved their mother and always would. Linda felt a sense of divided loyalty.

Linda and Amanda continued to argue and tussle with one another. When I saw them jointly to discuss this, Linda said perceptively, "I guess *we* should get a divorce!!" When I suggested that Linda draw her feelings (on a paper plate "mask") while I was speaking individually to Amanda, she drew a fearsome "Mr. Warewolf" with sharp teeth, which clearly depicted her anger (Figure 6.1).

Linda later gave me this drawing and I said that it certainly looked angry and scary; I offered to keep it for her in my office, where it would not get "on the loose" and hurt anybody. This obvious interpretation of the therapist's role was welcomed by Linda who smiled and accepted my offer without hesitation.

A separate session with Amanda included extensive doll play in which she played the nurturing caretaker to twin infant dolls. I did not interpret any of this play, but emphasized wherever possible "how lucky those babies were to be so well cared for." One time, in playing a card game, The Game of Feelings, with Amanda, she responded to an Angry card: "I felt angry when my parents split up." I agreed that this was understandable, but she declined my offer to talk and so we went on with the game.

Five Months after Death:
Summary of Family Session with Mother and Girls

Tension and arguments continued between Ann and Linda as Linda persisted in finding issues to present to Ann that suggested that she was being treated unfairly by her mother. For example, as a means of saving money and respecting Linda's growing "maturity," Ann had dismissed the regular after-school baby-sitter (Linda was now almost 11, and Amanda 9). This caused inevitable problems between the girls who complained to Ann about each other. Linda wanted the privilege of being left without supervision, while her sister would be expected to go to the sitter's house, as previously. Linda complained to her mother, "*I* went to the sitter when I was 9!"

My role in this was to point out that in view of the girls' difficulty getting along, that it was *not* a good idea to leave them alone together. I also reinforced the idea that it was, indeed, appropriate to treat them differently, respecting the age difference and giving Linda some added privilege due to her age.

I noted that at this time there was an absence of dissension about who would go first for therapy and I complimented the girls about their improved "maturity" with me.

Nine Months after Death:
Summary of Telephone Sessions with Amanda

When I went away for my usual 2-month summer vacation, I left my telephone number with Ann, clarifying with her that it was perfectly all right to call me, if the need arose. I received two phone calls from Amanda during this time. Amanda told her mother that she wanted to talk to me because she got worried when she was reading a book and the words "seemed to jump out at her." When I talked to Amanda she seemed very puzzled about this, and denied any event that might have been upsetting to her. I suggested that sometimes when we are reading our minds wander, and maybe that was what happened. I cannot recall the title of the book, but know I must have asked about it as well as about the content. I suggested to Amanda that she should not be overly concerned about what happened, but that I wanted her to call me again in a week. A week later when Amanda called she told me that she had had a dream about her mother dying. I said that must have been very frightening, even though it was only a dream. We had an upcoming appointment at the end of my vacation, and I made it clear to Amanda that we would try to understand more clearly these upsetting experiences when we met in person.

One Week Later: Session with Amanda

This was a very interesting session insofar as this 9-year-old came in to therapy having already figured out her own symptoms, which she then refused to explore further.

Content of Session	Analysis and Feelings
THERAPIST: It's good to see you in person, after those phone calls. I'm glad you called, but we need to take some time to try to understand what all of this means.	Wondering if some events in Amanda's life have changed, or whether she has experienced a delayed reaction to her traumatic year.
AMANDA: I think I know what happened. Those words on the page had "angry" voices. That must mean that I am angry inside of me.	Wow! This girl is really making some connections. Or has she discussed this with her mother?
T: It sounds like you've been thinking a lot about this. Were you really worried about what happened?	Trying to figure out the meaning of this experience to Amanda.
AM: It's been a very *rough* year!	Sounds like what she may have heard Mom or Dad say. True!
T: Yes. I know you've been through a lot, and I wouldn't be surprised if you were angry. You certainly have a *right* to be angry.	
AM: I'm not mad at anyone *right now*.	Back off. Even though she made her own interpretation, she cannot see herself as an angry person.

T: It sounds like you don't want to think
of yourself as having angry feelings, even
though part of you thinks that might be
the reason you had the experience of the
words in the book and the dream.

AM: It's okay now. I haven't had any
trouble for a long time now.

She wants to drop it. Shall I
go along with her, or pursue
it?

T: I'm glad you're feeling better. I do
agree with what you said before, that
some anger inside may be slipping out.
That's okay. Anger can't hurt you, and if
it happens again, we'll talk about it.

One Year after Death: Summary of Session with Mother and Girls

Father had let me know that he no longer wanted to bring the girls for
therapy and he had conveyed to them his doubts about whether they still
needed to come. Mother believed they did, and was willing to bring them.
In discussion with the girls, they seemed ready to terminate, and we discussed this in the process of reviewing the past year. Parents had now
decided to proceed with getting a divorce. The girls said they felt okay
about this, that it was now much better than before when the parents
were fighting all the time. Everyone agreed that there was less fighting
both between Linda and Amanda, and between Ann and Linda (and, of
course, between Ann and Jim!). The girls were doing well in their new
school classes, and they all seemed happy. The visitation plan had worked
well; they saw their father twice a week.

In the individual session with Linda, she asked to play with the wood-
en blocks (she had never used these before). She built an elaborate house
constructed on stilts, using all the blocks in my set. When I asked her
if she wanted to put some people in the house she used a male and female doll, referring to them as "the girlfriend" and "the boyfriend." She
declined my offer to make up a story about the house and the people,
but wanted to invite her mother and sister in to see it before she packed
it up, prior to leaving. In Amanda's separate session, she again played
with the baby doll, having the mother doll give birth.

Three Years after Death: Session with Amanda

Ann was planning to remarry, and Jim, who had kept the family home
up to now, planned to sell it. Ann and the girls moved out to live with

the maternal grandmother last year. Amanda asked her mother to see me to discuss some of her conflicts with her father, and her anxieties about her new school. Both girls continued to do well in school, and reported feeling very positive about their future stepfather.

CONCLUDING COMMENTS

In reviewing and writing about this case almost 4 years after the original referral, and approaching 3 years after the marital separation and death of the godfather, it is possible to identify and track the elements of mourning and its resolution as expressed by these latency-age girls. Insofar as they experienced two very stressful losses almost simultaneously, it was impossible to know how much of their anger was related to the parents' separation and how much was related to bereavement associated with the godfather's death. My own belief is that since the death was unavoidable, and thus "unpreventable" in Burgen's (1983) terms, the mourning associated with this resolved more completely and that "acceptance of the inevitable" became the operable family dynamic to which the girls also subscribed.

The separation and ultimate decision to divorce, however, presented greater challenges to the child grievers, since here, unlike in their godfather's death, there was the possibility of looking for someone to blame, and also there was the hope on the girls' parts (and sometimes on the father's part, as well) that the marriage could be saved. My own feelings about this possibility were very evident to me. I believe strongly in the value of marriage counseling, and had stated this recommendation to each parent. However, they were not open to this and I had to abide by their decision. In retrospect, my own self-critique makes me wonder if I was as effective as I might have been with regard to the conflict between Linda and her mother. Part of me was also angry with Ann. Although I liked her very much, I realized that the separation had been initiated by her, and I worried about the future impact on the girls of growing up in a divorced family. This points to the real challenge in family therapy for the therapist who may be pulled to identify with one or more members, despite sincere efforts for therapeutic neutrality. Fortunately, I had the opportunity to see Ann for one separate session at her initiation when her therapist was away. This meeting was tremendously beneficial to my understanding of the reasons for the marital break-up. It speaks, in retrospect, to the potential value in the therapist's conducting individual sessions with *all* family members from time to time, to facilitate professional objectivity.

At present, Linda and Amanda are proceeding with their development and I am optimistic about their future. Linda expressed her anger openly following the death and separation, and now seems to have moved beyond it. Amanda, who was younger and relied more on symbolic expression in play, currently seems to be experiencing some tension related to several life changes occurring simultaneously. Her positive past experience in therapy prompts her appropriately to seek assistance when she feels overwhelmed and vulnerable. I am confident that these girls will continue to develop normally, and now they will have the added benefit of living in a home with a happy mother and in a situation in which they can continue to have frequent contact with their father. Although the mourning of the loss of an intact family may never be "complete" (this may be an unrealistic goal), they have come to an acceptance of their life, and are enjoying their teenage years.

DISCUSSION QUESTIONS

1. Discuss the treatment plan with regard to the focus on the girls, rather than on the family as a unit. How else might the treatment have been structured, considering the advantages and disadvantages of other possibilities.

2. Discuss the issue of multiple therapists in a family where marital separation is occurring. Do you think it would have been helpful for the therapist treating the children to have been in touch with each of the parents' therapists? Explain your reasons.

3. Comment on the issue of sibling therapy. Evaluate how the therapist dealt with the sibling rivalry, and suggest how this might have been managed differently.

4. How do you interpret Amanda's phone calls over the summer? If you had been the therapist, how would you have handled the calls and the session that followed?

5. How do you evaluate the girls' respective play themes in the termination session? Do you agree with the therapist's decision about terminating at this time?

6. How successfully did these girls mourn (a) the death of their godfather, and (b) their parents' separation? Do you agree with the therapist's optimism about their prognoses?

REFERENCES

American Psychiatric Association. (1987). *Diagnostic and statistical manual of mental disorders* (3rd ed., rev.). Washington, DC: Author.

Bowlby, J. (1960). Grief and mourning in infancy and early childhood. *Psychoanalytic Study of the Child, 15*, 9–52.

Bowlby, J. (1961). Process of mourning. *International Journal of Psycho-Analysis,* 42, 317–340.

Bowlby, J. (1963). Pathological mourning and childhood mourning. *Journal of the American Psychoanalytic Association, 11,* 500–541.

Bowlby, J. (1980). *Attachment and loss: Vol. III. Loss.* New York: Basic Books.

Burgen, L. A. (1983). Childhood bereavement: Preventability and the coping process. In J. E. Schowalter, P. R. Patterson, M. Tallmer, A. H. Kutscher, S. V. Gullo, & D. Peretz (Eds.), *The child and death* (pp. 357–365). New York: Columbia University Press.

Falicov, C. J. (1982). Mexican families. In M. McGoldrick, J. K. Pearce, & J. Giordano (Eds.), *Ethnicity and family therapy* (pp. 134–163). New York: Guilford Press.

Furman, E. (1974). *A child's parent dies.* New Haven: Yale University Press.

Jewett, C. L. (1982). *Helping children cope with separation and loss.* Cambridge, MA: Harvard Common Press.

Moitoza, E. (1982). Portuguese families. In M. McGoldrick, J. K. Pearce, & J. Giordano (Eds.), *Ethnicity and family therapy* (pp. 412–437). New York: Guilford Press.

Raphael, B. (1983). *The anatomy of bereavement.* New York: Basic Books.

Viorst, J. (1986). *Necessary losses.* New York: Baltimore Books.

Wallerstein, J., & Blakeslee, S. (1989). *Second chances.* New York: Ticknor & Fields.

Wallerstein, J., & Kelly, L. (1980). *Surviving the break-up: How children and parents cope with divorce.* New York: Basic Books.

Webb, N. B. (Ed.). (1991). *Play therapy with children in crisis: A casebook for practitioners.* New York: Guilford Press.

Weiss, R. (1975). *Marital separation.* New York: Basic Books.

CHAPTER SEVEN

Accidental Sibling Death
Case of Peter, Age 6

CAROL P. KAPLAN
HANNAH JOSLIN

The bereavement of children who have experienced the death of a sibling has received far less attention than that of children who have lost parents, or parents who have lost children. Moreover, most of the literature on the effects of sibling death addresses instances of death from illness. This chapter focuses on the case of a 6-year-old boy, Peter, whose 2½-year-old sister died as a result of an accident. Thus, interwoven into the play therapy conducted with the youngster were his reactions to the circumstances of the death, as well as issues of sibling bereavement. Obviously, in the case of any child, age and developmental level, cognitive and emotional, will play a determining role. In this, as in a situation cited by Webb, "the crisis of a sibling's death [was] superimposed on the child's normal developmental process" (1991, p. 15). Accordingly, Peter's reactions, as well as the treatment itself, also exemplified many of the characteristics of play therapy with children in early latency.

ISSUES OF SIBLING BEREAVEMENT

A number of authors have pointed out that because the death of a child is such an overwhelming event for parents to endure, the impact on the surviving siblings may not always be noticed, especially since "children's mode of expression varies from adults' in many life situations" (Sourkes, 1980, p. 65). Yet the death of a child will inevitably affect the siblings in two ways: first, because children will necessarily have intense feelings about the loss of a significant relationship and, second, because stress on any part of the family system will affect all of its members (Cain, Fast, & Erickson, 1964; Binger, 1973; Gogan, Koocher, Foster, & O'Malley, 1977; Krell & Rabkin, 1979; Rosen & Cohen, 1981; Sourkes, 1980; Rosen, 1986). Whereas some researchers have focused on psychopathological reactions to sibling death (Cain et al., 1964; Rosenblatt, 1969), others have emphasized the importance of allowing children to express their feelings of loss and grief, verbally and through play, in the service of continued coping (Feinberg, 1970; Sourkes, 1980; Rosen, 1986). This case illustrates the latter approach, inasmuch as Peter was a normally developing child who manifested symptoms immediately following the death of his sister, and during the course of treatment appeared to resume his former level of adaptation.

A variety of reactions by children who have experienced the death or fatal illness of a sibling have been described in the literature. In virtually every study of children's responses to sibling death, the relevance of children's universal ambivalence toward their siblings has been noted. As Lindsay and MacCarthy (1974) point out, sibling relationships are "intense and complex," involving "loyalty, companionship, rivalry, love and hate, jealousy and envy" (p. 195). Thus, at the same time that children are grieving for their loss, they may also feel guilty because they believe that their earlier hostile thoughts and wishes caused the tragedy (McCollum, 1974). This is especially the case with younger children, who are more egocentric (Thunberg, 1977; Gogan et al., 1977) and prone to magical thinking. It may also be more prominent when the surviving child is older than the dead sibling (Lindsay & MacCarthy, 1974). Another source of guilt for children may be the fact that they have survived and their sibling has not (Sourkes, 1980). These themes appeared in Peter's therapy.

Other reactions frequently observed in children who have lost siblings are fear and anxiety, including separation anxiety (Cain et al., 1964; Krell & Rabkin, 1979; Rosen & Cohen, 1981). Sourkes (1980) has pointed out, with regard to the siblings of cancer patients, that the sibling relationship implies a sense of similarity and identification. For this reason, the sibling's death creates a particular fear in the child that the same fate could befall him/her. With regard to the separation anxiety seen in bereaved siblings, an additional factor may be at work. Many authors have noted that the parents, overwhelmed with their loss, may become emotionally unavailable to their surviving children, which causes them to feel insecure (Cain et al., 1964; Rosen & Cohen, 1981; Webb, 1991).

In the case of the Dawsons, Peter's parents, they were sufficiently attuned to their son's reactions after the death of his sister that they initiated and cooperated with his treatment. On the other hand, they were unwilling to engage in counseling for themselves, even though they were clearly suffering, and the father apparently became quite withdrawn. We may surmise, therefore, that their reactions played some role in Peter's separation anxiety.

ROLE OF RELIGIOUS BELIEFS

An important element in this case was the family's religious beliefs, and the way in which they were incorporated by Peter in working through his feelings about his sister's death. Some authors have viewed religious explanations about death, especially the concept of heaven, as potentially confusing or even counterproductive for the mourning process in young children because they foster denial and thus prevent the resolution of emotions (Furman, 1973; Lieberman, 1979; Rosen, 1986). Yet the death of a child has the potential to create tremendous guilt in the surviving children and the parents, in addition to blaming, which can be destructive to the whole family (Cain et al., 1964; Krell & Rabkin, 1979). Hence, the Dawsons' faith that their daughter's death "could not have been prevented," for "God wanted Kathy," appeared to provide comfort because guilt and blame were minimized. Clearly, as shown by his drawings, religious ideas and images gave some comfort to Peter. When these ideas did confuse him, the therapist enlisted the aid of the parents in clarifying reality.

ISSUES OF ACCIDENTAL SIBLING DEATH

Furman (1973) has written that for a child the deaths of either parents or siblings "are always premature and untimely, either because of illness or accident. The manner in which these premature deaths have occurred has a tremendous potential as a trauma in and of itself." Unlike the deaths of grandparents at an advanced age, "these potential traumata . . . must be taken into account in helping a child achieve some degree of freedom from untoward anxiety before he can utilize his capacity to mourn" (Furman, 1973, p. 229). In their discussion of traumatic grief, Eth and Pynoos (1985) agreed with Furman that "traumatic anxiety is a priority concern for the ego, compromising its ability to attend to the fantasies of the lost object that are integral to the grief process" (p. 175). They maintain that in a sudden, traumatic death a child experiences "traumatic helplessness" (1985, p. 180), which makes the circumstances of the death and the exposure of the child as important as its suddenness and its intrapsychic meanings. Thus, "the dual tasks of trauma mastery and grief resolution are critical, and therapeutic work can succeed when both are addressed" (Eth & Pynoos, 1985, p. 183).

In this case it can be surmised that Peter experienced "traumatic help-lessness," not only in the process of witnessing his sister being carried into the ambulance at the scene of the accident, but also by driving in the ambulance to the hospital with his parents while unsuccessful efforts were being made to revive her. In fact, it is possible that his parents' help-lessness in that situation exacerbated his own. Certainly, in therapy he expressed not only feelings about his loss and themes such as ambiva-lence, but also a preoccupation with danger; and such repetitive play ac-tivities as surrounding the dollhouse with clay may be seen as an attempt to master his anxiety. One may conclude, therefore, that the therapy was addressing his "stress overload" (Webb, 1991) at the same time that it permitted an opportunity to express his grief, cognitive confusion, and themes such as ambivalence and identification.

When a child dies the parents may attempt to "replace" that child, either concretely through pregnancy or else symbolically, with conse-quences that may be detrimental to the entire family (Krell & Rabkin, 1979). Similarly, to defend against the pain of loss, children may seek a replacement for the dead sibling, for example, by requesting a pet or a new baby (Feinberg, 1970; Lindsay & MacCarthy, 1974). In this case the fact that the mother became pregnant almost immediately after the accident, together with the reluctance of the parents to discuss their feel-ings about their daughter's death, suggests that the pregnancy may have represented such a replacement for them. Indeed, the desire to replace his sister was actually verbalized by Peter.

THE PLAY THERAPY

Children who have lost a sibling, whether or not the death involved a traumatic circumstance, need to grieve, and "opportunities for their mourning must be provided" (Sourkes, 1980, p. 68). As Rosen stated, "it is clearly beneficial to a child to be able to express his or her ideas, fantasies, and fears about death and to be in an environment that con-veys acceptance of his or her need to communicate about the loss" (1986, p. 76). Furman referred to "the need to present death realistically, meet a bereaved child's needs consistently, accept his feelings, support his reality testing, judiciously interpret his defenses, and assist him with mastering the inevitably terrifying reality which caused his premature loss" (1973, p. 229). Obviously, not every bereaved child will be seen in play thera-py; however, in Peter's case it was the play therapy that facilitated his mourning.

Sourkes states that in psychotherapy with bereaved siblings, "the aim is to make the covert overt in their mourning. Verbal interaction, draw-ing and dollhouse play are all means of inducing expression" (1980, p.

65). An interesting feature of this case is the way in which Peter utilized the therapeutic environment. Specifically, he was very much the director of his play, and he also tended to resist interpretations by the therapist that connected his fantasies with reality. Rather, he preferred to use fantasy for mastery of his feelings and concerns, and this appeared to be successful. In his seminal work on the developmental stage of latency, Sarnoff (1976) has defined the years 6 to 8 as early latency. During this phase "fantasy is the primary means of adjusting to emotional stresses and becomes a defense" (p. 33). Children can resolve their conflicts through fantasy, and the object of therapy is to enable them to do so. According to Sarnoff, reality-oriented interpretation is often unnecessary in early latency and may even be resisted by the child. This proved to be the case with Peter.

The treatment plan in this case was to see Peter for individual play therapy, and to provide parent counseling following Peter's sessions. In retrospect, family therapy might have been offered, although it is not clear whether the parents would have agreed to it. Krell and Rabkin (1979) have stated that "family therapy is the treatment of choice in these post-traumatic situations" because it provides the opportunity for family members to grieve together, which is "a painful but potentially solidifying experience." Moreover, "the demystification of communication and experience among family members is also most effectively handled in conjoint meetings" (p. 476). Play therapy was deemed appropriate for Peter, and did seem to be the "treatment of choice" for him, particularly since at his age the expression of feelings through play was more possible than the direct verbal expression used in family therapy with older children and adults. However, the question remains whether some family therapy sessions as an adjunct to the play therapy might have proved helpful in resolving certain issues.

THE CASE: PETER, AGE 6

Family Information

This was a white, middle-class family living in a house in the suburbs. In the home were:

> Peter, age 6, first-grader in a Catholic parochial school
> Jane Dawson, age 29, employed part-time as a secretary
> Bill Dawson, age 31, self-employed in a computer business
> Kathy, age 2½, died 10 days prior to referral

Religion

The family were devout Roman Catholics with a deep faith, observant of all Catholic religious practices. Typically, religious Catholics believe in an afterlife. Depending on the state of the soul at the moment of death, a person could go to heaven, hell, or purgatory. The soul of a young child, baptized at birth, would be considered innocent of sin, and would go to heaven in the event of an early death. The idea that a loved one is in heaven comforts the bereaved. It is usual that when any Catholic dies a funeral mass is held, and children may join the family in attending this service.

The Dawsons attempted to be flexible in adapting their religious beliefs for Peter. Two days after Kathy's death the family had a prayer service in their home. Mr. and Mrs. Dawson requested that the priest play down Jesus's resurrection for fear that Peter would hold onto the magical belief that Kathy would return. At the mass that was held on the following day, a closed coffin was presented. Afterwards, Peter was taken to the cemetery with the family and other mourners.

Presenting Problem

Mr. and Mrs. Dawson contacted the community mental health center because they were concerned about the way Peter was handling the death, 10 days earlier, of his 2½-year-old sister, Kathy. Previously an outgoing, sociable, and independent boy, Peter had become less gregarious and more sullen and was also showing separation anxiety. The Dawsons said that they were not interested in help for themselves, but wanted Peter to be evaluated and given treatment, if recommended.

Mr. and Mrs. Dawson gave the following account of the events surrounding Kathy's death, with Mr. Dawson in tears and his wife more emotionally constrained. On Sunday in the early afternoon Peter and Kathy went out to play with other neighborhood children, as they frequently did. The family lived on a cul-de-sac with little traffic and adjoining back yards. About 20 minutes later Peter came into the house telling his parents that he "lost Kathy." They went outside to look for her, calling her name, while Peter went over to a friend's house to play. The parents first checked the dry well at the back of their property, which was surrounded by a fence, and found no one; inadvertently, however, they apparently left the gate open. They went looking around the neighborhood and shortly afterwards returned to the well, where Kathy was discovered lying at the bottom. It is not clear whether she fell in while they were searching, or whether she had fallen in previously and they had failed to notice her in the well. Mrs. Dawson tried to administer first aid, while Mr. Dawson called the ambulance and then went to find Peter. He told Peter that Kathy was very sick and would have to be taken to the hospital. When the ambulance arrived Peter did not want to be separated from his parents, so he accompanied them to the hospital. He saw Kathy being carried into the ambulance.

In the ambulance Peter asked his parents numerous questions about Kathy; he seemed to be aware of the severity of her condition when he heard the paramedics making efforts to revive her. While the Dawsons waited in the hospital, Kathy received medical treatment for 12 hours before being pronounced dead. In the meantime, Peter was brought back and forth twice from home to the hospital by close family friends. Mrs. Dawson's sister flew in from out of town and was sleeping with Peter in Mr. and Mrs. Dawson's bed when they returned at 12:30 A.M. and told Peter that Kathy had died. Peter asked questions about the doctor's efforts to save her, cried, and fell asleep with his aunt.

After the second night, Peter resumed sleeping in his own bedroom and had a nightmare 5 days later which resulted in his calling for his parents. He dreamed that King Kong was in his room, coming to get him. After the funeral the parents were concerned that Peter might develop a fear of playing outside. He had made statements such as, "I wish we never bought this house" (the house had been bought 6 months previously), and "We should all pray more for Kathy." Mrs. Dawson explained that this accident could not have been prevented for "God wanted Kathy." At the time of intake, Peter was concerned about his mother going back to work part-time and wanted to sit in the office while she worked.

The Dawsons described Peter as being the "helper" in the family. Kathy had been born with a hip dislocation and required regular visits to the orthopedist. Peter would assist his mother in getting Kathy ready for these visits. Kathy was antagonistic at these times, biting and hitting her brother, but Peter would not retaliate, although on occasion he would complain to his parents. They added that they had expected sibling rivalry on Peter's part once Kathy was born, but were surprised to find little. Peter tore up Kathy's box of diapers once and scribbled on her toys, but that was the extent of his acting out.

Mr. and Mrs. Dawson acknowledged that religion had helped them cope with Kathy's death. Mr. Dawson stated, "It was meant to happen."

First Session with Child

The first session was held less than 2 weeks after Kathy's death. At intake the parents had been instructed to tell Peter that he would be coming to a special place where children came when something sad happened in the family; he would see a nice lady and play. This place would have toys, such as blocks and a doll house, and Mommy would go with him. In the session Peter was quite verbal and related in a free, spontaneous fashion. He did not seem depressed initially when speaking about neutral topics, but seemed dejected later when discussing his younger sister. The following is an excerpt from the latter section of the interview, with Peter talking to Dr. Joslin while exploring the toys in the playroom.

Content of Session	*Analysis and Feelings*
THERAPIST: Peter, can you make three magic wishes?	I want to help him start verbalizing.
PETER: Do you mean wishes on a star? I wish for a new sister because my sister died.	
T: What happened to her?	
P: She fell in the well—Mom found her laying flat. We took her to the hospital and Kathy was dead.	
T: That's very sad. What happened then?	
P: We had a prayer service at my house. (*In a disappointed tone.*) I didn't even see Kathy after she was dead. I saw the box she was in, it was white and holy water was sprinkled on it.	He has had a loss!
T: What does the holy water do?	
P: It makes her go to heaven. Kathy will be an angel in heaven.	
T: How do you feel about that?	
P: Sad, because I don't have a sister any more.	
T: Will Kathy ever come back?	Some notion of death as final.
P: No. Kathy and I used to play a lot together.	
T: Did you ever have little arguments, about toys and stuff?	
P: We *never* had fights! Can I play with these blocks?	Anxious, changes subject.
T: Sure. (*As he is playing.*) How do you feel lately? Are you eating all right?	

P: Yes, but Kathy was a faster eater than me.

Sibling rivalry.

T: Do you ever have any dreams?

P: Yes, a lot! I dream Kathy is with me playing and she fell, and we went to the hospital and I sat in the hospital. She was breathing on her own and her eyes closed and she died.

Revisiting the stressful event.

T: What happened the day Kathy died?

P: I was with Kathy in the ambulance. I got to turn the siren on. Mommy closed her eyes, I thought she fell asleep.

T: What do you think happened to Kathy?

P: Before, I was by the well with a ball. Mom and Dad were calling me. I came in the house and said Kathy fell in, that maybe Kathy began to play with the ball. I saw Kathy's hand but I couldn't reach her. I forgot to tell Mom to help Kathy. She knows how. In the ambulance I heard sounds, Kathy was clapping her hands. Can we play darts? (*Begins throwing darts.*) I used to play darts with my Grandpa. He was sick and old when he died. I miss him a lot.

Not what parents reported.

Guilty, confused, and anxious. I wonder what really happened.

Remembers earlier loss.

Preliminary Assessment and Treatment Plan

Peter appeared to be a bright and, until now, normally developing child who was reacting to the crisis of his sister's accidental death with reactions characteristic of both grief and "stress overload" (Webb, 1991, p. 20). He showed guilt, anxiety, depression, repetitive dreams, and cognitive confusion. From the parents' report, it could be surmised that he was also evidencing some social withdrawal. Hostile feelings for his sister were denied, in part due to an age-appropriate failure to differentiate between feelings and actions and perhaps also, in part, due to either spoken or unspoken parental prohibitions against such hostility. The egocentrism of his developmental stage led to his blaming himself for her death. These fantasies, suggesting the presence of ideas that he and other family members could undo the circumstances of the death, may also have served a defensive purpose. Dr. Joslin was uncertain exactly how the religious explanations given to Peter would affect his working through of the death.

The treatment plan was to see Peter on a short-term basis to enable him to express his feelings about the accident and about his loss, and to alleviate his guilt. Mr. and Mrs. Dawson were clearly motivated to help their son in this regard, as evidenced by their application for help for Peter very shortly after Kathy's death. It was felt that they themselves, having suffered an overwhelming loss, could also benefit from short-term counseling especially if they were to be able to remain emotionally available to Peter. However, although they were willing to cooperate by being seen collaterally around Peter's treatment, they were reluctant to engage in counseling for themselves. One might speculate that their reluctance was based in part on the ambiguity surrounding the circumstances of Kathy's death, and a fear that they would be considered neglectful for having left a 2½-year-old in the care of a 6-year-old.

Play Therapy Sessions

The following are key moments from Peter's therapy, which consisted of 20 sessions. After each session the mother, and occasionally both parents, would be seen for 10 or 15 minutes while Peter played in the supervised playroom at the clinic.

Session 2 (1 Week after the First Session)

Content of Session	Analysis and Feelings
PETER: I miss Kathy. Last night I was crying because I missed her. I wonder if she is an angel or if she is really a devil.	
THERAPIST: Why do you think she might be a devil?	
P: She used to do some bad things, like biting, pushing, and butting with her head like a goat. Sometimes she did that to me.	
T: Sometimes kids feel annoyed when their brother or sister does those things to them.	Permission for hostile feelings.
P: (*Continues to play, does not respond.*)	
T: When that happens, it is natural for kids to feel angry.	

P: (*Asks to paint. He paints a picture of the soldiers putting Christ on the cross, and a picture of Kathy as an angel with her head in God's lap. He explains these pictures, and Dr. Joslin echoes his explanations but does not make any interpretations.*)

It comforts him that Kathy is with God.

T: (*Later on.*) Did Mommy go back to work?

P: She's going back today. But I don't want to stay with the baby sitter because she's sad about Kathy and she has other children to take care of.

He feels vulnerable.

T: She's a grown-up, and she'll be able to take care of kids even if she is sad about Kathy. Maybe you still feel a little sad about Kathy too?

Reassuring him that he will be protected.

P: (*Does not reply.*)

Session 3 (1 Week Later)

Prior to this session Mrs. Dawson had phoned, very upset. Peter had refused to hold her hand crossing the street, stating he wanted to die and be with Kathy in heaven. The next night he had asked why God did not take him too, because he is also "special." Dr. Joslin directed her to tell Peter, "When you're dead you're dead, and if you're alive you're alive."

Content of Session

Analysis and Feelings

PETER: (*Asks whether Dr. Joslin still has the picture he made of Kathy, is satisfied to see both his pictures. Then goes to the doll house and uses clay to stand up the doll figures in the rooms. As he does this he chats.*) You know the angels took Kathy because she is special, and I'm here with Mom and Dad because I'm the big boy.

Did I keep something valuable of his?

He wants to feel special to me.

THERAPIST: Do you think you'd want to be with Kathy?

P: No, because when you're dead you're dead and if you're alive you're alive. The angels took Kathy because she fell in the

Parents told him and he believes them.

well. I know how to keep from falling in the well. You know, my grandpa died but he lived to be a very old man.

T: Most boys live to be old men.

P: I know some things that can't die: trucks, and toys. And I know some things that *can* die: people, animals, plants. (*Asks to play Candyland.*)	Working on understanding the concept of death.
T: Are you still dreaming about Kathy?	
P: No.	Some feelings resolved.

The parents were seen separately. They reported Peter was separating well to go to school, and to the sitter when Mrs. Dawson went to work. He had also resumed playing outside with his friends.

Session 4: 1 Week Later

Peter came in cheerfully, and asked to play Candyland. In contrast to the prior two sessions, he did not spontaneously mention Kathy. He also said that he had not been thinking or dreaming about her. Later on he asked to play darts.

Content of Session	Analysis and Feelings
PETER: (*Grasping a dart.*) You know, Jesus doesn't like it when you hold a dart carelessly. You might poke someone in the eye.	
THERAPIST: Jesus may not like someone hurting another person, but he understands we all may feel angry some of the time.	Addressing his guilt and separating out hostile feelings from actions.
P: (*Does not comment, throws dart.*)	

Mrs. Dawson, seen after Peter's session, indicated that Peter was playing well and sleeping well. He had expressed a little anxiety about being kidnapped, before going to sleep. Keeping a light on has helped.

Session 5: 1 Week Later

Content of Session	Analysis and Feelings
PETER: (*Makes an "angel hat" out of clay, in the shape of a halo.*)	

THERAPIST: I wonder if you've been
thinking about Kathy.

P: (*Annoyed.*) All you think about is Kathy! (*Goes to the doll house and puts pieces of clay around the edges.*) This is so the kids can't fall out. I had a friend, David, in my old neighborhood. He died because he fell out the window.	Resists interpretation, prefers fantasy. Play with clay masters the anxiety.
	Is this true?

Mrs. Dawson, seen after Peter's session, reported that David never fell out of the window, was never hurt, and did not die. Peter had recently told another child that a different friend "got his head chopped off." Dr. Joslin wondered whether this type of fantasy was another means of mastering his fears.

At this session, too, in view of his age and his limited appreciation of time, Peter was prepared for the fact that the following session would be the last one before his family's vacation. The family's plans were discussed, along with the fact that he would be returning to see Dr. Joslin after the vacation. He accepted this without reaction.

Session 7: About 1 Month Later, after the Family's Vacation

Content of Session	Analysis and Feelings
PETER: (*Denies any dreams or worries. Plays Candyland, then puts some clay on the head of a doctor puppet.*)	
THERAPIST: I wonder whether you feel angry at the doctor because he didn't save Kathy?	Is he also angry at me for vacation separation?
P: She's just a pain in the neck and she bit me and I don't miss her!	Now he is expressing anger at Kathy!

Mr. and Mrs. Dawson were seen after Peter's session. They spoke of a book on bereaved parents they had seen. Both seemed to be hurting, but were reluctant to open up and discuss their feelings.

Session 8: 1 Week Later

Content of Session	Analysis and Feelings
PETER: (*Puts clay all over the edges of the doll house.*) I used to be afraid that Kathy would fall out of the window, but now I'm afraid that *I'll* fall out.	Fear represents wish. Guilty, also identifies with sister.

THERAPIST: Sometimes when Kathy was a pain in the neck, I wonder if you ever wished *she* would fall out the window?

I try to interpret his hostile wish but he resists my interpretation.

P: You're full of baloney!

When the parents were seen, Mrs. Dawson cried. She explained that her husband had been away on a business trip, and she had felt very lonely when Peter was in school.

Session 12: 4 Weeks Later, after Several Sessions with Neutral Content

Content of Session

Analysis and Feelings

PETER: (*Sets up doll house with family dolls, and manipulates a puppet.*) There's a big giant coming to get someone. (*Picking up dolls.*) He's dead, he lost his head, he's only clay. His mouth is coming out, his hair, now his eyes. (*Manipulates the puppet.*) The big giant came to life. Now he feels like playing in the stupid house. Mess 'em up in the house. (*He messes up the doll furniture, then takes the puppet again.*) Bam, naughty boy, put him up for a nap. (*Asks Dr. Joslin to help him put clay on the sides of the house.*) Let's do the sides to keep the monster from climbing up.

Guilt about aggressive feelings. He wants to use play to master his fears.

THERAPIST: Ever think about monsters, or dream of them?

P: You're full of baloney! Do you think a first grader would think that? Finished! He wakes up. (*Puts away the puppet. Helps Dr. Joslin put clay on the windows. Asks to go to the bathroom.*)

I need to just facilitate the play and not comment!

Mrs. Dawson was seen after Peter's session. She reported that she was pregnant and Peter knew about the pregnancy. He told her, "I wish you would hurry up and get a baby 'cause it would help me to get over Kathy." She also revealed that her husband had been very withdrawn, and she had thought of leaving him until she read the book on bereaved parents, which explained his behavior.

Session 13: The Following Week

Content of Session	Analysis and Feelings
PETER: Help me put clay on the doll house to keep the monster out. No, to keep the people from falling out.	A way to master his fears.
THERAPIST: Why would people fall out of the house?	Joining with him in his theme instead of intruding with reality.
P: When there is a fire people jump into a net. I'm making a big hose for the daddy to put the fire out, I'm making hoses for every room.	He wants father to protect the family.

Session 14: 2 Weeks Later

Content of Session	Analysis and Feelings
PETER: (*Paints a picture of Kathy as an angel, then asks to use black finger paints.*) Kathy watches me from heaven. Angels tell God things to help Him save people.	
THERAPIST: Tell me more about that.	
P: I'm just 6 years old. Even grown-ups don't understand this stuff!	It *is* hard to comprehend death!

Session 16: 2 Weeks Later

Content of Session	Analysis and Feelings
THERAPIST: (*Brings up mother's pregnancy.*)	I know he thinks about it.
PETER: I don't want a sister because girls are a pain in the neck. Kathy used to hit me and bite me.	He is now much more comfortable with his hostile feelings toward Kathy.

Mrs. Dawson reported that Peter was doing very well, and it was decided to prepare him for termination. Dr. Joslin encouraged Peter to verbalize any feelings of rejection, and the reasons for termination were clarified. She told Peter: "You came here right after your sister died. You were sad and missing Kathy. Now I see you are feeling better, not missing her so much. You are busy with school and playing with friends. It seems you don't need to come any more. I'm going to miss you. I like playing with you. Maybe you can come back once in a while, but you don't *need* to come here. I'm sure you have many things to do, like riding your bike and playing outdoors. I'll see you two more times, and then maybe Mommy will bring you back once in a while so I can see how you are doing." Peter accepted this explanation and the termination process proceeded without any regression on his part.

At the last session Mrs. Dawson said that she would like Peter to be re-evaluated around the time of her delivery, but the parents did not recontact the mental health center.

CONCLUDING COMMENTS

During the 6-month period of Peter's treatment the original presenting symptoms of guilt, anxiety, and depression abated, and the repetitive dreams and thoughts about Kathy and the accident virtually ceased. He was no longer socially withdrawn and had resumed his formerly good functioning. He was more comfortable with his ambivalence toward his sister, as evidenced by his willingness to express hostile thoughts and feelings about her. With the help of his parents he had resolved the original confusion about death by adopting from his religion an image of Kathy in heaven, which was comforting but did not involve denial of the finality of death.

At the same time, we admit that Peter's longer-term adaptation cannot be known. The fact that the parents refused counseling even though they were suffering, and that Mrs. Dawson became pregnant so quickly, leaves open to question their continued emotional availability to their son. Furthermore, if in fact they circumvented their own mourning by means of a "replacement baby," and if Peter, too, regarded the new baby as a replacement for his sister, this suggests the possibility of unresolved grief and family dysfunction that might resurface in the future. Dr. Joslin regretted that she did not have the opportunity to continue seeing the family before and after the baby's birth, or at least to follow up afterwards.

In retrospect, it seems that in view of the parents' reluctance to be seen alone, one or more family sessions with Peter and both parents might have been helpful in clarifying the ambiguity surrounding the accident, as well as feelings of guilt and self-blame on the part of both parents and child. During the first session with Peter he described a scenario of the accident that was drastically different from the one presented by the parents—one that implied he blamed himself for Kathy's death. Specifically, when asked by the therapist what had happened, he replied: "Before, I was by the well with a ball. Mom and Dad were calling me. I came in the house and said Kathy fell in, that maybe Kathy began to play with the ball. I saw Kathy's hand but I couldn't reach her. I forgot to tell Mom to help Kathy. She knows how." In the parents' version of the story, on the other hand, their failure to close the gate during the search for Kathy led to the child falling into the well. While Peter's general improvement tends to suggest that he did not continue to blame himself, a conjoint family session early in his treatment could have emphasized for him that Kathy's death was not his fault. In addition, an exploration of the circumstances of the accident could have revealed whether the parents harbored feelings of guilt and self-blame, and they might have become more willing to engage in treatment for themselves.

An interesting feature of the play therapy with Peter is that he was almost completely self-directed in his use of fantasy. A variety of play and art materials were made available to him and he selected and used them very purposefully. For example, his drawings depicted Kathy in heaven safe with God, and his repetitive use of clay around the doll house appeared to serve the purpose of assisting him in mastering his feelings of anxiety and helplessness. Moreover, he let Dr. Joslin know clearly when he felt that her suggestions, interpretations, or interpretative questions were intrusive, for example, by saying such things as, "You're full of baloney!" or by closing himself off. In point of fact he did a great deal of the work himself, even to the extent that at times Dr. Joslin felt as if she were interfering with him. Using this countertransference reaction as a guide, she learned that, while clarifying comments could be made at appropriate moments, often the most useful position was one of participant observer in Peter's play. Furthermore, he was more likely to accept her comments when they built on the language and content of his fantasy material than when she attempted to make direct interpretations of reality issues (e.g., his ambivalent thoughts and feelings about Kathy).

Being of a different religion, Dr. Joslin also experienced countertransference reactions when Peter initially manifested some confusion about death based on his understanding of the parents' religious beliefs. Essentially, she felt frustrated. Her goal was to straighten out the child's misconceptions without contradicting the parents' beliefs, both out of respect for these beliefs and because she knew that they provided some comfort to Peter. She wanted to understand better what they said to him and why, but she did not share a religious common ground. For this reason, and also because she realized that parents' statements make a significant impression on children, she enlisted their help. When, at her suggestion, they told Peter, "When you're alive you're alive and if you're dead you're dead," this satisfied the dual purpose of establishing the finality of death and permitting the religious conceptions to remain and to comfort. This statement by the parents also put to an end Peter's fantasies of joining Kathy and his wanting to be "special" to God in the process. Needless to say, it would have been interesting to follow Peter and to assess whether, and in what way, these religious ideas continued and whether they underwent any changes as his development proceeded.

DISCUSSION QUESTIONS

1. If family sessions had been held with Peter and his parents, how might the therapist have guided the interactions to maximize a 6-year-old's participation and understanding?

2. Can any other themes, aside from those identified in this chapter, be seen in Peter's fantasy or verbalizations?

3. Discuss the "normal" grief reactions of a 6-year-old who has experienced the loss of a family member. In what respects do Peter's symptoms reflect "normal" grieving, and/or do you consider his symptoms to be pathological? How would you differentiate Peter's symptoms upon referral from those of posttraumatic stress reaction?

4. Do you think Peter had resolved the issues surrounding his sister's death at the termination of therapy, or will it continue to be an issue for him in the future? If so, in what way(s)?

REFERENCES

Binger, C. M. (1973). Childhood leukemia—emotional impact on siblings. In E. J. Anthony & C. Koupernik (Eds.), *The child in his family* (Vol II, pp. 195–209). New York: Wiley.

Cain, A. C., Fast, I., & Erickson, M. E. (1964). Children's disturbed reactions to the death of a sibling. *American Journal of Orthopsychiatry, 34,* 741–752.

Eth, S., & Pynoos, R. S. (Eds.). (1985). *Post-traumatic stress disorder in children.* Washington, DC: American Psychiatric Press.

Feinberg, D. (1970). Preventive therapy with siblings of a dying child. *Journal of the American Academy of Child Psychiatry, 9,* 664–668.

Furman, R. A. (1973). A child's capacity for mourning. In E. J. Anthony & C. Koupernik (Eds.), *The child in his family* (Vol. II, pp. 225–231). New York: Wiley.

Gogan, J., Koocher, G., Foster, D., & O'Malley, J. (1977). Childhood cancer and siblings. *Health and Social Work, 2*(1), 42–57.

Krell, R., & Rabkin, L. (1979). The effects of sibling death on the surviving child: A family perspective. *Family Process, 18*(4), 471–477.

Lieberman, F. (1979). *Social work with children.* New York: Human Sciences Press.

Lindsay, M., & MacCarthy, D. (1974). Caring for the brothers and sisters of a dying child. In L. Burton (Ed.), *Care of the child facing death* (pp. 189–206). Boston: Routledge & Kegan Paul.

McCollum, A. T. (1974). Counselling the grieving parent. In L. Burton (Ed.), *Care of the child facing death* (pp. 177–188). Routledge & Kegan Paul.
Rosen, H. (1986). *Unspoken grief: Coping with childhood sibling loss.* Lexington, MA: D. C. Heath.
Rosen, H., & Cohen, H. (1981). Children's reactions to sibling loss. *Clinical Social Work Journal, 9*(3), 211–219.
Rosenblatt, B. (1969). A young boy's reaction to the death of his sister. *Journal of the American Academy of Child Psychiatry, 8,* 321–325.
Sarnoff, C. (1976). *Latency.* New York: Jason Aronson.
Sourkes, B. M. (1980). Siblings of the pediatric cancer patient. In J. Kellerman (Ed.), *Psychological aspects of childhood cancer* (pp. 47–69). Springfield, IL: Charles C. Thomas.
Thunberg, U. (1977). Death and the dying adult. In R. C. Simons & H. Pardes (Eds.), *Understanding human behavior in health and illness* (pp. 387–394). Baltimore: Williams & Wilkins.
Webb, N. B. (1991). Assessment of the child in crisis. In N. B. Webb (Ed.), *Play therapy with children in crisis: A casebook for practitioners* (pp. 3–25). New York: Guilford Press.

CHAPTER EIGHT

Suicidal Death of Mother
Cases of Silence and Stigma

NANCY BOYD WEBB

A suicide stops time. Before it happens, it is unimaginable. When it does happen, it feels unreal, out of time. . . . You can't get angry at a suicide, and you can't grieve. If you ask *why?* any possible answer seems to implicate you. Your questions become guilty: *How did I fail her? What could I have done?*

—HAMMER (1991/1992, p. 16)

The death of a parent is a cruel loss for a child to endure, but when it is the result of the parent's own actions, the child's feelings churn in a confused mixture of disbelief, fear, helplessness, rage, and profound sadness. the mother, more than any other adult, usually holds the key to the child's sense of security and well-being. Even in times of war or of great personal danger, the child feels safe in the mother's presence. Whereas the father also provides protection, the mother typically spends more hours of the day feeding, comforting, bathing, and disciplining the child. Therefore her significance to the preschool- and school-age child looms very large. The normal narcissism of young children focuses them on the private worlds of their own bodies and families, and in this world the mother reigns as sovereign. When she abdicates her role, the child fears that his/her physical needs may no longer be met, and that no one else will ever provide the same unconditional love.

It has been estimated that annually between 7,000 and 12,000 children in the United States have a parent who commits suicide (Small & Small, 1984). Because deaths by suicide are notoriously underreported, the actual number is undoubtedly higher. Regardless of the precise figure, however, the legacy of suicide bequeaths to the survivors many negative feelings and thoughts regarding their own actual or possible role in having precipitated the suicidal act or having failed to abort it. *It can be a heavy load* (Shneidman, 1975).

SUICIDE BEREAVEMENT

Several factors contribute to the belief that "suicide is the most difficult bereavement crisis for any family to face and resolve in an effective manner" (Cain, 1972, p. 11). McIntosh (1987) enumerates the following three features as pronounced in families with child survivors of parental suicide:

1. Guilt
2. Identification
3. Information/communication distortion

We know that feelings of guilt and of identification with the deceased may occur after any death. Among those bereaved by suicide, however, these reactions may be more extreme.

Guilt

Worden comments that "guilt feelings are normal after any type of death, but in the case of death by suicide they can be seriously exacerbated" (1991, p. 94). Children, because of their magical thinking, may ascribe exaggerated influence to the power of their thoughts. This leads them to the unfounded conclusion that wishing for something can make it come true. For example, if, in anger, the child felt a fleeting death wish toward the parent who later committed suicide, the child may believe that his/her wish caused the death. It is ironic that the young child can feel simultaneously so helpless and so powerful in the aftermath of death!

Identification

McIntosh (1987) elaborates that the child's identification with the deceased parent may take the form of assuming the parent's former role within the family, or of displaying similar behavior or symptoms as the suicidal parent. Some children even identify with the deceased parent to the extent that they become resigned to the probability or certainty that they will also die by suicide (McIntosh, 1987, pp. 78–79). These children may, in fact, be at risk and should be monitored closely.

Information/Communication Distortion

Denial, evasion, lack of open discussion about the suicide, and even fabrication and distortion of the facts have been reported by many researchers who studied child survivors of parental suicides (Cain & Fast, 1972; Shepherd & Barraclough, 1976; Pfeffer, 1981; McIntosh, 1987; Worden, 1991). Due to family members' wish to protect the young child and themselves from the truth, they may participate in what Cain and Fast (1972) refer to as a "conspiracy of silence" about the facts surrounding the death. They present the death as accidental, and then they create a myth about what really happened to the victim. Worden explains that "if anyone challenges this myth by calling the death by its real name, they reap the anger of the others, who need to see it as an accidental death or some other type of natural phenomenon" (1991, p. 96).

The young child, of course, is very confused by this misinformation. When the child later learns the facts about the death, he/she may feel an intense sense of betrayal and erosion of trust because of the deception, Pfeffer (1981) suggests that lack of open discussion, denial, and distortions can result in serious psychological problems for the child, in addition to hindering the mourning process and the child's normal development.

Distorted communications may have been the pattern in the family long before the suicidal death, however. Hurley states that "pretraumatic family conditions are generally problematic in families in which suicide occurs" (1991, p. 237). The reasons for these problematic conditions may relate to alcoholism, child abuse, marital discord, or psychiatric illness such as depression. Worden states that "within this context ambivalent feelings may already exist among family members, and the suicide only serves to exacerbate these feelings and problems" (1991, p. 96).

A suicidal death is a stigmatized death, causing the family to feel shame and humiliation because of the expectation of social disapproval when the true facts become known. The family that alters information about a suicidal death is trying, either deliberately or unconsciously, to protect itself from the personal implications of admitting the truth, and from the withdrawal of social support it expects to accompany the revelation of the facts. Christopher Lukas, whose mother fatally cut her throat when he was 6 years old and who was not told the true cause of her death until he was 16, comments that "socially, suicide is considered to be an aberrant act, and the family of the person who kills himself comes in for some powerful public opprobrium. . . . It is only recently that organized religions have changed from a punitive approach toward the suicidal person to a relatively beneficent one. For centuries, people who killed themselves were buried at crossroads, their hearts often pierced with a stake.

Survivors were shunned, excommunicated and robbed of the suicide's possessions" (Lukas & Seiden, 1987, p. 19).

The use of secrecy, silence, and even distortion to protect the familial "survivors" of suicide must be understood in the context of society's views about such deaths. The term "disenfranchised grief" (Doka, 1989) refers to losses, such as suicide, that are not socially sanctioned and, therefore, cannot be openly acknowledged or publicly mourned. When the adults cannot speak frankly about the death, children sense that something is wrong, and that they should not ask questions. It is too terrible to discuss. In the absence of correct information children supply their own fantasized explanations, frequently implicating themselves in their parent's death because of something they said or did. Open discussion about the circumstances of the death would permit the child to ask questions and to relive his/her guilt.

Anger

Since suicide represents a *voluntary* act, the survivors often feel rejected and abandoned by the deceased. The question "How and why did he/she do this to *me?*" may not be articulated as fully by the child survivors as by adult family members, but children are, nonetheless, vulnerable to feeling abandoned. They may wonder whether Mommy really loved them, and if she did, how could she have left them? Often the child concludes that he/she was "bad," with resulting negative impact on his/her self-esteem.

Expression of anger toward the deceased parent, however, would create even more anxiety for the child. Instead, the anger frequently becomes detoured onto other targets, such as therapists, teachers, babysitters, and other whom the child may resent for any similarities to the lost mother. This was an important factor in the response of 9-year-old Jimmy, whose mother had killed herself when he was 5 and who resisted all my best efforts to engage him in therapy. He could not permit himself to form a relationship with another woman. Worden warns therapists that suicide survivors may act out in counseling as a way to cause the counselor to reject them "in order to fulfill their own negative self-image" (1991, p. 98). The unique treatment challenges in working with the child bereaved by suicide will be discussed more fully later.

TRAUMATIC COMPONENTS
OF SUICIDE BEREAVEMENT

Although the death of a parent may not necessarily qualify as a "traumatic" event in the strict sense of the definition of posttraumatic stress disorder (PTSD) (see Chapter 11), there is little doubt that the *suicidal death* of a parent frequently leads to responses in survivors that meet the necessary criteria for PTSD. Depending on the manner of death, the possible disfigurement of the body, whether or not the child witnessed the death or discovered and/or viewed the body—all these factors can contribute to intrusive memories about the death that can seriously delay or interfere with grieving. Eth and Pynoos state that "reminiscing, so essential to the bereavement process, may be drastically inhibited because the intrusive images of the violence interfere with the child's efforts to recollect pleasant memories of earlier parent–child interactions" (1985, p. 175). They argue for early treatment that initially focuses on the circumstances of the trauma in order to pave the way for more open expressions of grief. The child needs to express and deal with feelings of horror connected to the manner of the death before he/she can deal with grief reactions of sadness and guilt. Thus, *the treatment of the child suicide survivor includes dual tasks of trauma mastery and grief resolution* (Eth & Pynoos, 1985, p. 183; emphasis mine).

It is common for children whose parent committed suicide to engage in re-enactments and imitation in play of the parent's suicidal behavior. This may be the result of their identification with the deceased parent or it may indicate their own symptoms of depression. Since statistics attest to increased risk of depression and suicidal behavior among children of survivors (Adam, 1973; Brown, Harris, & Bifulco, 1986), it is imperative that all child survivors of parental suicide receive prompt intervention by a professional trained in grief counseling, in crisis intervention, and also in play therapy.

TREATMENT OF THE SUICIDE-BEREAVED CHILD

Few forms of bereavement present more challenges to the therapist than that of intervention with a child who has lost a parent to suicide. The therapist/counselor must draw from an extensive knowledge base including a thorough understanding of child development and family dynamics as well as experience in working with children who have been traumatized. In addition, the therapist should be knowledgeable and experienced in the area of grief counseling and regarding the expectable pattern of *children's* grief, as distinct from that of adult bereavement. Funeral directors and hospital and school personnel should be prepared to refer families with suicide-bereaved children to mental health professionals who possess this specialized training.

One of my motivations in publishing this book is to call attention to the special needs of bereaved children that are all too often overlooked. A former student, now an M.S.W. and a Certified Grief Counselor with more than 10 years' experience working with bereaved families in a hospice setting, confided that he was extremely uncomfortable and felt ill-prepared to work with bereaved *children*. Indeed, there is no reason to expect that a therapist/counselor who is expert in treating adults would automatically be able to work successfully with children, any more than we would expect a gerontologist to feel equipped to work on a pediatric service! Intervention with the *child* client requires experience in the specialized method of play therapy, whether the setting is a hospital or hospice. When the child is bereaved by a parent's suicide, the need for specialized treatment is even *more* imperative.

Chapter 3 discussed Worden's (1991) distinction between "counseling" and "therapy," clarifying that grief *counseling* intends to facilitate the tasks of uncomplicated grief, whereas grief *therapy* focuses on helping resolve disabling or traumatic grief. The experience of Dunne-Maxim, Dunne, and Hauser (1987) in their work with suicide survivors leads them to conclude that the suicide of a close relative or friend constitutes a psychic trauma in children who feel emotionally overwhelmed and helpless in the throes of this event. These clinicians contend that "some form on interventions with children is *always* necessary following the suicide of a relative or friend, and that failure to provide it does a grievous disservice to the child" (1987, p. 244; emphasis mine). The need for prompt intervention with child survivors following a suicide is also emphasized by Fox (1985) and Hurley (1991). I repeat here my opinion that the intervention should be provided by a child therapist who is trained in trauma and grief counseling.

Challenges in Therapy with Child Survivors

Avoidance

The child whose parent has committed suicide may attempt to avoid the pain of this loss by refusing to discuss it. Hurley points out that the child may resist therapy because the therapist talks and asks questions about the deceased parent: "the child protests the incursions of the therapist into his or her inner space and denies that there are feelings that bother him or her other than the therapist's questions. A typical response is: 'I'm doing fine' " (1991, p. 241).

The therapist who is trained in play therapy can invite the child to draw or play and thereby develop a relationship with the child through nonverbal, symbolic expression that is less threatening to the child's defenses. It is important to move at the child's pace, keeping in mind that children can tolerate only *limited* exposure to painful feelings.

The Therapist's Reaction

It may be difficult for the therapist to withstand his/her *own* intense feelings that emerge in working with a child whose mother has voluntarily ended her life. The therapist must guard against over identification with the survivor's feelings of anger toward the "abandoning" parent. There is a fine, but crucial, line between accepting the child's anger and joining with it.

Feelings of sadness may also threaten both the child and the therapist. Children consider crying "babyish" and do not agree with adult beliefs that crying will bring relief. At times, the therapist's conviction about the value of expression of feelings may be shaken by the child's indignant accusation that talking and crying "just make me feel *worse!*" Again, moving at the child's pace, gives the child a measure of control over his/her life under circumstances in which he/she has felt totally powerless.

Developmental Considerations

Always important in therapy/counseling with children, the understanding of the child's developmental level is *crucial* in working with the suicide-bereaved. Because of the nature of the death and the intense reactions (both expressed and masked) of family survivors, the young child can become immobilized with confusion. Worden quoted Polombo in noting that children between 5 and 7 years of age are particularly vulnerable to a parent's death. This is because their cognitive development permits some understanding of the permanence of death, yet "their ego skills and social skills are insufficiently developed to enable them to defend themselves. This particular group should be singled out for special concern" (Polombo, 1978, quoted by Worden, 1991, p. 25). If this holds true for parental death, in general, it is all the more relevant for the young child whose parent died from suicide.

Various Treatment Options

The decision about how to intervene in a helping role with the bereaved child and family always depends on a number of factors, including the willingness of the family to involve the child, in addition to the pragmatics of the counseling treatment options available at a given time and place. Some schools, for example, routinely offer bereavement counseling groups on a biannual basis for any child who has experienced a death in the intervening period (see Chapter 13). However, the decision about whether or not to include a child who is bereaved by *suicide* in a group of children whose parent or other relative died from natural or accidental causes must be very carefully weighed. Dunne-Maxim et al. (1987) are not in favor of including young suicide survivors in bereavement groups because of the "potential for additional trauma when children are exposed to a variety of 'horror stories,' which are the inevitable legacy of a suicide death" (p. 244). Whereas it might be very supportive for a child to know that one or more other children besides him/herself have also suffered the suicidal death of a parent, it is unlikely that the incidence and timing of such deaths would permit the formation of a group of children who are bereaved exclusively by suicide. The possibility that the child suicide survivor might feel stigmatized or ostracized in a heterogeneous group due to the circumstances of his/her parent's death represents a potential obstacle that could override the anticipated benefits of group membership.

Because of the numerous potential pitfalls in bereavement groups for child suicide survivors, my preference is for family therapy, individual therapy, and peer-pairing as intervention options that, singly or in combination, can best meet the needs of the young child bereaved by a parent's suicide.

Family Therapy

As an antidote to the secrecy, shame, and distortion that often surround a suicidal death, family therapy is clearly the treatment of choice. An example of this form of intervention can be found in Chapter 3 following the death of a grandmother, although this was a natural, not a suicidal, death. The goal in bringing the family together after a death is to facilitate the grieving process through active reminiscing about both positive and negative characteristics of the deceased. For reasons already discussed, this process may be delayed in the case of a suicidal death, until traumatic elements connected with the suicide have been aired.

Frequently, a combination of family therapy and individual play therapy is appropriate following a suicidal death. Hurley (1991) discusses a multilevel intervention in work with a family of three children ages 12, 8, and 4½, after the suicidal death of the father. The 12-year-old boy was experiencing anxiety and disturbing nightmares, the 8-year-old boy was angry and aggressive, and the 4½-year-old girl was tearful, clinging, and insistent on sleeping with her mother. The father, a psychiatric patient with a diagnosis of psychotic depression with paranoid features, shot himself while on leave from the hospital.

The treatment plan for this bereaved family included weekly family therapy sessions focused on bereavement counseling, parent counseling for the mother who had difficulty providing the children's care and discipline, plus individual play therapy sessions for the children. In the individual play therapy, the young girl, Cathy, revealed that she "knew how her daddy had died but that her mommy said she did not want her to talk about it" (Hurley, 1991, p. 245). It was important for the therapist to clarify with the mother that Cathy needed permission to talk about her father during the therapy sessions.

In situations where the family is unwilling or unable to come together for family therapy, the therapist must, nonetheless, maintain contact with the parent in order to help the parent help the child: Sometimes the therapist uses a psychoeducational approach guiding the parent according to the child's needs. This goal may be achieved only marginally, however, as in the family presented by Hurley, due to the mother's need to preserve the myth that father's death had been "a sacrifice on behalf of the family." Despite the mother's defensiveness, however, Cathy benefited greatly from individual play therapy in which she was able to explore some of the feelings of loss, confusion, and guilt about her father's death.

Individual Therapy

Young children generally are confused by death. As reviewed in Chapter 1, they may not understand that it is final and irreversible, and they do not understand what causes it. In a family session, many of the child's misunderstandings may be glossed over, in the face of the adults' greater verbal skills, unless the therapist is especially sensitive to children's typical concerns. Also, the child may be unwilling to expose his/her fears in the presence of the surviving parent, either because the child wants to spare the parent pain, or because the child understands the parent's implicit message "not to talk." For all of these reasons it is important for a trained play therapist to see the young child on an individual basis, assuming that the parent has given the child *permission* to talk freely with the therapist.

In the first three individual play therapy sessions with Cathy (Hurley, 1991, pp. 242–251), the following issues/themes were broached via play in sand, with Plasticine, and with dolls:

- Bad and happy dreams about daddy, "out of the coffin"
- Wishing that daddy would come back
- Disfigured "cookie faces" ("broken/messed up"—like father's wounds?)
- Burial of dolls in sand (verbal connection to father in coffin)
- Tells therapist she is not allowed to say father shot himself

- Anger toward brother (Plasticine figure), who is "bad" (possible blame for father's death?)

The child, through play, communicates feelings symbolically and frequently nonverbally. The transcript of the play therapy sessions with Cathy reveals several points when the child closed up, asked to leave, or refused to talk when the therapist tried to move too quickly into *verbal* connection between what the child was playing out and her life experience related to her father's death. My preference in this instance would have been to conduct the therapy within the metaphor of play, without attempting interpretative comments.

It is highly unlikely that Cathy would have been able to express her concerns in a family session, especially in view of her mother's prior admonition *not* to talk. The mother's needs to protect her own feelings about her husband's death would have interfered with allowing the young child to question and to explore *her* unique concerns. This situation prevails frequently in families with a suicide, and it therefore behooves therapists/counselors to arrange *individual* treatment for the young child, whose needs otherwise may be totally overlooked.

Peer-Pairing

Peer-pairing is a method of providing support while also facilitating grieving. It consists of matching individuals who have certain characteristics in common and offering therapy to them conjointly. This helping method can be beneficial "when group or individual therapy proves to be too overwhelming or threatening" (Bluestone, 1991, p. 257). Mervis states that

> pairing is also effective in working with children who feel they are very different from others or who have severe family problems. These children need the opportunity to share feelings and experiences, but it can be too risky to expose them to a group setting in which they might be vulnerable to ridicule or rejection. Through peer-pairing, the children gradually can learn to trust others and to share some of their feelings and experiences in a more controlled and accepting environment. *When the sharing becomes mutual, the sense and isolation these children feel can be greatly reduced.* (1985, p. 125; emphasis mine)

Bluestone paired a 9½-year-old girl whose mother committed suicide by shooting herself with a 10½-year-old girl whose father died suddenly of a heart attack. Despite the differences in ages and in the manner of death of their parents, these girls developed a strong, supportive relationship with the help of the school social worker who brought them together for this purpose. Their shared characteristics were the sudden loss of a parent and the fact that each had been socially isolated.

The peer-pairing technique for helping children bereaved by suicide has yet to receive the attention it deserves. There may be an intrinsic danger in pairing a suicide-bereaved child with a child whose parent died of natural causes, as happened in Bluestone's case when Cindy expressed horror to Rosa about the manner of her mother's suicide death. If two children, both suicide-bereaved, could be paired together, the possibility of support would be greatly enhanced even as the possibility of stigma would be irrelevant.

AUTOBIOGRAPHICAL CASES: CHRISTOPHER, AGE 6, AND SIGNE, AGE 9

In contrast to the rest of this book, both of the cases presented below are based on published autobiographical accounts, used here with the consent of the authors (see Lukas & Seiden, 1987; Hammer, 1991/1992). Both adults, in childhood, suffered the suicidal deaths of their mothers and each wrote about the impact of this experience retrospectively.

Christopher Lukas, Age 6 (at Time of Mother's Suicide)[1]

Family Information

> Mother, age 33, history of manic-depressive illness; previous treatment with electroconvulsive therapy; currently in psychotherapy; killed self following therapy session, by cutting her throat in psychiatrist's garden
>
> Father, successful lawyer; in conflict with mother-in-law regarding modality of wife's treatment (wanted wife to have another course of electroconvulsive therapy; disapproved of psychotherapy)
>
> Brother, age 8, away at summer camp at time of suicide
>
> Christopher, age 6, told that mother was "ill"; sent to friends house overnight, and then to brother's camp for 10 days following mother's death
>
> Mother's mother, age 50, "domineering"; in conflict with son-in-law regarding daughter's therapy, and, later, regarding what to tell Christopher and his brother about the death

[1]I am grateful to Chistopher Lukas for permission to reprint material from his book, *Silent Grief: Living in the Wake of Suicide*, 1987, New York: Scribner's. Copyright 1987 by Christopher Lukas and Henry Seiden.

Presenting Problem

When Christopher Lukas's mother killed herself there was a disagreement between his father and his grandmother about what to tell the children. The father evidently could not endure facing the truth, and he convinced the family to keep the nature of the death a secret for 10 years. When Christopher finally was told by his father, the explanation given to the 16-year-old boy was that his mother had been "sick." Not until many years later, after a "prolonged psychoanalysis," did Lukas seek out the police and hospital reports documenting the graphic and distressing details about his mother's traumatic death.

Within a year of his mother's death, Christopher's father contracted tuberculosis and went away to a sanitarium in a distant state. This necessitated enrollment in boarding school for Christopher and his brother, who thus became further removed from their family and the possibility of discussion about their mother and disclosure about her death.

Comment: Familial "Bargain of Silence"

Lukas writes as follows about the implicit pressure he felt *not* to talk about his mother nor to ask questions about her death:

> The bargain between family members not to talk about the suicide was in full force. I did not violate its terms for many years; I did not make any attempts to penetrate the silence. Why? Because I felt the pressure *not* to ask questions. No one volunteered anything, so the rule appeared to be that you weren't supposed to talk about that particular death. . . . That silence has been maintained remarkably well for forty years. With rare exceptions, no one in my family has brought up my mother's suicide. . . . In fact, the dictum of silence is so strong that I encountered numerous depressions and anxieties during the writing of this book. Only with a lot of soul-searching did I realize that they were due to the fact that I was breaking the rule of silence that had been established over forty-five years ago. (Lukas & Seiden, 1987, pp. 198–199)

Psychosocial Development (Ages 6–20)

Cognitive Confusion. Because there had been no funeral, no memorial service, or any concrete *evidence* that his mother had died, Lukas says that he created his own myth of disbelief. He had no proof that his mother had been ill and, therefore, he did not believe that she was dead. He says that he invented ways to explain how or why his mother had left, and believed, also that she would return.

Lukas states that he believed that if he avoided doing anything "wrong," his mother might come back. This contributed to perfectionsistic behavior that Lukas, in retrospect, describes as "goody-goody" and prudish. He further believes that this effort prevented his ability to engage in normal playful behavior, typical of childhood and adolescence.

Affective Relationships. It is not uncommon for survivors of suicide to experience difficulty in establishing trust. When one's primary love relationship inflicts pain from abandonment, the expectation of similar hurt prevails in future relationships. Lukas states that his relationships with both male and female peers suffered. He could not trust men since his father had lied to him, and his expectation of rejection by women led him to reject them first.

Somatic Symptoms. Lukas states that he had severe stomach aches that often kept him from going out. These were especially pronounced when he had a date. He views them now as a form of punishment related to his guilt about his mother's death.

Forty Years Later

Lukas went into psychoanalysis when he was 22, which led to alleviation of his stomach problems, and gradually to improvement in his relationships with people. His book represents the working through of many of his feelings about his mother's death, and it certainly constitutes a removal of the silence barrier in his family. The fact that several others of his relatives died of suicide may have proven a further impetus to his examining the literature on the topic of suicide with the intent of understanding the impact of suicidal death on himself and his family.

It is a testament to therapy that Lukas has been able to marry, and to achieve happiness as a husband and father of two daughters. It is interesting that his choice of career, as a writer and director in public and commercial television, puts him in a role in which *communication* is essential!

Signe Hammer, Age 9 (at Time of Mother's Suicide)[2]

Family Information

> Mother, Agnes, age 44, of Norwegian ancestry; legal secretary prior
> to marriage; currently a homemaker; depressed, thin, anxious, per-
> fectionistic, shy, nervous; unhappy in her marriage; wanted a
> divorce, but was unable to face the family and social disapproval
> this would create; killed self in own kitchen by breathing fumes of
> gas oven
> Father, John, age 46, of German ancestry; civil engineer; retired Army
> officer; army service for 2–3 years during World War II, during
> which time he was away from family; employment necessitated
> many family moves
> Brother, Arno, age 18, a freshman in college; away from home; had
> been high school football player and had sung in chorus
> Brother, Hal, age 15, a Boy Scout; interested in guns; liked to hunt
> and skeet shoot
> Brother, Eric, age 13, mother's favorite; jealous of Signe
> Signe, age 9, successful in school; taking French and piano lessons
> until Father eliminated them; variety of friends; sensed mother's
> withdrawal and depression and the tension between parents

Presenting Problem

At the time of her mother's suicide, Signe Hammer's parents' marriage
was evidently under great stress due to a recent job transfer that motivated her father to want to move. The family had moved frequently
throughout the marriage. As Hammer reconstructs these events almost
40 years later, her mother was greatly attached to the house they had
lived in for 4 years, and could see no way out after her father purchased
another house and insisted that the family move yet again in order to
reduce his commuting time.

The father's single-handed house purchase may have been the last
straw in a relationship in which the partners had been in conflict for several
years following the father's return from the war. During his absence the
mother had managed to run the home, although Hammer remembers her
mother as being depressed at times.

[2]I am grateful to Signe Hammer for permission to reprint material from her book,
By Her Own Hand: Memoirs of a Suicide's Daughter; hardcover, 1991, New York: Soho
Press; paperback, 1992, New York: Vintage. Copyright 1991 by Signe Hammer.

Despite the problems in the parents' relationship, the children appear to have been developing normally. Hammer was very aware of a lack of support from her father for both her mother and herself. A general tone of misogyny pervaded family interactions. Hammer now believes that her father stopped her French and piano lessons in order to "get at" her mother (1991/1992, p. 130).

Comment: A Family Systems View of Suicide

Hammer, a writer and editor who has published journalism, poetry, and fiction as well as nonfiction books, sensed intensely the inner dynamics of her family tragedy. She writes: "This suicide, like all real tragedies, was a family affair. The Greeks and Shakespeare understood what we deny; that, in families, actions almost always have a reason" (1991/1992, p. 19).

Of course, the real tragedy is that the young child finds the reason in his/her *own* behavior, rather than in that of the adults. Hammer writes: "The questions haunt me, past all the family speculations: Could any of us—myself, for instance—have saved her, and was one of us—myself, for instance—therefore responsible for the fact that she died? Or for the fact that she turned on the gas in the first place?" (1991/1992 pp. 20–21).

Developmental Considerations

Hammer captures the spirit of *the middle-latency-age child* as follows: "By the time my mother killed herself. . . . I had reached high childhood, when a girl is both competent and mobile, and had not yet been betrayed by her flesh into sexuality and death. I was immaculate, and free. . . . My mother was in her up period. . . . We were all acting like a family. . . . I came into my own as a child at last. . . . My buoyant mood made me a success" (1991/1992, pp. 101–105).

These idyllic memories partly explain the young girl's understandable anger toward her father, whose life-long egotism and chauvinism prevented any consideration of his wife's or children's feelings.

Although Signe and two of her brothers found her mother's body, and Signe had been given the choice about whether or not to attend the funeral (she declined), there was never any discussion in the family about her mother's suicide or death. Hammer writes: "When I was with other kids, it sometimes felt as though nothing had ever happened. I was floating through a dreamy landscape, a never-never land of sweet trivialities. . . . We had no words for feelings, but even if we had, I would not have been able to use them. . . . Behind the terror I felt very small and very empty, completely inadequate to deal with such an immensity. Above all, I felt intense shame, for myself and for her, and a terrible dread. She had made a huge mess and implicated me. Sooner or later, I would have to pay for it" (1991/1992, pp. 150–151).

The Scapegoat Role

As with the most children after a death, the young Signe tried to figure out the reasons: "After the suicide, the scapegoat coat fit me like a second skin. My aunts had been telling me my mother was an angel. When an angel commits suicide, you can't get angry at her for leaving you, for throwing away her life and ruining yours. I believed I must have done something terribly wrong to provoke her rage, to make her reject me so completely" (Hammer, 1991/1992, pp. 169–170). Furthermore, she believed that her mother monitored her behavior from heaven: "I could no longer sneak away, because my mother's view was no longer confined to the angles commanded by the front and side windows of her bedroom. *Now she sat next to God and saw everything*" (Hammer, 1991/1992, p. 154; emphasis mine).

Forty Years Later

Among Hammer and her brothers, "one is manic–depressive; on lithium, the classic drug. The other three . . . are, to varying degrees, chronically depressed. All of which could be the work of an inherited trait or disease" (Hammer 1991/1992, p. 17). Psychoanalysis helped Hammer understand her parents' marriage and its tragic outcome. She wrote her memoirs partly to discover why her mother committed suicide and partly to break the family silence.

CONCLUDING COMMENTS

Of all the chapters in the book, this one has been the most difficult to write. Helping the child following the suicide of his/her mother is analogous to providing temporary shelter following the total destruction of home and community in a violent earthquake: We do what we can to pick up the pieces, but life will never be the same again. The therapist/counselor in this situation has to face and accept limits of his/her ability to help.

The two autobiographical accounts give us hope. Both child survivors of their mothers' suicides have developed into productive, creative adults, who still bear scars, but whose lives hold meaning. The fact that both are highly intelligent, and had some extended family support and the financial resources to afford psychotherapy as adults, perhaps sets them apart from many survivors without such opportunities. However, they represent an attainable ideal.

The unanswered question for me remains whether it might have been possible to have provided therapy to these children when they were younger and if that might have made a difference in their lives. In thinking about this we need to consider the family context including, especially, the closed communication system which, in part, may contribute to the suicide as a "cry for help." However, suicides *do* occur in families such as Christopher's in which a therapist is involved. Again, we must accept the limitations of therapy.

Intervention with the child whose mother has committed suicide must focus on helping the child understand that he/she was not responsible. This message will need many repetitions. The therapist also should help the family find a way to reinforce this fact. The family may need assistance in recognizing the child's form and timing of grieving to be different from that of adult grief. Because of the discontinuous nature of children's grief, the child therapist can plant the seed with the family that the child may benefit from therapy to sort out his/her feelings either now or *in the future*. If the therapist can "normalize" the child's need to speak with someone outside the family, it may facilitate an appropriate future referral.

Because the family itself is in grief, it may be appropriate to follow up after 6 months to again offer therapeutic intervention. The process of suicide bereavement will take many years, often requires professional intervention and, even then, will leave lasting scars.

DISCUSSION QUESTIONS

1. Discuss some of the typical reactions in families of suicide survivors, analyzing the dynamics that contribute to the "conspiracy of silence" which often prevails.

2. How would you help a family talk with a 4-year-old about the suicidal death of his/her mother? Be specific, indicating what facts and feelings the family should be prepared to communicate.

3. Answer the question above with respect to a 9-year-old child.

4. How can the counselor/therapist deal with his/her own reactions in working with a family in which a suicide has occurred?

5. What is the special contribution of a play therapist in working with a child bereaved by suicide?

REFERENCES

Adam, K. (1973). Childhood parental loss, suicidal ideation and suicidal behavior. In E. J. Anthony & C. Koupernik (Eds.), *The child and his family: The impact of disease and death* (pp. 275–297). New York: Wiley.

Bluestone, J. (1991). School-based peer therapy to facilitate mourning in latency-age children following sudden parental death. In N. B. Webb (Ed.), *Play therapy with children in crisis: A casebook for practitioners* (pp. 254–275). New York: Guilford Press.

Brown, G. W., Harris, T. O., & Bifulco, A. (1986). Long-term effects of early loss of a parent. In M. Rutter, C. Izard, & P. Read (Eds.), *Depression in young people: Developmental and clinical perspectives* (pp. 251–296). New York: Guilford Press.

Cain, A. C. (Ed.). (1972). *Survivors of suicide.* Springfield, IL: Charles C. Thomas.

Cain, A. C., & Fast, I. (1992). Children's disturbed reactions to parent suicide: Distortion and guilt, communication and identifcation. In A. Cain (Ed.), *Suvivors of suicide* (pp. 93–111). Springfield, IL: Charles C. Thomas.

Doka, K. (1989). *Disenfranchised grief.* New York: Free Press.

Dunne-Maxim, K., Dunne, E. J., & Hauser, M. J. (1987). When children are survivors. In E. J. Dunne, J. L. McIntosh, & K. Dunne-Maxim (Eds.), *Suicide and its aftermath* (pp. 234–244). New York: Norton.

Eth, S., & Pynoos, R. S. (Eds.). (1985). *Posttraumatic stress disorder in children.* Washington, DC: American Psychiatric Press.

Fox, S. (1985). *Good grief: Helping groups of children when a friend dies.* Boston: New England Association for the Education of Young Children.

Hammer, S. (1992). *By her own hand: Memoirs of a suicide's daughter.* New York: Vintage. (Original work publishd 1991)

Hurley, D. (1991). The crisis of paternal suicide: Case of Cathy, age 4½. In N. B. Webb (Ed.), *Play therapy with children in crisis: A casebook for practitioners* (pp. 237–253). New York: Guilford Press.

Lukas, C., & Seiden, H. (1987). *Silent grief: Living in the wake of suicide.* New York: Scribner's.

McIntosh, J. L. (1987). Survivor family relationships: Literature review. In E. J. Dunne, J. L. McIntosh, & K. Dunne-Maxim (Eds.), *Suicide and its aftermath* (pp. 73–84). New York: Norton.

Mervis, B. A. (1985). The use of peer-pairing in child psychotherapy. *Social Work, 30*(2), 124–128.

Pfeffer, C. (1981). Parental suicide: An organizing event in the development of latency-age children. *Suicide and Life Threatening Behavior, 11,* 43–50.

Polombo, J. (1978). *Parent loss and childhood bereavement.* Conference on Children and Death, University of Chicago.

Shneidman, E. S. (1975). Postvention: The care of the bereaved. In R. O. Pasnau (Ed.), *Consultation–liaison psychiatry* (pp. 245–256). New York: Grune & Stratton.

Shepherd, D. M., & Barraclough, B. M. (1976). The aftermath of parental suicide for children. *British Journal of Psychiatry, 129,* 267–276.

Small, A. M., & Small, A. D. (1984). Children's reactions to a suicide in the family and the implications for treatment. In N. Linzer (Ed.), *Suicide: The will to live vs. the will to die* (pp. 151–169). New York: Human Sciences Press.

Worden, W. (1991). *Grief counseling and grief therapy. A handbook for the mental health practitioner.* New York: Springer.

CHAPTER NINE

Violent Deaths of Both Parents
Case of Marty, Age 2½

TERESA BEVIN

One month after the tragic news hit the papers, Marty was being protected by his grandparents from the fallout of having witnessed his father shoot his mother to death. Police found him covered with blood, cuddled against his mother's body, his arms around her neck and his cheek pressed against hers. She was still alive, but her heart stopped as soon as they took Marty off her. His father was found in the locked bathroom, shot in the head by his own hand. Two neighbors had seen Marty's father enter the apartment with his key, then they heard three shots, and then another that seemed to come from deeper with the apartment.

Marty's father had a history of abuse as a child, had suffered from depression most of his life, and often talked about suicide. He was frequently absent from the home and spent very little time with his son. During the short periods of time that he spent with Marty, he yelled at him and called him "stupid" for romping or making noises. Marty's mother was an active, hard-working, and intelligent young woman caught in an unhappy marriage to a man who had physically abused her at least twice. She spent all her spare time with her bright and inquisitive 2-year-old son. He was included in most of her socializing, went with her to the grocery store, to the beauty parlor, to church, and sometimes she would even take him to her office, where Marty was spoiled by the staff. Marty's mother was very close to her parents, who were always willing and ready to be involved in the upbringing of their grandson.

156

BEREAVEMENT IN EARLY CHILDHOOD

Marty's anguish and desolation after the deaths was immediately apparent, but his grandparents thought that because of his young age, he would become accustomed to the situation. Eventually, they realized that both Marty and they needed help in coping with the tragic events that had altered their lives so drastically. Through the use of toys, activities, and guided play, Marty began slowly to reaffirm his self-image, leading, it is hoped, to understanding and, eventually, acceptance of the finality of his mother's abrupt departure from his world.

The work of several practitioners and researchers provides a framework for understanding this case. Raphael (1983) projects the process of bereavement through the entire life span, focusing especially on the bereaved infant and child. Raphael states that a child in the 2- to 5-year-old age range can experience grief similar to that of adults, "but others may not perceive his responses as bereavement." Because others find "his recognition of death and his painful mourning intolerable they may deny him his feelings and their expression" (1983, p. 95).

The work of Malmquist (1986) also bears on this case, particularly as it is centered around the posttraumatic aftermath related to children who witness parental murder. Aside from the obvious trauma connected with the murder of the prime attachment figure, the issue of delayed intervention is mentioned. In his investigation of 16 children who had witnesses parental murder, "most of the cases seem to have had a minimal or no psychiatric intervention prior to the raising of legal issues" (1986, p. 321). In Marty's case, the grandparents waited 1 month before seeking help for him.

Krueger (1983) addresses the developmental consequences of loss as they relate to diagnosis and treatment. In reference to pre-Oedipal loss between the ages of 2 and 4, Krueger states that when the child is "unable to register or comprehend the concept of permanent loss," restitutive fantasies are imposed in order to maintain "an idealized image of the parent who is hoped to return" (1983, p. 585).

Terr (1988) discusses how memories of terrifying events during the preschool years may manifest themselves in later years. She observes that studies show that memories of nontraumatic experiences can be later modified, but "studies do not establish what happens to a childhood memory of real trauma." In her study she establishes the differences between behavioral and verbal memory and discusses approximate ages at which a trauma can be recalled verbally. Her findings show that the age of 2½ to 3 years "appears to be about the time most children will be able to lay down, and later to retrieve, some sort of verbal memory of trauma" (Terr, 1988, p. 97).

THE CASE: MARTY, AGE 2½

Family Information

Mother, Galiana Vega, age 25, legal secretary
Father, Martin Vega, age 28, computer specialist
Only child, Martin Vega, Jr. ("Marty"), age 2½
Grandmother, Demetria Gonzaga, age 55, retired teacher
Grandfather, Melchor Gonzaga, age 54, businessman

Religion and Culture

Marty's family is of Spanish origin. His mother's family was originally from Andalusia, and his father's was from Castille. Historically, both families had been actively involved in the Spanish Civil War and were Socialist in their ideology. Religion had not played an important part in their lives, except for Galiana, Marty's mother, who had embraced the Catholic church after her marriage, perhaps in search of counsel and solace over her problems with her husband. However, the Spanish Catholic church is rich in tradition, and Marty's grandparents did adhere to this. They observed Catholic holidays and religious customs. This meant that the funeral was Catholic, and a memorial mass was offered 1 week afterward. Normally, children attend these ceremonies, but Marty's grandparents protectively decided to keep him away from it and sent him to spend a week at the beach with family friends.

Presenting Problem

Marty's grandparents were trying to help their grandson with his tragic loss, even as they, themselves, were grief-stricken. They distracted him, bought him toys, took him out often, indulged and pampered him. They had never been involved with any kind of therapy. When they realized that Marty needed more than their love and care, they began to make phone calls in order to find someone who could help them in their first language. Marty's family functioned in Spanish at home, so they had always wanted the child to learn Spanish before English.

By the time Marty came to me, 1 month had passed since the murder of his mother and his father's suicide. Marty had lost weight, appeared lethargic and whiney, and had abandoned his favorite toys. Malmquist noted how common it is that psychological attention is so often late or nonexistent in cases like this, perhaps because of "the need to deny some of the aftereffects of traumatic events" (1986, p. 321). For Marty's grandparents, this negligence is very understandable, since they were identifying with Marty's pain. As Raphael indicated, to avoid painful memories the surviving adult may deny that the child is affected by the loss, "then he may be left with residual vulnerabilities to separation and loss" (1983, p. 80).

Marty was told that his mother had gone to heaven because God loved her and had called her. Of course, Marty could not conceive of his mother leaving without him. He would call her, look for her all over his grandparents' home, and would fantasize that he was talking with her on the phone. He begged his grandfather to take him "home" where he used to live with her. It was difficult for him to fall asleep, and then he would wake up calling her. Tantrums were a daily occurrence, and Marty regressed to baby talk whenever he was frustrated or tired. "It is at this age that the infant is first unconsolable for his 'own and only mother' whom he has lost." There is no consolation because "no other person can take away the anguish of his screams. . . . He wants simply her" (Raphael, 1983, p. 82). Bluestone noted that "the death of such a loved one leaves the bereft child with a world that may never again be as secure and safe a place as it was before" (1991, p. 254).

Marty became very attached to his grandmother's cat and wanted to sleep with him, perhaps for added security. Once the cat spent the night outside the home and Marty was inconsolable. Krueger warned that the trauma of loss has implications for intrapsychic organizations during development, as "the loss frequently provides a sensitizing precursor for any subsequent experiences of loss" (1983, p. 582), and this can impact on natural losses that occur in adult life. I was keenly aware of this child's terrible tragedy and his vulnerability as I began my work with him.

First Sessions

The first session was focused on earning Marty's confidence. His grandmother stayed in the room and Marty seemed comfortable, playing, running around, asking many questions, and behaving like any 2-year-old. His most outstanding quality was that he spoke very clearly and loudly, although not often, giving the appropriate inflection to his questions. He indicated he needed to go to the bathroom at the proper time, and gave no signs of disturbance.

For the second session, 6 days later, Marty was alone with me. He cried a little at the beginning but his attention quickly moved to a bright clown that had not been in the room the previous time. Marty went to it and grabbed it. He played with the clown, moved around the room holding it, and then "walked" it. He later moved from one toy to the next, dragging the clown, then sat on a small chair, sucked his thumb and looked at me, with his arms around the clown. I asked him if he was sleepy but he did not answer. I moved toward him, patted him on the knee, invited him to play, but he suddenly burst into tears, threw the clown on the floor and walked toward the door, calling his grand-mother.

When the time came for the third session, 1 week later, Marty was throwing a tantrum and had to be carried in by his grandfather. Marty's grandfather told me that every time they drove past a McDonald's restaur-ant, Marty would scream for them to stop because he had "seen" his mother. She used to take him there once a week for burgers, soda, fries, and to play on the colorful swings. One their way to this particular ses-sion, their route took them past a McDonald's. Not only did Marty in-sist that his mother was outside the restaurant waiting for him, he also said he could see her, and called out to her, punching his grandfather's arm when he wouldn't stop the car.

As stated by Krueger, the lack of cognitive development to compre-hend the concept of death as final, causes the child to conceptualize the loss as a reversible departure: "It is a common fantasy of the child who loses a parent to expect a return . . . "; this expectancy is first "consciously and later unconsciously experienced" (1983, p. 584). Bowlby (1963) in-dicated that the typical grief reaction begins with shock, protest, and anger. The individual cannot believe that the person is really dead, and chil-dren are likely to remain in denial for a very long period of time.

Once in my office, Marty continued to cry for about 10 minutes. Finally, he noticed a group of toys on a low table and stopped crying. He looked at the toys, then at me, all this while hanging on to his grand-father's shirt. It took a while for him to let go and walk toward the toys. Then Mr. Gonzaga walked out of the room.

Content of Session	Analysis and Feelings
THERAPIST: (Sits on the floor, close to the toys.)	Wondering if he will be able to focus. The memory of the "lost" mother is so terribly painful.
MARTY: (Approaches the table with his hand behind his back. Looks at me.)	
T: We can play with that. Go ahead.	
M: (Walks around the table, picking one toy, then another. Sits on a small chair, carefully, checking around for boundaries. Grabs a hammer. Bangs the table.)	

Touches and grabs toys, asking what they are.) What's this? (*Smiles easily. Moves his chair closer to me, seems to expect directions.*)

T: (*Moves closer to Marty.*)

M: (*Gets up, looks for a new toy, wheels a little wooden dog around the room. Stops and looks around.*)

T: There are more toys in that box. (*Points to a large wooden box.*)

M: (*Picks up a set of family figures using both hands, places them on the table. Goes back to the box and picks a toy gun. Presses the trigger several times, pointing in different directions.*)

T: What do you have there?

M: Gun. (*Turns toward me and shoots several times.*) Bam! Bam!   A moment that was expected and feared at the same time.

T: Ouch! (*Takes hands to chest and leans against the wall.*)   I am not sure about what to do here.

M: (*Moves toward me, aims at my head at close range.*) Bam! Bam! Bam! (*Frowns, seems to concentrate on what he is doing. He shoots many times.*)   His mother had been shot in the head at close range.

T: (*Stays still for a few seconds.*)   I doubt whether this is a good idea.

M: (*Moves toward the chair quietly and sits down, leaving the toy gun on the table.*)   He seems overwhelmed by the memory of the traumatic event.

T: (*Sits up.*) What happened?

M: (*Shrugs his shoulders.*)

T: (*Walks toward Marty. Sits next to him.*) What happened?

M: (*Sucks his thumb, stares into space. Does not talk again during the session.*)   My heart goes out to him but I cannot reach him.

Preliminary Assessment and Treatment Plan

Because witnessing the murder of a parent is a rare event, it is very difficult to draw conclusions. The attempt at making any generalization is hindered by the absence of statistical support (Malmquist, 1986). In cases when a child has been the witness of a parent's murder, the differences in circumstances can significantly complicate research efforts. Krueger states that "the loss event is important as well as the loss process: the chain of events preceding, set in motion by, and subsequent to the loss" (1983, p. 583). The perpetrators vary greatly as they may be known or unknown; the witnessing may be only auditory, or only part of the scene may be witnessed. In some cases, the child may be hurt him/herself. The reaction of the family after the murder is another important variable, both in the way they conduct themselves and the way they handle the child witness, including the period of time that passes before consulting a professional.

In Marty's case, not only did he see his mother die violently, but his own father committed the murder. Despite the father figure's "distance" from Marty and his mother, a young child focuses a great deal of attention on the male identification model. In addition, this father was dragged from the bathroom, in front of Marty, bloody and limp. Hurley (1991) explored the particular complications in the death of a parent by suicide, in which the grief process is affected by the manner of the loss. The difficulty in treating Marty was compounded by this twist of fate. Another factor in this case is that the grandparents were very close to Marty, but their own grief got in the way of the attention they could give him and their ability to perceive or understand his signals.

Marty's sadness, intrusive thoughts, fitful sleep, tantrums, and fear of separation from his grandparents fulfilled the *Diagnostic and Statistical Manual of Mental Disorders* (DSM-III-R; American Psychiatric Association, 1987) criteria for posttraumatic stress disorder. This case is further complicated by the possible repercussion of the criminal act performed by the father, which Marty attempted to imitate in a session with the toy gun as he tried to communicate what he saw. He may have found some relief in this replay of the traumatic scene, as stated by Webb: "Through replay of the crisis experience the child transforms the passivity and impotence he or she experienced into activity and power" (1991, p. 30). However, the nature of the criminal act leaves many questions as to how such an early memory may manifest itself as the child gets older. Terr found that "repeated and/or variable events (as in child abuse) are less fully remembered than are single episodes of trauma" (1988, p. 97) and that events that are short in duration are recalled more fully than longer events. Consequently, Marty's re-enactment of the shooting itself may signal a more vivid memory than the subsequent bloody scenes, and may remain imprinted for years to come.

The positive side in the aftermath of these events resided in Marty's grandparents, who were dedicated to him, committed to making him feel secure, loved and needed. His grandmother often recruited his help in making cookies, and always complimented him, saying how grateful she was for his help. His grandfather, in turn, would take Marty with him on his errands, soliciting his cooperation in carrying little bags, holding doors open for him, and also showing a great deal of appreciation for Marty's help.

It was obvious to me that Marty might need long-term therapy; my intervention was limited to stabilizing the crisis and referring him to a long-term therapist. It was difficult to find a Spanish-speaking professional, but 2 months from the initial session a suitable referral was located. My focus, then, was to strengthen Marty's self-image, address the finality of his loss and ultimately, yet very carefully, transfer the case to another therapist who would stay with it for an indefinite period of time. Through play therapy, I was planning to proceed intuitively, because there was very little in the way of research to which I could refer that could help me treat this child.

Play Therapy Sessions

The session described below was crucial in Marty's reconciliation with reality. He had been attending weekly sessions for 2 months. Each session was 1 hour in duration. Sometimes one or both of his grandparents would have to be present because he felt insecure and feared he would not see them again if they left the room. The need for their presence, however, diminished with each session.

On this occasion, not only was Marty able to be alone with me without discomfort, but anticipating his arrival, I seized what I hoped might be a therapeutic opportunity: a dead goldfish. One of my colleagues had a fish bowl with several goldfish in it. One fish had just been found dead, so I asked my colleague to lend me the bowl with the dead fish in it. About 5 minutes into the session, Marty noticed the fish bowl in front of the window. I had placed it on a low table so he could see it up close. I then pretended to be surprised in finding the dead fish.

Content of Session   *Analysis and Feelings*

THERAPIST: Oh, my! . . . I'm afraid this fishy is dead. (*Takes it out of the water and places it on a paper towel next to the bowl where the other fish were alive and well.*)

MARTY: (*Looks at the dead fish intently.*)

T: It's dead, see? (*Touches the fish, lifts it, puts in the palm of her hand.*) Do you want to touch it?

Wondering how he will respond.

M: (*Reaches out, very carefully receives the fish in his hands, stares at it while he strokes it with index and middle fingers.*)

T: It is dead, Marty, you see? It can't swim anymore, it is like he's asleep, but he can't wake up.

M: (*Keeps stroking the fish.*) No. twimmin'.

T: No, no swimming. We have to put him in the earth. We have to bury him. See the others. They are going to be sad because they miss him, but he can't swim with them anymore.

M: (*Shifts attention to the live fish while still holding the dead one.*) They sad.

T: Yes, they're very sad because their brother is dead, and now they don't have him anymore. He can't swim, he can't do anything. So we have to bury him. Do you want to help me bury him?

M: (*Nods, with a very serious facial expression, as if in deep thought.*)

T: We are going to need a few things. (*Finds a spoon to use a a shovel, and a tiny box for the fish. Gives the box to Marty.*) That's so you can put him in the box.

Not sure if there is any point in doing this, since the child did not attend the funeral. But his grandparents had tried to explain to him what had happened to his mother's body.

M: (*Puts the fish in the box. Looks toward me for directions.*)

T: Now we can go to the yard to bury him. (*Tries to take Marty by the hand, but he prefers to carry the box with both hands. We go to the yard, to a large planter.*) You see, Marty? This is what happens when somebody is dead. Everybody is very sad, and they have to bury the one who's dead. Do you want to make a hole in the dirt with the spoon?

Hoping on some level that the symbolism/metaphor will be meaningful to him.

M: (*Nods, gently puts the box on the ground, takes the spoon, and carefully begins to spoon loose dirt out. Makes a huge hole and seems to get lost in the activity.*)

I wonder if he understands the meaning of the procedure.

T: That's very good, you have made a very big hole for the fish. Now you have to put the box in the hole.

M: (*Lowers the box in the hole with care. Once again expects directions from me.*)

T: Now we have to cover the box with dirt.

M: (*With his hands, begins to scoop dirt and put it over the hole.*)

T: (*Helping Marty.*) Now maybe we should find a stone to put here so we know where the fish is.

M: (*Looks around and quickly finds a stone which he puts on top of the small mound.*)

T: Very good. How about a flower?

M: (*Quickly finds a flower and half buries it on the mound.*)

T: Well done, Marty. You know that's what happened with your mommy when she was dead.

M: Shot. Daddy shoot Mommy.

T: Yes, when Daddy shot her, it was like she was asleep and she couldn't wake up. Then Granny and Grampy had to take her and bury her, and they were very sad. It also happened with your daddy.

M: Where's my mommy?

Shows no interest in his father.

T: You want to know where she is? Where they put her?

M: (*Nods.*)

T: We have to ask Granny and Grampy.

Apprehension about the reaction the grandparents may have to this idea.

As I found out later, Marty's grandparents were receptive to the idea. They had not visited their daughter's grave since the burial and thought

it would be good for all of them. They had started to talk about the funeral
and burial in front of Marty and he had asked many questions about
where his mother may be "asleep."

During the following session, Marty seemed cheerful, even when he
told me about the visit to his mother's grave:

Content of Session	Analysis and Feelings
MARTY: Mommy has flowers and flowers.	Relieved by his reaction after visiting the grave.
THERAPIST: Did mommy like flowers?	
M: (*Nods.*) The fishy like flowers.	
T: Do you want to put a new flower for the fishy?	
M: (*Nods.*)	

This did not mean acceptance, but it was a beginning. Marty's grandparents observed that after visiting the grave, he seemed less restless and
had begun to sleep better. He still looked out the window as if waiting
for her, and when he heard the turn of the key he would often expect
her to open the door. Then he would throw a tantrum out of disap-
pointment.

On a subsequent session, I experimented with some fingerpaints.
Marty enjoyed wearing an apron "like Mommy's." He focused on the
red fingerpaints, ignoring other colors; he smeared paint on his chest and
arms, and remained quietly staring at his arms for a few minutes; he
smeared some on a large piece of paper, smelled it, and tasted it. His
movements were deliberate and slow. After approximately 15 minutes,
he insisted on washing himself completely, putting away the paints, and
playing with something else. On later sessions, whenever the paints were
offered, he rejected them. The red paint seemed to provide Marty with
the opportunity to re-enact his experience of being covered with his
mother's blood.

Mr. and Mrs. Gonzaga continued to visit the grave with Marty and
to talk about the incident at home. They reported that Marty would listen
without asking questions, as if trying to reach his own conclusions.

The next challenge was termination and transfer. It was time for
Marty's new therapist to take over the case. I knew that (fortunately)
I had not become a substitute for the lost mother. This was probably
due to the nurturing and dedication of his grandmother. However, Marty
had felt very comfortable in the last five sessions, had been affectionate
toward me, and had obviously given some emotional meaning to the time
he spent in session. In order to make the transition as easy as possible,
I requested the cooperation of his new therapist.

She attended the last two session with Marty and me to establish a bond. It was explained to Marty that he would be going to her office instead of mine. He was told that I was not going away, that he could visit me from time to time if he asked his grandparents. He did not seem uncomfortable at all, and seemed to accept his new therapist quite well.

CONCLUDING COMMENTS

According to Krueger, "a mourning process is initiated by the perception of loss as well as an acceptance of its permanence and irreversibility. One factor precluding mourning is the maintenance of the fantasy of the retrievability of the loss" (1983, p. 590). Had Marty really initiated his mourning process? For children, the mourning process takes years "because children can only tolerate small does of painful feelings" (Bluestone, 1991, p. 255).

In dealing with this case, I often felt I was in the dark because there is a paucity of literature on the subject of the very young child witness to violence. In Marty's case, the violence of the event, the identity of the perpetrator, and the child's age made it impossible to follow any particular guidelines. It is certain that Marty will need ongoing help as he grows and understands more fully how his parents died. The grandparents also will benefit from ongoing assistance to help them convey to Marty that both his parents loved him and that he did not cause, nor could he have prevented the tragedy that occurred. The outcome for Marty may depend strongly on the support of those who love him and their willingness to put time and energy in raising him in a loving home, nourishing him with security, making him feel important and needed.

DISCUSSION QUESTIONS

1. Discuss the normal grief of a 2½-year-old child related to the death of a parent. What explanations about the death are appropriate in working with a child this age?

2. If the therapist had not utilized the burial of the dead goldfish as part of her work with this child, what other play therapy materials or experiences would you consider introducing?

3. What counseling issues do you consider important in work with the grandparents?

4. How would you assess Marty's prognosis? At what developmental stages do you consider that he might be "at risk" and why? What interventions might serve as a preventive purpose?

5. How would you avoid becoming a substitute for the lost parent while establishing a strong relationship with a preschool-age child?

REFERENCES

American Psychiatric Association. (1987). *Diagnostic and statistical manual of mental disorders* (3rd ed., rev.). Washington, DC: Author.

Bluestone, J. (1991). School-based peer therapy to facilitate mourning in latency-age children following sudden parental death. In N. B. Webb (Ed.), *Play therapy with children in crisis: A casebook for practitioners* (pp. 254–275). New York: Guilford Press.

Bowlby, J. (1963). Pathological mourning and childhood mourning. *Journal of the American Psychoanalytic Association, 11,* 500–541.

Hurley, D. J. (1991). The crisis of paternal suicide. In N. B. Webb (Ed.), *Play therapy with children in crisis: A casebook for practitioners* (pp. 237–253). New York: Guilford Press.

Krueger, D. W. (1983). Childhood parent loss: Developmental impact and adult psychopathology. *American Journal of Psychotherapy, 37*(4), 582–591.

Malmquist, C. P. (1986). Children who witness parental murder: Posttraumatic aspects. *Journal of the American Academy of Child Psychiatry, 25*(3), 320–325.

Raphael, B. (1983). *The anatomy of bereavement.* New York: Basic Books.

Terr, L. (1988). What happens to early memories of trauma? A study of twenty children under age five at the time of documented traumatic events. *Journal of the American Academy of Child and Adolescent Psychiatry, 27*(1), 96–104.

Webb, N. B. (1991). Play therapy intervention with children. In N. B. Webb (Ed.), *Play therapy with children in crisis: A casebook for practitioners* (pp. 26–42). New York: Guilford Press.

CHAPTER TEN

Play Therapy Group for Bereaved Children

DONNA CASEY TAIT

JO-LYNN DEPTA

The mourning of children is often unrecognized or minimized. Adults frequently see children as being "too young to understand" and "quick to recover" following a death. Children may be shamed about crying when tears are interpreted as a sign of weakness. Faith may be used inappropriately to replace mourning. Whereas grieving adults are consoled, bereaved children by contrast are passed over.

Children deserve open and honest information about death, grief; and mourning. It is not in the child's best interests to withhold information and details in the name of protection since children cannot cope with what they do not know. The child's recovery may be seriously compromised by withheld or inaccurate information.

Children's grief differs from that of adults' in the manner in which children express it. They miss their deceased father on Father's Day or their deceased mother on Mother's Day, but children may act out their feelings and the misunderstood behavior may result in discipline or punishment.

Sometimes children may harbor guilt about the death as a result of their magical thinking. For example, they may have wished in a moment of anger that their parent would disappear, go away, or die, and if that occurs they may believe that their thought made it happen (Wolfelt, 1991). Regression may enable the child to gain a sense of safety and security as the child returns to earlier developmental behavior, such as talking baby talk, wanting to be held and rocked, sleeping with a parent, and resistance to separation from the living parent. The regression precludes the child's taking over some of the roles and responsibilities of the deceased, as sometimes expected and encouraged by family members.

PLANNING THE BEREAVEMENT GROUP

The literature on children's grief and mourning is quite sparse; in fact, this field is still in its infancy! In preparing this play therapy group, we studied the work of Wolfelt (1991), Worden (1991), and Segal (1984).

Wolfelt (1991) has identified the following six tasks of grieving children:

1. To experience and express outside of oneself the reality of the death
2. To move toward the pain of the loss while being nurtured physically, emotionally, and spiritually
3. To learn to convert the relationship with one who has died from one of interactive presence to one of appropriate memory
4. To develop a new self-identity based on a life without the person who has died
5. To relate the experience of the death to a context of meaning
6. To experience a continued supportive and stabilizing adult presence in future years

We also reviewed Worden's (1991) four stages of mourning which involve these four basic tasks:

1. To accept the reality of loss
2. To experience the pain of grief
3. To adjust to an environment in which the deceased is missing
4. To emotionally relocate the deceased and move on with life

The development of our bereavement group was based on Worden's and Wolfelt's concepts which we synthesized into four central themes:

- The pain of grief
- Exploration of roles and changing roles
- Reinvestment of energy into the current world
- Closure

To incorporate these themes into action we adapted activities from Segal's (1984) article "Helping Children Express Grief through Symbolic Communication." We planned the structure and format based on the guidelines of the Family and Community Development Program (Rude-Weisman, Todd, & Lilja, 1992). Table 10.1 presents the agenda of activities for this grief group.

TABLE 10.1. Children Dealing with Loss Group: Agenda of Activities

Session 1	Focus:	Introduction.
	Activities:	Define death. Introduce question box. Draw death as peaceful and harsh while listening to music. Draw the family (if time available).
Session 2	Focus:	Express feelings.
	Activities:	Clay: Design something related to death.
Session 3	Focus:	Express feelings.
	Activities:	Feeling charades, body movements as animals, and connecting feelings to a small body map.
Session 4	Focus:	Explore roles and changing of roles.
	Activities:	Family sculpting: past, current, and future.
Session 5	Focus:	Explore roles and changing of roles.
	Activities:	Family sculpting: past, current, and future. Design a future-wish poster.
Session 6	Focus:	Reinvest missing energy into the current world.
	Activities:	Read children's storybook about death. Puppet play: Since the death what has changed and will change for the future?
Session 7	Focus:	Closure.
	Activities:	Saying good-bye in action with message to the deceased inside a helium balloon. Message box to self.
Session 8	Focus:	Closure.
	Activities:	Graduation party. Pizza, certificates, graduation pictures, star bookmarks, and evaluation form completed.

Rationale for Group Approach

This group was developed to meet needs of bereaved children that could not be accommodated as effectively in an individual therapy approach. Our rationale rests on the following premises: groups tend to facilitate normalization; groups provide peer support; groups break the sense of isolation; and a cohesive group creates a safe place to share taboo issues.

A cofacilitation approach was used for this group because we wanted to ensure that the ratio between supportive adults and actively grieving children would be as low as possible. Having two facilitators enables one therapist to focus and meet the needs of a child in stress, while the other facilitator is able to continue with the group process.

CASE EXAMPLE: CHILDREN'S BEREAVEMENT GROUP

The children we worked with were in pain as experienced in nightmares, anger outbursts, academic and social difficulties; they were withdrawn, cautious of others, hurt, abandoned, and depressed. They were trying to cope with a traumatic event that had drastically changed their lives. The group members were as follows:

Name	Age	Person who died	How long ago
David (DV)	7	Father	3 yrs.
Jordan (JD)(sibling of ML)	7	Father	4 yrs.
Justin (JS)	8	Mother, sister	9 mos.
Joel (JL)	10	Father	3 mos.
Adam (AM)	10	Mother, grandmother, two family friends	3 yrs.
Andrea (AN)	10	Mother	3 mos.
Melissa (ML)(sibling of JD)	11	Father	4 yrs.
Dan (DN)	11	Uncle	18 mos.
Aaron (AR)(sibling of TO)	11	Stepfather (5 years)	18 mos.
Tom (TO)(sibling of AR)	11	Stepfather (5 years)	18 mos.

Two children (Andrea and Adam) observed death in a parent with a prolonged illness involving long hospital stays, a gradual deterioration of health, and preliminary family discussions regarding the inevitable death. The other eight children had no warning. They experienced death as a sudden, traumatic, unexpected event. One child (Andrea) lost everything in her life including a pet she left behind when she moved in with relatives. Five of the children were witnesses to the frightening discovery of their parent's death. Two children experienced multiple deaths in the family.

Screening Procedures

Prior to the group each child was screened for his/her ability to benefit from the group experience and to identify the best possible service to meet the current needs of the child. Five children were referred to the grief group by school teachers or principals, four children were currently receiving services at the Family and Community Development Program, and one child was referred by a government agency. Screening information was gathered individually from parents or guardians. Screening questions focused on the child's relationship to the deceased, the length of time since the death, current difficulties exhibited by the child, parental expression of grief, and whether or not the child was given an opportunity to say good-bye to the deceased.

Nine of the ten children experienced the death of a *parent*. The length of time since the death ranged from 3 months to 4 years. Most of the children either were having difficulty expressing their anger in ways that were safe to themselves and others, or were withdrawn, depressed, and unable to express any emotions. Most of the parents had difficulty talking about the death objectively, with the exception of one parent who spoke of the death experiences with an apparently angry denial that the death of a spouse would generate an emotional response.

The proposed group activities listed on the agenda were described to the parents in order to allow them to make an informed decision regarding parental consent for their child to attend the group sessions. The parents were directed to describe the activities to the children and to encourage them to attend the first two sessions before allowing the children to decide against attending further group sessions.

Cotherapist Facilitator Preparation

Prior to the first session, both facilitators met to discuss the implications of this therapy group since death is a difficult and taboo issue impacting on therapists as well as "clients"/participants. We each discussed our awareness regarding death and losses in our own lives. *The importance of this task cannot be understated as unresolved issues, particularly in this area may hinder the healing process for those we are trying to help.*

First Group Session

As each child arrived, they were welcomed by one of the facilitators. Each was asked to make a name tag and they were directed to the free-play area where all the children would play for 15 minutes as we circulated, conversing with the children. After the initial period, the group proceeded to a big table for snack time. We introduced the grief group by saying that everyone here has experienced the death of a loved one and that the purpose of the group was to help each other. We began by inviting the children to come up with a group rule. After several replies the rule was decided and summarized as "Be kind to each other in words and actions."

One of us (J.L.D.) introduced the issue of death by asking, "What does death mean?" We adopted a nonjudgmental stance while focusing on this sometimes scary topic. Some of the responses included heaven and hell, darkness, goblins, and ghosts. The other therapist (D.C.T.) stated that each of us has a right to believe or disbelieve what we choose. The children were invited to discuss family beliefs at home. We introduced a question box during this discussion, explaining that any question about death and dying could be written anonymously and placed in the box and that the facilitators would answer to the best of their ability. We wanted to let the children know that we do not have all the answers, that some areas of death remain a mystery to us, and that we were comfortable in not knowing all the answers.

With the topic introduced, we explained the activity of drawing two pictures, one expressing what they felt was harsh about death and another picture of what they might feel is peaceful about death. The children began by drawing peaceful expressions of death while listening to Handel's Water Music. After 10 minutes they were asked to switch to what they felt was harsh about death. The song "The Storm—the Destruction" from Disney's *The Little Mermaid* was played during the time period for the second drawing. To enable a sense of safety for this exercise we general-

FIGURE 10.1. One child's drawing of death as peaceful.

ized the topic by not naming the deceased. Our intention was for the drawings to be symbolic.

The pictures of peace included flowers, heaven, angels, crosses, cemeteries, and coffins, and tended to be still (see Figure 10.1); harsh pictures included airplane crashes, guns, blood, darker colors, murders, and action and motion. A couple of the children drew a mix of personal information and symbols. Three children questioned their peers regarding the identity of the person in their family who had died, and some children copied ideas from others. We observed this exercise to be safe, expressive, and enjoyable for the children. The exercise seemed somewhat abstract for the younger children. The music was not essential but assisted in the atmosphere.

Session 2: Clay

Prior to this session the group engaged in 15 minutes of free-play time and 15 minutes of snack time. The first 10 minutes of the theme activity follows:

Content of Session

(THERAPIST 1 = D.C.T.; THERAPIST 2 = J.L.D.)

T1: Today we are going to play with clay. You will each get a piece of clay to work with and you can use any of these tools you would like. I am asking you to design with your clay something related to death—death in general, like making a gravestone, or create something that makes you think about the death in your family or the person you lost.

MELISSA: What should we make?

T1: You could make something that reminds you of your loved one, like a book if they read, or a football if they like sports.

DAVID: I don't know what to do.

AARON: What are you making (*to neighbor*)?

DAN: Hmm.

JOEL: What?

Analysis and Feelings

The children ask for clarification and begin to show some anxiety. We attempt to break down the task to make it easier.

T1: Make something that reminds you about death.

ANDREA: I like clay.

MELISSA: It feels sticky.

AN: Can I add water?

T1: No, please stay in the room.

AN: This is too hard. We add water at school to soften it. Can I?

> Avoidance of task of testing limits.

T1: No. Try your best. You can use any of the tools.

JORDAN: I don't know what to make.

> Need for support.

T1: You can do it. Just make anything that makes you think about death.

T2: (*Quietly to Joel.*) You have started working. Tell me about your design.

JL: This is my Dad's face.

T2: I like how you are working so well. (*Time lapse of a few minutes while both therapists quietly approach each child individually to give attention and feedback on the clay work and behavior.*)

T1: (*Quietly to Justin who has not spoken yet and is wearing his coat zipped up.*) Hmm, tell me about your clay.

JUSTIN: (*Silence for a minute then he begins to speak in a shaky voice.*) It is the train that hit Mom and Susan in our car and killed them. (*He begins to cry, tears rolling down his face, then opens into sobs with his head resting on his arms on the table.*)

> Justin moves directly into the intense experience of feeling the pain of the loss.

T1: You took great care in making your design. You miss them very much don't you.

JS: Yes. (*Sobbing increases.*)

T1: Justin, I'm so sorry that you have this big hurt. You are such a neat boy. I feel your hurt. It is good to have tears. They help us let out some of that pain and hurting inside of our bodies.

> I am in tears and begin to feel swallowed up by Justin's heartache. I look around and make eye contact with J.L.D. I sense her support and strength. She is available to the other

JS: (*Continues to cry openly, he accepts my embrace of an arm around his shoulders. He stops briefly then swells into another round of tears.*)

ML: I remember those tears.

AN: I'm so sad. What can we do to help?

ML: I don't know.

DN: Poor guy.

JL: That's hard.

children so I feel safer and stay with Justin. As my strength returns I slowly become aware of the whispered support the other children are giving to Justin and myself. They are whispering. Maybe as a way to show their respect for the pain and not to disturb Justin. As I again look around the room I can see the children notice my tears. They do not look away quickly, instead I sense a feeling of belonging to the group. I sense we have all just now become a group, united in our hurts, pain, and the freedom to express this to each other.

Summary of Sessions 3, 4, 5, and 6

In *session 3* we played feeling charades, a guessing game involving nonverbal acting out of descriptive words by one group member while others guess the feeling word that is being charaded. We followed the charades game with another feelings exploration game we call body movements as animals. One group leader calls out the name of an animal while the group then tries to make appropriate body movements and sounds which mimic the animal, such as shark, lion, kitten, monkey, puppy, and alligator. These two games served as warm-up exercises for the children to each complete a body map of feelings. *The Body Map of Feelings* (Gregory, 1990) lists six feelings: happy, sad, angry, worried, love, and afraid. The children were asked to identify and illustrate on a doll-type drawing by color-coding feelings they felt in different parts of their bodies (see Figure 10.2). In their drawings, two children surrounded their bodies with fear (see Figure 10.3). We observed these siblings to be cautious in their approach to others and immobilized at times, unable to risk new activities. Four children drew anger in their hands and feet; these children had presenting problems of anger outbursts and temper tantrums (see Figure 10.4). Three children placed love and happy feelings on their heart but surrounded the heart with a shield of sadness and fear. One child drew a thick, heavy belt of fear across the stomach (see Figure 10.5); this child wore a coat zipped up to the neck throughout most of the sessions.

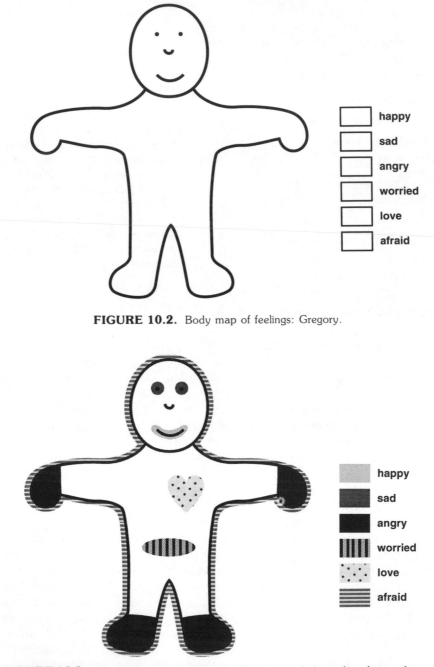

FIGURE 10.2. Body map of feelings: Gregory.

FIGURE 10.3. One child's feelings of surrounding fear and physical readiness of anger as coded on a body map.

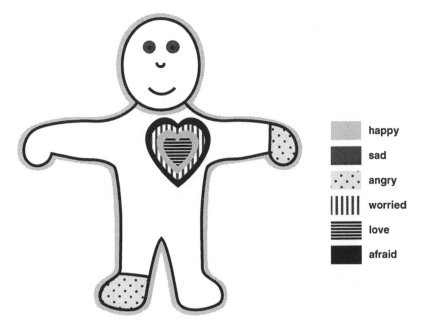

FIGURE 10.4. One child's feelings of anger shown in his dominant limbs, and feelings of worry, fear, and anger shielding a heart of love.

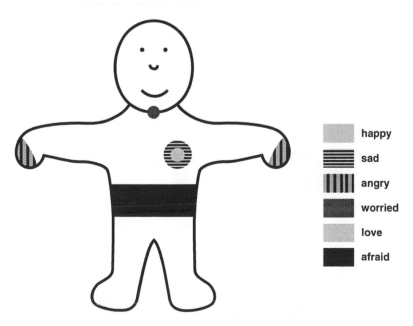

FIGURE 10.5. One child's thick belt of fear.

In *sessions 4 and 5* we asked the children to do family sculpting by using each other as actors and sculpt or show us what a typical day is like in their family at three points in time: as it was in the past, as the family is currently, and as a wish for their family in the future. When their poses were ready we took instant pictures of the family sculpting and gave these pictures to the children to take home. Our intent was to "walk" the children through the changes in family roles and activities before and after the death, and to include a wish for the future of the family. We were interested in whether the children could make a future wish. Most of the children made wishes for the future which included stepparents and more family time spent together. A few of the children posed their family as it was in the past, then were unable to go any further with the exercise. One child chose not to participate at all, possibly finding the exercise too revealing or difficult.

In *session 6* we read a children's storybook about the death of a parent (Vigna, 1991). The children were silent, attentive, and sober. We believe this book was symbolically cathartic, reliving the process of death, grief, and mourning. We then asked the children to present puppet plays to each other telling a story of what has changed in their lives since the death and what changes they would like for the future. The children had difficulty with the puppet plays. They teamed up in groups of three or four and the stories appeared to be unrelated to their personal experiences. We question if it was too hard for the children to move on to a new activity following the reality and power of the storybook. Possibly a focus on only the storybook or the puppet play would eliminate the need for a transition of play techniques.

Session 7: Saying Good-Bye in Action

This exercise was developed to assist in letting go while demonstrating that saying good-bye does not mean forgetting. The activity gives a child

FIGURE 10.6. Saying good-bye in action with message-filled balloons.

a taste of converting a real life relationship into an appropriate memory. The children began by writing a message to the deceased. They were asked to write anything they would want or need to say to the deceased if they were able to communicate with them. The note was placed inside a helium balloon with a string attached. When everyone completed the process the whole group proceeded outside with each child holding his/her own balloon(s) (see Figure 10.6).

Content of Session

T1: Let's form a circle.

T2: At the count of three everyone let go. One, two . . . (*A few children are not in the circle yet.*) Let's start again. One, two, three! (*The balloons are let go, and J.L.D. begins taking pictures with a camera.*)

DAVID: Look, look! (*Silence.*)

TOM: There's my balloon.

ANDREA: Can I have a picture?

T1: Yes.

MELISSA: Can I take a picture?

ADAM: They're getting higher and higher. (*Everyone watches and watches until the balloons are out of sight. A moment passes. We return to the group room.*)

Analysis and Feelings

With a lump in my throat I say good-bye to Grandpa (J.L.D.).

There is once again a sense of group cohesiveness and peace.

Comments on the Session

Our plan for the next session was to invite the children to write a message from the deceased in response to the message the children had sent. We asked the children to use the week between this session and next to think about what that person might want to say to them if they could.

Summary of Session 8

We organized this session around the purpose of a formal good-bye of the members to one another. We hoped that this would bring a sense of closure and healing related to the death. We held a graduation party including pizza, certificates, and picture taking. We asked the children to complete an evaluation form and then passed bookmarks around the circle, one for each child on which everyone wrote a positive characteristic they liked about each group member. At the end of the session, each child took home a certificate and photograph, a bookmark, and all their artwork and crafts created during previous sessions.

Self-Critique and Concluding Comments

Transference and Countertransference.

The facilitators defined transference/countertransference as "ghosting," meaning that someone or something triggered a ghostlike memory of an unresolved issue of grief or other issues. Ghosting by the children was not apparent during the sessions; the children seemed clear about the source of their own displayed grief and little projection took place.

The facilitators, however, were aware of their own ghosting. J.L.D. writes: "One young lad was picked on at school and attended the same school as my own children. The issue that ghosted was my memories of being bullied as a young child in elementary school which resulted in my feeling protective toward the child in the group, which was not necessarily helpful to him."

The death of my (J.L.D.) grandfather occurred during the course of this group. In contrast to the childhood memory, this was a current loss that enabled me to empathize and share my experience, yet remain objective. D.C.T. writes: "Facilitating this group reminded me of a recent loss due to a miscarriage and brought me closer to some feelings I was denying and repressing."

The danger of ghosting in bereavement support and counseling is the issues of which the facilitators are unaware and the feelings that arise which may inhibit facilitation of the *children's* pain. Protection from feelings due to the facilitator's or therapist's discomfort impedes the necessary expression of grief.

GUIDELINES FOR BEREAVEMENT GROUP THERAPISTS/FACILITATORS

Prior to beginning a play therapy grief group for children we recommend that the group therapists/facilitators take into account the following key factors.

Grief History

Explore your own grief history prior to facilitating a grief group. Grief work will undoubtedly bring up personal pain experiences associated with

TABLE 10.2. Personal Death History: Epp

1. The first death I experienced was the death of _____
2. I was _____ years old.
3. At the time I felt _____
4. I was most curious about _____
5. The things that frightened me most were _____
6. The feelings that I have now as I think of *that* death _____
7. The first funeral I ever attended was for _____
8. The most intriguing thing about the funeral was _____
9. I was most scared at the funeral by _____
10. The first personal acquaintance of my own age who died was _____
11. I remember thinking _____
12. I lost my first parent when I was _____ years old.
13. The death of this parent was especially significant because _____
14. The most traumatic death I ever experienced was _____
15. The most recent death I ever experienced was _____
16. At age _____ I personally came closest to death myself when _____

your own past grief. In preparation meetings the cofacilitators can explore with each other their personal death histories, discussing past experiences with death and current feelings of grief. Table 10.2 presents the Personal Death History for facilitators (Epp, 1992). Identifying these hurts prior to the group experiences can benefit facilitators by allowing them to discuss how they might handle overwhelming emotions experienced during group sessions. It was our decision to share answers to personal and direct questions from the children regarding our own grief experiences, but not to dwell on these responses. We chose to share our tears with the children as modeling for healthy and appropriate grief.

Parental Grief Information

Be prepared to provide grief support and information for the parent or guardians of the child. During the screening interview and over the telephone the parents showed their struggles to cope with their children's grief. An information package was presented to the families regarding local services and resources on grief and mourning for children and adults.

Group Preparation Time

Allow a few months for preparation and contact time prior to beginning the group. The therapists/facilitators need to explore together their grief histories, the community needs to be informed about the grief group, screening questionnaires and parental consent forms need to be completed, and assessment and evaluation forms need to be prepared and administered,

Evaluation

Measure and assess the effectiveness of the group. The use of a play therapy grief group for children is a recent innovation with few available guidelines. These groups require assessment as to the value and benefits of the sessions for the children. We chose to ask a parent to complete a 26-item pre- and posttest questionnaire regarding the child's behavior, and the children were asked to complete a four-item open-ended form. Results from the evaluation of this initial group were encouraging. We hope to offer this group again to further test the effectiveness of play therapy groups for bereaved children.

DISCUSSION QUESTIONS

1. Comment on the composition of this group in terms of diversity in ages, varying time interval of members' bereavement, and gender mix. One child who had *not* experienced the death of a parent was included with the others who had. Discuss the issue of heterogeneity versus homogeneity in the formation of a children's bereavement group.

2. How can the therapists/facilitators balance structured and unstructured activities in a children's play therapy bereavement group? Do you think an appropriate balance was achieved during these eight sessions? If not, what changes would you suggest?

3. Comment on the duration of this group. Do you think that the 8-week interval was an adequate time frame? What accommodation might be appropriate given the varying needs of individual children?

4. What are the advantages and disadvantages of the therapists'/facilitators' open expression of their feelings through crying? Do you think this was helpful or detrimental to the children in the group described?

REFERENCES

Epp, D. (1992). *Palliative care training manual.* Lethbridge, Alberta: Lethbridge Family Services.

Gregory, P. (1990). *Body map of feelings.* Lethbridge, Alberta: Family and Community Development Program.

Rude-Weisman, B., Todd, J., & Lilja, J. (1992). *Intake and assessment group format and procedures.* Lethbridge, Alberta: Family and Community Development Program.

Segal, R. (1984). Helping children express grief through symbolic communication. *Social Casework: The Journal of Contemporary Social Work, 65*(10), 590–599.

Vigna, J. (1991). *Saying goodbye to daddy.* Morton Grove, IL: Albert Whitman.

Wolfelt, A. (1991). Children. *Bereavement Magazine, 5*(1), 38–39.

Worden, J. W. (1991). *Grief counseling and grief therapy.* New York: Springer.

PART THREE

DEATH IN
THE SCHOOL
AND COMMUNITY

CHAPTER ELEVEN

Traumatic Death
of Friend/Peer
Case of Susan, Age 9

NANCY BOYD WEBB

The death of a friend is a crisis—a danger and an opportunity—for
surviving children. The danger is that the youngsters will be
emotionally overwhelmed by the death. The opportunity, however, is
the possibility of mastering the crisis and emerging with new
emotional strengths. . . . Children who must deal with the death of a
friend are indirect victims, at risk for emotional and behavioral
disturbances both at the time of the death and in the future.

—Fox (1985, pp. 3–4)

Accidental deaths occur randomly, sometimes striking even a 9-year-old
boy. Many children of this age know about death through their personal
experience of a pet's or a relative's death, and most have witnessed countless television deaths involving cartoon characters and "celebrities" in news
broadcasts. A few 9-year-olds may know a peer who is terminally ill with
cancer or AIDS. For the typical 9-year-old child, the concept of death
is an event that happens to someone who is remote in terms of age, ge-
ography, or state of health. The idea that death could strike a neighborhood friend on a weekday afternoon while being driven to an after-school
activity by his mother, is simply beyond the child's belief!

This chapter presents precisely this tragedy: the sudden, accidental,
mutilating death of a 9-year-old boy who died instantly when the car,
driven by his mother, went off the road into a ditch. The grieving survivors of this terrible accident included not only the dead child's immediate
family, but also the circle of school, church, and family friends who were
stunned by the sudden, irrevocable loss of a fun-loving, fourth-grade
student.

What reactions would we consider "normal" for the boy's 9-year-old friend, Susan, who had known him since nursery school, and whose mother was an intimate friend of her own mother? Susan did not cry, even at the funeral, nor had she spoken about her dead friend, Carl, since the accident. She refused to enter his house and waited outside in the car while her mother stopped to see Carl's mother. Susan was having nightmares and her mother was very worried about her because she "was holding all her feelings in." Susan's mother brought her for an evaluation 3 weeks after the accident.

It is sometimes difficult to distinguish between the reactions of "normal" grief and the symptoms of "posttraumatic stress disorder" (PTSD) (American Psychiatric Association, 1987). The following section discusses the topic of PTSD in children so that the reader can join me in determining whether Susan's response was within the range of "normal" grief, or more aptly diagnosed as PTSD. The case presentation also invites the reader to consider whether or not Susan "needed" therapy, and, if so, what kind and for how long. Because Susan returned for two follow-up play therapy sessions a year after the accident, we will also consider the topic of delayed mourning and its subsequent eruption in anniversary reactions.

POSTTRAUMATIC STRESS DISORDER IN CHILDREN

The diagnosis of PTSD has been used since 1980 to describe a group of reactions that occur following a distressing event "outside the range of usual human experience." Table 11.1 outlines the criteria necessary for designating this diagnosis, which "can occur at any age, including during childhood" (American Psychiatric Association, 1987, p. 249). We will examine these criteria with reference to Susan's symptoms at the time of her referral.

A. *Distressing experience.* The sudden death of Susan's friend, Carl, whose body was mutilated, clearly qualifies as a "distressing event outside the range of usual human experience." The "mutilation" involved severe damage to the head; this was not discussed openly by Susan's family in order to protect their own feelings of horror, as well as those of Carl's family. However, because rumors about the nature of Carl's injury circulated at school, Susan must have been aware that her friend's head suffered extensive damage in the accident.

B. *Re-experiencing the traumatic event.* Susan was waking nightly with distressing dreams of being chased by a monster. Although

TABLE 11.1. DSM-III-R Diagnostic Criteria for Posttraumatic Stress Disorder

A. The person has experienced an event that is outside the range of usual human experience and that would be markedly distressing to almost anyone, e.g., serious threat to one's life or physical integrity; serious threat or harm to one's children, spouse, or other close relatives and friends; sudden destruction of one's home or community; or seeing another person who has recently been, or is being, seriuously injured or killed as the result of an accident or physical violence.

B. The traumatic event is persistently re-experienced in at least one of the following ways:

   (1) recurrent intrusive distressing recollections of the event (in young children, repetitive play in which themes or aspects of the trauma are expressed)
   (2) recurrent distressing dreams of the events
   (3) sudden acting or feeling as if the traumatic event were recurring (includes a sense of reliving the experience, illusions, hallucinations, and dissociative [flashback] episodes, even those that occur upon awakening or when intoxicated)
   (4) intense psychological distress at exposure to events that symbolize or resemble any aspect of the traumatic event, including anniversaries of the trauma

C. Persistent avoidance of stimuli associated with the trauma or numbing of general responsiveness (not present before the trauma), as indicated by at least three of the following:

   (1) efforts to avoid thoughts or feelings associated with the trauma
   (2) efforts to avoid activities or situations that arouse recollections of the trauma
   (3) inability to recall an important aspect of the trauma (psychogenic amnesia)
   (4) markedly diminished interest in significant activities (in young children, loss of recently acquired developmental skills such as toilet training or language skills)
   (5) feeling of detachment or estrangement from others
   (6) restricted range of affect, e.g., unable to have loving feelings
   (7) sense of a foreshortened future, e.g., does not expect to have a career, marriage, or children, or a long life

D. Persistent symptoms of increased arousal (not present before the trauma), as indicated by at least two of the following:

   (1) difficulty falling or staying asleep
   (2) irritability or outbursts of anger
   (3) difficulty concentrating
   (4) hypervigilance
   (5) exaggerated startle response
   (6) physiologic reactivity upon exposure to events that symbolize or resemble an aspect of the traumatic event (e.g., a woman who was raped in an elevator breaks out in a sweat when entering any elevator)

E. Duration of the disturbance (symptoms in B, C, and D) of at least one month.

   Specify delayed onset if the onset of symptoms was at least six months after the trauma.

Note. From *Diagnostic and Statistical Manual of Mental Disorders* (3rd ed., rev., pp. 201–251) by the American Psychiatric Association, 1987, Washington, DC: Author. Copyright 1987 by the American Psychiatric Association. Reprinted by permission.

the dreams were not a precise replication of the accident, they nonetheless caused Susan intense anxiety. She had not had any such dreams prior to the accident, so it appeared probable that they were related to Carl's death.

C. *Avoiding trauma-related stimuli/numbing.* Susan would not enter Carl's house; this appeared to be a way of avoiding memories about him (item #2 in criteria under C, Table 11.1); she was sleeping more than usual (possibly item #1, avoiding thoughts associated with the trauma, or #5, feelings of detachment from others); she also appears to have restricted affect (item #6), as evidenced in her absence of tears.

D. *Increased arousal.* Susan's mother reported that her daughter was very irritable (item #2, Table 11.1); Susan later told the therapist that she was experiencing some headaches in school (item #6).

E. *Duration.* The criteria specify that the symptoms must have been evident for at least 1 month. Susan's mother referred her after 3 weeks; however, the symptoms continued for several weeks following the initiation of therapy.

Preliminary Assessment

There is certainly enough evidence to consider a tentative diagnosis of PTSD based on the information reviewed here which was given by the mother over the telephone. Susan's sessions with me which will be reported later, subsequently confirmed this preliminary impression.

Before proceeding with the case, we will focus briefly on two elements of Susan's symptoms, the nightmares and her isolation of affect, and also on the topic of incomplete mourning and its relationship to anniversary reactions.

Posttraumatic Nightmares

According to Terr, who studied 26 children after their traumatic kidnapping and burial for 29 hours, "children who have been psychologically overwhelmed dream that they themselves die . . . because they no longer believe in their personal invulnerability. They are entirely convinced of their helplessness once they accept the 'fact' during an event that they might die at any moment" (1987, pp. 239–240). Although Susan did not dream of dying, she felt very threatened by being chased by the monster in her nightmares, and that fear awakened her. Perhaps she felt that if Carl could die suddenly, she might be next. Even when a trauma has not been witnessed first-hand it can stimulate nightmares, as happens following frightening television programs, and scary movies. It is possible, therefore, that merely hearing about Carl's tragic death proved traumatic to Susan. Terr states that "horror is contagious. It can be experienced by those who never themselves were directly horrified" (1987, p. 241).

During the latency age of development, the bad dreams of the preschool years are usually less frequent and bothersome; Terr comments that "nightmares at this calmer, more organized stage of childhood may . . . often occur at times of severe outside stress" (1987, p. 237). Clearly this seems to be the case with Susan.

Absence of Grief/"Masked" Grief

Susan's mother was very concerned about her daughter because she was "holding all her feelings in." In Lindemann's classic article about acute grief he refers to the tendency to avoid the syndrome (physical sensations of grief) "at any cost . . . and to keep deliberately from thought all references to the deceased" (1944, p. 8). If this is a characteristic of "normal" grief, then Susan's restricted affect should not cause concern. However, we must consider that her entire family, including her father, were visibly shaken, sad, and tearful about Carl's death, so that Susan's lack of reaction seemed puzzling to them. Furthermore, if we interpret the nightmares as the nighttime expression of the repressed daytime anxieties, then these reactions may qualify as evidence of "masked" grief. Worden (1991) defines this term as related to symptoms and behaviors that cause difficulty, but which are not recognized by the bereaved individual as related to his/her loss. Susan, thus, can admit that she is having nightmares, but she cannot enter Carl's house, because she would then have to face the reality of the grieving mourners and his absence. Helene Deutsch suggests that absent grief reactions may occur in individuals whose ego is not sufficiently developed to bear the strain of grief and mourning and who therefore employ self-protective mechanisms to circumvent the process (Worden, 1991). Deutsch's belief is that "every unresolved grief is given expression in one form or another" (Deutsch, 1937, quoted in Bowlby, 1963, p. 531).

Anniversary Reactions

When grief is not fully expressed, it may find an outlet in symptom formation, as described above, or it may return at some future time, stimulated by a memory of the loss triggered by a significant date or time of year that stirs up the repressed feelings. The clinical literature views anniversary reactions as manifestations of incomplete mourning (Gabriel, 1992). Susan's inability to deal with her feelings about Carl's death at the time it occurred made her vulnerable to a strong reaction about a year later when her fifth-grade class was reading a story about the tragic death of a young person. This gave her and me another chance to deal with some of her feelings associated with her traumatic loss. Because children's grief is usually sporadic and protracted, this case permits us to appreciate more fully the gradual unfolding of grief, with anniversary reactions "conceptualized as normative and expectable, perhaps, existing on a continuum . . . unfolding over decades" (Gabriel, 1992, p. 189).

THE CASE: SUSAN, AGE 9

Family Information

> Mother, Dina, age 43, former teacher, currently at home
> Father, Don, age 43, stockbroker
> Susan, age 9, fourth grade, active in Girl Scouts
> Becky, age 7, second grade, described by Mother as "loud and boisterous; takes a lot of my time because she is so 'hyper' "

Maternal and paternal grandparents live on the West Coast, as do the mother's and father's siblings. The James family has lived on the East coast for about 12 years. They maintain telephone contact with their Western relatives and visit occasionally. Carl's family has been very close since prior to Susan's birth when Dina and Carl's mother taught together in the same school. Susan and Carl were born the same year, and the two young mothers spent many hours together during their children's preschool years. Susan and Carl went to the same nursery school and have been in the same elementary school, although not the same class.

Religious/Cultural Heritage

Susan's family is Protestant and is very active in their church; they attend church weekly, and the girls attend Sunday School. Carl's family attends the same church. All went to Carl's funeral together where a closed casket, covered with flowers, rested in front of the altar. Because Carl had once expressed negative feelings about cemeteries to his mother, his family selected the option of entombment in a mausoleum for his body, rather than burial in a cemetery.

Background on Referral

The referral came to me, a child and family therapist, through a former social work student who knew Carl's family through the church and who was told by Carl's mother that Susan had become "angry, cranky, and mean."

My usual procedure with a new case is to see the parents alone prior to seeing the child. The purpose is to obtain a detailed history of the problem and to discuss with the parents how to prepare the child for the upcoming evaluation session. In this instance I decided to arrange an appointment for the child, with one or both of her parents right away because I viewed this situation as one in which the child was in considerable discomfort, which merited an immediate response in the form of crisis intervention. I therefore spoke with the mother at length on the phone and obtained the information that has already been reviewed. I suggested to Susan's mother that she tell her the day before our scheduled appointment that she had spoken to a doctor who helps children and their families after a death, and that she would be taking Susan to speak with me after school the next day. I advised the mother to not go into great detail about the appointment but that she should convey through her manner a "matter-of-fact" firmness that the appointment was definite, and not something Susan could decline. In turn, I conveyed to Mrs. James my own conviction that I wanted to see Susan because I knew that it would be helpful for her to speak with someone, although I understood that Susan might find this very difficult initially.

First Session with Child

At the agreed-upon time my buzzer rang and the mother came into the waiting room all flustered, stating that Susan was in the car refusing to come in. My immediate response was to tell the mother that I would go out to the car and speak with her. Without thinking about the 30° temperature of February in New York, I left the office without my coat and immediately spotted Susan in the car by the entrance. The motor was still running and Susan was sitting in the back seat. I walked over to the car window, smiled, and introduced myself, and invited Susan to come in to the office. She seemed reluctant, but nevertheless was aware that I did not have a coat on and that it was very cold. I remember saying to her, "Please come in so we can talk inside; it's freezing out here!" Susan got out of the car and accompanied me into the office while her mother proceeded to park the car. My feeling was, "Well, at least we got to first base, let's see where things will go from here." Excerpts from the session follow:

Content of Session

THERAPIST: Hi! I'm certainly glad you agreed to come inside. It was *very* chilly out there! I guess you didn't want to come in, but now that you're here we might as well try to get to know each other. (*At this point the mother comes in and I invite her to join us. To Susan.*) I know that you've been having a rough time lately. Do you understand why your mom brought you to see me?

SUSAN: I'm having bad dreams that wake me up every night. Then in the morning I don't want to get up. I'm tired all the time, even when I go to bed at 8 o' clock.

T: That sounds pretty bad! Can you tell me what the dreams are like?

S: I dream that there is a gorilla in my closet and that he is going to sneak up to my bed and grab me and then take me away and roast me on a barbeque.

T: That must be pretty scary! Does the dream wake you up?

S: Yes, and then I run into my mom's bed.

T: I know that your friend was killed in an accident. You've been through a terrible experience! Can you tell me how you found out about it, and what you were told?

S: Mom and Dad told me. I was home from school with the flu that day.

T: What a terrible thing to hear! I know that you can Carl were good friends.

S: I didn't invite him to my birthday party this year.

MOTHER: Susan had an "all-girls" bowling party.

T: I know that a lot of 9-year-olds do that. I'm sure Carl understood.

Analysis and Feelings

This is hard for both of us, but she is probably more scared and uncomfortable that I am. It is *my* job to put *her* fears at rest.
Grateful that mother was able to carry out my instructions and get Susan here.
Wondering how Susan will respond.

Sounds like she is worn out!

Stay with *her* concerns.

I sense that Susan feels my empathy. She has pretty good eye contact. I am ready to risk asking her directly about the death.

She does not give any of her reactions. Seems well defended.

Is she denying their friendship, or feeling guilty?

Wanting to universalize/ normalize the situation.

At this point I believed that Susan might be ready to spend some time alone with me. I invited her mother to wait in the adjourning room while Susan and I talked alone. I pulled out some drawing paper and markers, wondering whether Susan would communicate symbolically as much, or more, than she had done verbally.

Content of Session	Analysis and Feelings
THERAPIST: Did your mom tell you what kind of doctor I am?	
SUSAN: (*Looking uncertain.*) A therapist?	So far so good. Does she have any understanding about my role?
T: That's right. I'm a therapist. Do you know what a therapist does?	
S: (*Shrugs shoulders, and looks uncertain.*)	
T: I help kids and their parents with their worries; sometimes we talk and sometimes we play. I know you have a lot of worries right now. How about taking a break from talking for a while. I usually invite kids to draw something when they are here. How about drawing a picture of a person? (*Susan eagerly selects a piece of paper and begins drawing a figure of a Girl Scout; there are a lot of markings around figure*	This is obviously a self-portrait, since Susan is dressed in her Girl Scout uniform.

FIGURE 11.1. Susan's drawing of herself as a Girl Scout.

suggesting rain?/wind?/turmoil? [Figure 11.1].) I see she's a Girl Scout. You draw very well. Our time is up for today, but I'd like to see you again and will set up an appointment with your mother.

I deliberately do not comment on the markings since I do not want to make Susan self-conscious about her work.

S: Okay. Thank you.

This was a fairly good beginning, considering Susan's reluctance. Her motivation for help was because of the nightmares, which she did not connect to her feelings about Carl's death. Our alliance initially would be around helping her with her discomfort about the dreams.

Sessions 2 and 3

The next two sessions occurred at weekly intervals. Susan reported that she continued to have nightmares. Her description of the dreams varied from saying that they were "scary" to giving fairly good detail. In one dream she was "in a mansion with lots of doors and windows and rooms. I was with my friend and a monster was chasing us. I was so scared I woke up and ran into my mother's bed."My response was to empathize with her feelings and to suggest to her that "sometimes our daytime worries come back to chase us at night." Susan's usual response to a statement like this was to say that everything was fine, and that she wasn't worried about *anything*. In her opinion, her only problem was the nightmares and some headaches she had sometimes in school. My role certainly was not to argue with her but to give her the opportunity to express some of her feelings symbolically in play.

Drawings and Games

In the second session I invited Susan to draw a family. She quickly drew five figures with a pen, then colored their clothes with a green marker and added hats and facial expressions in blue. None of the faces looked happy. In conclusion, Susan drew a circular spiral "whirlwind" around the figures (Figure 11.2). When I asked Susan to tell me about this family she responded breezily, "It's my Girl Scout troop. Can we play a game now?" The game she selected from the wide range of available choices on my game shelf was Battleship, a game consisting of two players guessing the location of their opponent's ships, with correct guesses causing the ships to "sink." In my experience, this game is rarely selected by latency-age *girls,* and, as we played I began to wonder about its significance to Susan. I guessed that possibly the randomness of the "bombs" resembled

FIGURE 11.2. Susan's drawing of her Girl Scout troop.

the unexpected quality of Carl's death. My comments to Susan tried to convey this feeling. I made statements such as: "Boy, you never can tell when or where a bomb will fall! This is really scary! You never know when you number is going to be picked." Susan's mood during the game was very animated; she seemed to enjoy it greatly, and to be totally oblivious to the underlying meaning of the statements I was making.

FIGURE 11.3. Susan's drawing of the therapist in a garden.

After completing one game we still had some time remaining in the session and Susan asked to draw again. She said she would draw a surprise, and, indeed, it was. She drew a picture of me holding a watering can and watering flowers in a garden. I thanked her for the picture, and felt optimistic about our work, despite what I had perceived as unwillingness on Susan's part to talk openly about Carl's death. This was the first picture drawn by Susan in which she used a variety of colors and in which the mood seemed cheerful, including a bright sun shining in the sky (Figure 11.3).

Session 4

Content of Session

Mother has brought Becky to this session and, upon arrival, she announces that she also had brought some pictures of Carl. I invite Mother and Becky to join me and Susan. Mother spreads out the pictures on the coffee table. Neither Becky nor Susan appears to take any interest.

THERAPIST: (*To Susan and Becky.*) It must seem strange to look at these pictures now. I bet it's hard to believe that Carl is dead.

BECKY: He died *instantly* when the car went down the cliff.

T: Susan, you're not saying anything. Would you like to speak with me alone? (*Mother and Becky get up to leave without waiting for Susan's response.*)

SUSAN: (*After the others have gone.*) Can we play Battleship again?

T: This is your time to use any way you want to. I could see that you didn't want to talk about Carl. It must be *very* difficult for you!

Analysis and Feelings

Mother has told me that she is not concerned about Becky; therefore I do not attribute any special meaning to her presence. I am very interested in seeing how Susan will react to the photos.

I am watching Susan, but her face does not convey any emotion.

Becky can talk about this. It occurs to me that *she* expresses what Susan cannot bear to say.

I want Susan to know that I am there for *her* even though she cannot talk.

She wants to move away from any discussion about Carl.

I feel I must at least make some acknowledgment that we are moving away from direct discussion of Carl's death.

As we played the game I was more deliberate in my comments than I had been the week before. The fact that Susan asked for the game again tended to reinforce my hypothesis that it represented to her the random violence of sudden death. I decided to "play this for all it was worth" in the hope that we could talk about Susan's feelings about death in the metaphor of play, since she could not tolerate direct discussion about her traumatic experience.

Content of Session	Analysis and Feelings
THERAPIST: (*After Susan has bombed one of my boats.*) What about the people on the ships? What is going to happen to them?	
SUSAN: They are swimming. They're going to swim to shore.	
T: It's out in the *ocean*. Can they make it to shore?	Deciding to press a bit.
S: Kennedy swam to an island and then went back to get his buddy. He was very courageous. We had it in school.	Denial of death is strong.
T: He was very lucky. What if there had been sharks in the water?	Am I pushing to hard?
S: He made it to the island okay.	This denial is very important for Susan. She cannot imagine death, even in fantasy.
T: Well, I just worry about those people in the boats when they get bombed. I hope someone rescues them.	

As we talked, we continued to play the game and Susan won. She was quite animated. She asked if she could have *two* snacks today, because she was "starved." I permitted this, realizing that the game and my comments probably were stirring up anxious feelings. Susan then asked to draw. She drew a picture of her and me playing Battleship, with her calling out the winning number, and me indicating that she has "hit" one of my ships (Figure 11.4).

FIGURE 11.4. Susan's drawing after playing Battleship.

Comment on Session

I was struck by Susan's unwillingness to consider the reality of death, even in a game situation. Neither she nor Becky wanted to look at the pictures of Carl and to be reminded of the reality of his death. I was aware of Susan's anxiety through her almost manic mood: Her eating and her speech seemed more rapid than previously and she drew and moved from one activity to another with a sense of haste. I believe that she was afraid that if she lingered she might be drawn into a discussion that would overwhelm her. I wondered how long she could keep up the evasiveness.

Session 5

This session occurred 3 weeks after the previous sessions because of a prearranged parent counseling session, and a cancellation because Susan had "turned her ankle" and had been advised by her doctor to "stay off her foot."

Content of Session	Analysis and Feelings
THERAPIST: It's been a while since I've seen you How are you?	Wondering if the break in continuity will result in Susan's "distancing" further from any grief work.
SUSAN: I'm not having any more nightmares or headaches.	How will this affect Susan's motivation to come for therapy??
T: That's great! So your life is sort of getting back to normal, except for your foot.	
S: I'm really mad about my foot, because now I can't do stuff for my Girl Scout camp-out. I'm not supposed to run around.	Could her injury possibly reflect anger turned against herself?
T: How did it happen [that you hurt your foot]?	
S: It just happened. Nothing special. We were doing relay races in gym and I slipped and twisted my ankle. The doctor X-rayed it and it's not broken.	Sounds like an accident.
T: Well, I'm sorry you have to go through all of this. As if you didn't have enough to cope with already.	

S: You don't even know the whole story. My guinea pig died and my friend's father died (*conveyed in a very matter-of-fact tone, as if she were reciting events that had little meaning to her*).

The reality of death continues. Maybe the cumulative effect will force Susan to talk about her feelings.

T: Tell me about this.

S: Well, I came home from school and found my guinea pig dead, and we buried it in the backyard. Now I want a bird.

This girl is *so* literal, and cut off from her feelings. I am not sure which death to explore.

T: Were you sad? How did you feel?

S: It's okay. I'm not going to worry about it.

This is her mantra.

Susan was equally blasé in responding to my expressions of concern about her friend's father's death. When I would reach for a feeling response, Susan would reply with some bit of factual information. She did tell me that Becky had asked, "Why is everyone dying?" further confirming my hunch that Becky expressed anxieties that Susan felt, but could not admit.

Play Therapy Modalities

When I invited Susan to select an activity, she did not ask to play Battleship nor did she ask to draw. I suggested that she might be interested in making something out of clay. Her high energy level and sense of tension continued and I thought that working with clay might relieve some of the tension. Susan made a mushroom out of clay, and continued to ask for food during this session. After eating a box of TicTacs Susan asked to play the board game Candyland, a game usually selected by preschoolers.

Comment on Session

The interruption in treatment had occurred during a number of significant events. Sudden deaths and accidents seemed to recur in this child's life, yet her response remained ostensibly unemotional. She was now "symptom-free" which made me wonder, given her great need for denial, how much longer she would be willing to come to therapy. I decided to bring this up with her in the next session, half-hoping that she would find some value to continuing therapy. I was pleased that her symptoms had abated and was fascinated by the possibility that the reason for this rested primarily with *play,* not talking therapy.

Session 6

Susan began this session all smiles. She reported that she had received
an A + on her science test. She also told me about Becky's birthday party
the previous weekend, and referred to what she wanted to do for *her*
next birthday, several months hence. She had had no more trouble with
nightmares or headaches. When I asked her about how she felt about
coming to see me now, Susan said, "It's okay, but I don't really think
I need to come any more." I asked her what she thought the reason for
coming had been, and Susan said, "My friend died and my mom thought
I was acting different. Now everything is fine; I don't have to run into
her bedroom at night any more."

I suggested that we taper off our sessions, and plan to have our next
session in a month. For the remainder of the session we made squiggle
drawings and Susan made up a story about the figures she created. Two
of the squiggle drawings and the story follow (see Figures 11.5 and 11.6).

Susan's Story of the Rabbit/Dog and the Castle
(Dictated to the therapist)

Once upon a time there was a castle in the woods. The king was scared
of a mean, ugly rabbit/dog who was trying to eat the princess. The
princess didn't know that he was trying to get her. The king heard
the rabbit/dog talking while he was riding in the forest. The king decided that he had to kill the rabbit/dog in order to save his daughter.
When the rabbit/dog is sleeping the king is going to sneak up on him
and shoot an arrow through his heart.

FIGURE 11.5. Squiggle drawing of the rabbit/dog.

FIGURE 11.6. Squiggle drawing of the castle.

The rabbit/dog hears him coming and wakes up and runs away.
He will never go near the castle again. The moral of this story is: Find
a better way to deal with your problems than killing people.

Comment on Session

I was not surprised that Susan wanted to terminate, and in many respects
I agreed with her own assessment that her life was more or less back on
course. I was somewhat resigned to the fact that Susan could not openly
talk about her feelings about Carl's death, and I realized that if I had
helped her experience therapy in a positive way she would be more likely to consider it as an option in the future. I reminded myself that children grieve differently than do adults, and that for Susan this may be
a process that will require many years of "bits of work." I did feel that
we had made a good beginning.

With regard to Susan's squiggle story, I noted that the threat of death
was an ever-present theme. However, in her story, the princess is protected by her father. Although he contemplates using violence to protect
his daughter's life, the threatening creature manages to escape. There is
a sense at the end of the story that everyone is safe, although they had
been close to danger. I commented on that to Susan.

Termination Session

The most significant aspect of this session held 1 month later, was that Susan's mother announced at the beginning that they had all gone to visit the mausoleum that weekend, because it was Carl's birthday. Mrs. James said that she was proud of Susan for agreeing to go, even though she did not want to. My discussions with Susan about this follows.

Content of Session	Analysis and Feelings
THERAPIST: I'd like to hear about your visit to the mausoleum.	
SUSAN: It was a big room with names on the walls and something like an altar at the front with flowers.	Susan gives a factual description. Does she realize the bodies are there?
T: Did you see Carl's name?	
S: Yes I put some flowers on a shelf in front of it.	
T: What did it *feel* like for you to be there?	Wondering if there is any possibility Susan will describe her feelings.
S: I'll draw a picture of it for you. (*Proceeds to draw, and indicates the place where she put the flowers* [Figure 11.7].)	Susan really "uses" art and games rather than verbal means to communicate.
T: It must be sad to think that Carl's body is there.	Trying to help her verbalize.
S: (*Brightly, with no hint of sadness.*) Carl's mom told me that his soul is in heaven, and that we will all see him again sometime.	She is totally closed off to any feelings of loss or sadness. I am almost concluding that this my be functional for her. She must go on with her life. I am struggling with whether to accept her denial that Carl's death is final and irrevocable. Here it becomes evident to me that the religious view of afterlife may, in fact, discourage expression of grief.
T: Still, I'm sure you miss not having him here with you *now*.	
S: You can keep the pictures if you like.	
T: Yes, I'll keep it in your folder with your other drawings. This is the last time	Wanting Susan to consider this a real "open door" policy.

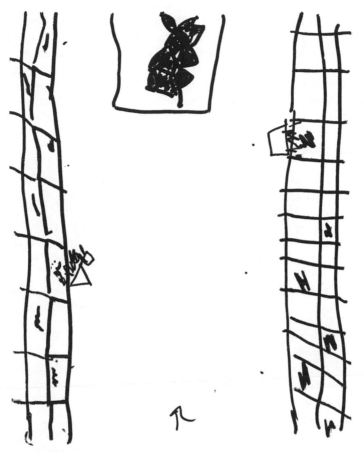

FIGURE 11.7. Susan's drawing of Carl's mausoleum.

we're going to meet for a while, but I'll
save your drawings in my file drawer.
You might come back again some time in
the future if you have worries, or just
want to talk. If you ever do, ask your
Mom to call me and I'll always be glad to
see you.

S: Okay. Good-bye.

Nine Months Later

Mrs. James telephoned because Susan's teacher had notified her that
Susan's school performance had deteriorated seriously in the past 5 weeks.

She had evidently stopped doing all of her homework and failed several tests. This was a drastic change for Susan, who typically was a superior, highly motivated student. In discussions with the teacher, Mrs. James learned that the class had read and discussed a very sad story involving the sudden, tragic death of a fifth-grader. There had been some references made by one of the students in Susan's class to Carl's death approximately 1 year previously.

I suggested that Mrs. James tell Susan that she was concerned about her and she had called me to make an appointment.

Content of Session	Analysis and Feelings
THERAPIST: (*To Mother and Susan.*) Hi! It's been a while. Why don't you both come in together, then I'll spend some time alone with Susan. (*After in office.*) It's good to see you, tell me what brings you here today.	Susan smiles at me and seems comfortable. Wanting Mother to clarify in Susan's presence the reason for her concerns.
MOTHER: I told Susan I called you because her teacher is worried about her; she failed science, and that's her best subject. The teacher says she had stopped turning in her homework.	Susan watching her Mom without expression.
T: (*To Susan.*) Don't I recall that science used to be your favorite subject?	Trying to establish some continuity with the past.
SUSAN: Yes. It's already getting better. I'm improving already, since the teacher called.	
T: Was something bothering you? Sometimes when we get preoccupied with a worry or concern we neglect our work.	Trying to universalize, to make it easy for Susan to admit worries.
S: I just got so interested in reading I forgot to do my assignments. (*To Mother.*) You shouldn't let me get so many books from the library, because I just can't stop reading them.	
T: Was there any book in particular that grabbed your attention?	
S: I just like to read.	
M: (*Pulling out book* [*Bridge to Terabithia;* Paterson, 1987].) Miss Robbins [Susan's teacher] said that this book is about a girl who died in fifth grade in an accident and that it reminded some of the kids about Carl.	Glad Mom came in since Susan has blocked this out.

FIGURE 11.8. Susan's drawing of Girl Scout and cookies.

I suggested that Susan and I spend some time alone together, and Mrs. James waited in the waiting room. I commented to Susan that it has been just about a year since Carl's death, and that it is *very* common for people to think about someone who died around the same time of the year. In her case, reading that story must really have stirred up some memories.

Susan denied that her lapse in school performance had anything to do with Carl. She kept repeating that her work was already improving and that she would be more careful "not to read too much" in the future. We played the "Deck of Feeling" card game. Not surprisingly, Susan gave rather stereotyped responses. I invited her to draw and she drew a figure of a Girl Scout with a package of cookies (Figure 11.8). This drawing, in contrast to the first Girl Scout drawing that Susan made in her first session a year ago, had no cloud around the figure and the figure looks happier.

Two Weeks Later

Susan reported that she had made up most of her school work. When I asked her what she thought went wrong, she stated that she "just wanted a vacation from homework."

I told Susan in her mother's presence that I thought it was just too much of a coincidence that she stopped working when she read a sad story about a child dying at the very time of year Carl had died. I said that this might happen to her again sometime, and, if it did, she or her mom should react sooner and call me or find someone else to talk with. I clarified my belief that Susan's reaction came from holding her feelings inside, and that talking and playing with a therapist really can help.

No further appointment was given, and there has been no further contact in 3 years, apart from receiving written permission from Susan and her mother to write about her therapy in this book.

CONCLUDING COMMENTS

This case is a textbook example of a child who could be classified as a "reluctant griever" (Crenshaw, 1992). This term, coined by Crenshaw to refer to children who have experienced multiple losses and trauma, seemed also applicable to a child like Susan who experienced the sudden, traumatic death of her friend, and who subsequently seemed totally unable to talk about her loss.

In thinking about my work with Susan from the perspective of a 3-year interval, I wonder if I might have somehow managed to involve her more in an active grieving process. If I could return again to my early sessions with Susan I would now invite her to draw a picture of her and Carl doing something together. I would have worked harder to involve Susan in telling me about Carl, what he was like as a person, what she liked about him and, also, what she might not have liked.

As I review my work from a current vantage point, I wonder why I did not ask more questions along these lines. I know that I felt some sense of trepidation about the circumstances of Carl's death, and about the nature of his head injury. This had been described to me in graphic terms by school personnel who felt horrified by the injury. Even in this chapter I have avoided giving details. As I think about this now, it suggests the concept of "vicarious traumatization," a term referring to therapists' reactions to client's traumatic material (McCann & Pearlman, 1990). My conscious intent was to proceed at Susan's speed, and not to rush her prematurely into painful memories that might drive her away from the therapy. It is also possible that I was protecting myself. In the future in a situation that generates mental images of gruesome details, I will be more alert to find ways to debrief my own reactions so I will be freer to tune in and explore the child's fears. Although I am not certain that a different approach would have been more successful with Susan, I am certain that a fearful therapist is working under a major, self-induced handicap.

DISCUSSION QUESTIONS

1. Do you concur with the diagnosis of posttraumatic stress disorder and, if not, how would you assess Susan's presentation of symptoms at the time of referral?

2. Do you believe that Susan's symptoms would have subsided without therapy? Give reasons for your response.

3. How do you feel about the termination in Session 7? Do you think there would have been value to continuing to see Susan? If so, how might this have been structured?

4. What do you predict with regard to Susan's future adjustment? If you anticipate future difficulties, specify at what age and under what circumstances Susan might be vulnerable to relapse.

5. Do you believe that the therapist avoided Susan's feelings of traumatic grief? Specify where this occurred and suggest alternative interventions.

REFERENCES

American Psychiatric Association. (1987). *Diagnostic and statistical manual of mental disorders* (3rd ed., rev.). Washington, DC: Author.

Bowlby, J. (1963). Pathological mourning and childhood mourning. *Journal of the American Psychoanalytic Association, 11,* 500–541.

Crenshaw, D. (1992). Reluctant grievers: Children of multiple loss and trauma. *The Forum, 17*(4), 6–7.

Deutsch, H. (1937). Absence of grief. *Psychoanalytic Quarterly, 6*(12), 12–22.

Fox, S. (1985). *Good grief: Helping groups of children when a friend dies.* Boston: New England Association for the Education of Young Children.

Gabriel, M. (1992). Anniversary reactions: Trauma revisited. *Clinical Social Work Journal, 20*(2), 179–192.

Lindemann, E. (1944). Symptomatology and management of acute grief. *American Journal of Psychiatry, 101,* 141–148. [Reprinted in Parad, H. J. (Ed.). (1965). *Crisis intervention: Selected readings* (pp. 7–21). New York: Family Service America.]

McCann, I. L., & Pearlman, L. A. (1990). Vicarious traumatization: A framework for understanding the psychological effects of working with victims. *Journal of Traumatic Stress, 3*(1), 131–149.

Paterson, K. (1987). *Bridge to Terabithia.* New York: Harper Trophy.

Terr, L. C. (1987). Nightmares in children. In C. Guilleminault (Ed.), *Sleep and its disorders in children* (pp. 231–242). New York: Raven Press.

Worden, J. W. (1991). *Grief counseling and grief therapy* (2nd ed.). New York: Springer.

CHAPTER TWELVE

Sudden Death of a Teacher
Multilevel Intervention in an Elementary School

GAIL DOSTER
CAROLINE Q. McELROY

In a large elementary school, a teacher died of what, at the time, seemed to be a mysterious illness. Her death created a crisis situation for the staff, children, and parents.

This chapter will focus on the effect of the loss of a remedial reading teacher on the lives of latency-age children in a school, and the interventions intended to support and help the children and staff. This includes both the formal actions taken by the school administration and teaching staff as well as individual and small and large group interventions conducted by the two school counselors. The school interventions, in cooperation with parental support, helped these children grieve and learn new coping mechanisms which they could use in the event of future losses.

TASKS OF GRIEVING

As a basis for our work with the children, we relied on the principles developed by Sandra S. Fox, founder of The Good Grief Program at Judge Baker Guidance Center, Boston, Massachusetts. The program's purpose is to help groups of children cope with death and provide crisis intervention and consultation to schools and community groups when a death occurs. Fox's book (1988), *Good Grief: Helping Groups of Children When a Friend Dies,* outlines four psychological tasks that children need to accomplish at the time of a death: (1) understanding, (2) grieving, (3) commemorating, and (4) going on.

Both authors contributed equally to this chapter. Order of authorship is alphabetical.

Understanding

To facilitate the first task children need to be given honest and accurate information about the death in words that they can understand. The child needs to understand what it means to die: The body stops working, the heart stops beating, the person stops breathing. The child must understand that the teacher will never be part of the school again, he/she will never be seen again, and another teacher will take his/her place. The child also needs to know what caused the teacher's death.

Children often need assistance in sorting through all the true and false information that they hear from a variety of sources. When a death occurs in a school there are many sources of information—parents, staff, and peers. As a result, often the information children hear is inaccurate and even distorted. Children may be confused by seemingly contradictory information, such as what it means to be buried in the ground and living in their memories simultaneously.

Grieving

Many child psychiatrists and thanatologists (e.g., Nagy, 1948; Grollman, 1967, 1990; Bowlby, 1980) believe that children do not completely grieve a loss until adulthood. They grieve off and on throughout their growing-up years in a "hit and run" style. Because children have difficulty acknowledging, understanding, and dealing with the painful feelings that come with a death, they may remain in shock or denial for a long time. They will, however, deal with "bad" feelings in spurts, allowing a little bit of pain at a time and vacillating from acknowledging the pain to denying it. These painful feelings include anger, sadness, guilt, and blame. Children grieve differently at different periods in their growing-up years. A child's grief can look very different from that of an adult; one minute the child may be teary and the next minute the child will be immersed in play.

Children need help to make sense of the many, varied, and often conflicting feelings that arise as a result of a death of a teacher and they need the opportunity to work through these feelings. Their feelings need to be acknowledged, accepted, and respected. Children have difficulty knowing how they feel, why they feel that way, and talking about their feelings. Adults can help children make sense of their feelings by giving the clear message that it is okay to feel whatever they are feeling. By communicating in language that the children can understand, they provide an opportunity for children to explore their varied feelings.

In order for children to grieve successfully, they need to accept the reality of the loss and the pain that it evokes in them. Then they can begin to adjust to the change in the environment that the loss has created. They need to withdraw the emotional energy they have invested in the loss and reinvest it in a new situation and new relationships. The child's movement through the tasks of grieving is not a smooth or predictable one; it is an ongoing, erratic, and sometimes lengthy process.

Commemorating

Commemorating the death of a teacher provides closure for the child. It allows the child to show that he/she cared for the individual, to feel the support of others, and to say good-bye to the deceased. It provides a time and place for the child to confirm the reality of the loss, to realize that a change has taken place and to acknowledge the value of the deceased's life. There are formal and informal ways to commemorate a death.

Formal commemorations are funerals, burials, memorial services, or dedications. Children need information about what will happen at a formal commemoration, why it happens, and what will be expected of them. Adults should be prepared for a variety of very specific questions from the child. For example, it is typical for the child to ask what happens to the dead body. It is important to answer such questions in a calm and matter-of-fact way, giving only the details which are requested. Children should be given the choice about attending a service or not. The parent is often the one who is involved in this process with the child; however, the school staff is in a position to offer some assistance in the explanation.

Examples of *informal commemorations* are planting a tree, making a garden, or hanging a picture or plaque which provides a physical reminder of the person who has died. Informal commemoration of a teacher involves giving equipment or books to the school, or establishing a fund in the person's name to be used to meet future needs of the children. School children should have a part in the planning and implementing a commemoration that should be meaningful to them. Staff in a school should also participate in commemorating their colleague. Finally, the family and friends of the deceased should be consulted and be in agreement with the commemoration.

Going On

The child goes through three tasks for "good grief" and is now free to move on. Going on, as described by The Good Grief Program (Fox, 1988), means that the child has a basic understanding of the death and has worked through many of the feelings aroused by the loss. The child may continue to think about the person who died, but will have increased energy for other aspects of his/her life. The beginning of the school year, returning to the classroom, special events, or anniversaries may, however, continue to arouse memories of the deceased. Adults need to be sensitive to the child's more vulnerable times and be available to children at these times.

THE LATENCY-AGE CHILD'S UNDERSTANDING OF DEATH

The child's ability to reason, solve problems, think about cause and effect, and recognize beginnings and endings develops during latency. Children at this age (roughly ages 6–11) think very logically and concretely and approach tasks in a very practical way. There is a thrust toward developing competency in school and mastering his/her world. The desire to do things well and to persist in tasks through completion becomes evident in latency-age children.

By the time children reach latency age, they understand that death is final, that all living things will die, and that death causes important and disruptive changes. However, some do not believe it will ever happen to them. They see themselves as invincible and therefore, think that *they* will never die. As the latency-age child matures, he/she begins to develop a more realistic view of death and begins to realize that it will someday happen to him/her, but not until he/she gets old. "Death may be envisioned as a space invader, or a ghoul, a kidnapper, a crook, any sinister shadow figure that hints at personal destruction. This figure is neither infallible nor omniscient, and only the stupid child allows himself to be snared" (Carroll, 1985, p. 154).

Because death is a difficult concept for children to understand, they may use magical thinking as a way of making sense of it. They feel responsible for what goes on, and some children believe they did something to cause the death such as being angry at the deceased.

Children understand, react, and deal with death uniquely based on their intellects, learning styles, temperaments, and experiences. It is sometimes hard to read how children are feeling or how they are coping. They may become withdrawn and quiet, noisy and boisterous, or aggressive and oppositional; they may displace their feelings onto others; they may speak little about their feelings surrounding the death, but they may ask lots of specific, seemingly gruesome questions; they may have difficulty talking about their feelings. A death may stimulate fear of their own death or the death of someone in their family.

Some typical behaviors of grieving children include angry outbursts, acting-out behavior, and/or "model" behavior that attempts either to reverse what has happened or to relieve feelings of guilt. A child may ask the same question of many different people in an attempt to make sense of the loss. A child may tell his/her story to a complete stranger as a way of releasing his painful feelings and in an attempt to feel better. Regression may occur, socially, emotionally, or behaviorally. A child may have physical symptoms of headaches, stomach aches, or other psychosomatic complaints. All of the above behavior represent the child's attempt to cope. As the child moves through the grieving process, he/she will learn more appropriate ways of coping.

IMPACT OF TEACHER'S DEATH

The teacher–student relationship is very powerful for a child. The elementary school child spends roughly 30 hours per week in a classroom with his/her teacher. Children develop a sense of competency from their teacher as they accomplish academic tasks and, also, the teacher helps students define themselves as social beings outside their own families. Often children will look to their teacher for emotional support. Brooks, in *The Self-Esteem Teacher,* states that "every educator is capable of being a 'charismatic adult' who truly infuses in students a feeling of excitement and self worth, who helps them see more clearly the positive in themselves and in others" (1991, p. 13).

The impact of the death of a teacher on students will vary depending on the individual needs of each child, but no child in the classroom will be left unaffected. The child who complains the most about his/her teacher can be as devastated by this loss as the child who has a positive, nonproblematic relationship with the teacher.

Children outside the classroom will also be impacted by the death of a particular teacher. Students come in contact with other teachers throughout the school day at recess, lunch time, and for special projects and programs. A child may have a sibling who was a student of the deceased teacher. Also, there will be students in the general population who have no relationship with the teacher, but they will be impacted because of their own experiences with loss.

The following factors all contribute to the impact of a teacher's death on the school community:

- Age of teacher
- Circumstances surrounding his/her death (length of illness; nature of medical care; where and how death occurred)

- Length of service in the school
- Perception of teaching duties (this may differ depending on who defines these duties)
- Degree of authority teacher conveyed (real or imagined)
- Quality of relationship to staff and to students
- Involvement in community outside the school
- Role as parent of school-aged children

This Teacher's Death

Children reacted to Mrs. Tobin's death in many different ways. They had little time to prepare for her death, they never saw a change in her, she did not look sick, nor did she look like she was going to die. This made it very difficult for them to process her death. Many felt very sad; some were relieved, angry, or guilty for they did not perceive her as a perfect teacher; some were in total denial, acting like nothing happened; others were in shock and disbelief.

Mrs. Tobin's death impacted the teachers in the building in a variety of ways. Her closest friends were most touched by her death, as were the younger teachers of similar age and also parents of school-aged children. Classroom teachers who had a close professional relationship with her and in whose classes she assisted on a regular basis also felt deeply affected.

Illness and Death in the School

An elementary school is a public institution whose mission is to educate children in the areas of academic and life skills. The educational staff, made up of teachers, administrators, counselors, and special educators, guide children through difficult life experiences, but the staff is cautious not to take over the role of the parent. Educators must help children to understand why negative things happen in life and teach them positive coping skills, but this must occur while respecting the religious and moral values of the individual families.

Illness is an occupational hazard for teachers who work with grade-school children. Midwinter in an elementary school can seem more like a pediatric medical center than an educational setting due to the number of runny noses, coughs, colds, and stomach viruses. Teacher folklore claims that eventually one builds up immunities to these illnesses. Nonetheless, teachers do fall victim to the germs in their classrooms.

In our school building most of the staff attempt to keep working when they are sick with such viruses and feel that they should not give up easily to these ailments. However, if a teacher does call in sick for a few days it is understood that the "bug got the best of him/her." Therefore, no one was overly concerned when Mrs. Tobin called in sick with flu-like symptoms; people assumed that she had one of the several viruses that had been circulating through the building. Her death 2 weeks later was all the more painful because all who knew Mrs. Tobin believed her sickness was minor in nature.

Just as our society in general has a difficult time talking about death, so do some adults in the school. The school's job is to develop children's minds and teach new ideas in a safe and protected atmosphere. Death education is not always considered part of that job. Some educators may feel inadequate in talking about death to their students. When there is a death in a school, the natural attitude of teachers is one of protection of their students and that protection may take the form of avoiding discussion of painful topics. Their view may be that talking about a death only makes it harder for children and maybe if it is not talked about, it will just go away. Other staff members may feel that the school is the natural forum for learning about and discussing painful topics and that the school can help children grieve in a healthy way.

Counselor's Role in the School

The support services offered to children in a school setting are best described as psychoeducational. Generally, the goal of school counseling is to help the child have a happy, successful educational experience. Children are referred to the school counselor when it appears that issues, difficulties, or worries are interfering with learning. Counseling occurs in the school in the form of individual, group, parent, and crisis counseling, as well as mediation. The focus is to help the child to develop coping skills and behavioral strategies to manage academic, social, and family stress. School counselors tend to be on the "front line" when there is a crisis. The counselor at school helps the child through the immediate crisis, but children and families are referred to community services for ongoing psychotherapy.

THE CASE: SUDDEN DEATH OF MRS. TOBIN, AGE 35

Much of what we did when Mrs. Tobin died was to act promptly as in any crisis situation. We realized that the death of Mrs. Tobin would affect the whole school community. We needed to prioritize our focus and our energies. First, we targeted the teachers; second, the children who were friends of Ruth, Mrs. Tobin's child, Ruth's classroom and day-care group; third, the children whom Mrs. Tobin serviced; fourth, the children in whose classrooms she worked; fifth, all the classrooms in the grade level that she serviced; and finally, the children who had experienced previous losses.

The Teacher

At our school Mrs. Tobin was not a traditional classroom teacher. Instead, she was a remedial reading teacher who serviced children on a one-to-one basis, in small groups, and sometimes in a large classroom setting. She saw her students three to five times per week for a couple of hours per day. When she serviced her students in their full classroom settings, other children in those classrooms would receive help from her as needed.

Mrs. Tobin shared a room called the Reading Room with several other colleagues, so she had contact with other children receiving academic help. Also, Mrs. Tobin administered academic testing to children who were referred for extra help. Mrs. Tobin worked in this position at our school for 3 years.

Her students ranged in age from 7 to 10 years old. Students with reading deficits often have concerns about their intelligence and performance. Some children may feel good about themselves and their academic abilities, and they may perceive a teacher like Mrs. Tobin as a tutor. Other children, however, may be more academically or emotionally impaired. Some children may see their reading teacher as someone to whom they can admit their academic weaknesses. Often children are too proud to admit their shortcomings when they are in their own classroom. There are some children who act out in the large classroom rather that acknowledge that they are less capable than their fellow students. For children like these, Mrs. Tobin's room was an essential "safe-haven."

Mrs. Tobin's students felt safe when working with her and many enjoyed her dry sense of humor. She had a good working relationship with them. She was supportive, and she set firm, fair limits. In doing so, she encouraged the children to challenge their abilities. The message she gave to her students was that there was a time for work and a time for play.

Mrs. Tobin's life was that of a single parent of three school-aged children. Only her youngest daughter, Ruth, attended our school. Mrs. Tobin socialized with many of the parents in the community whose children were in our school. Her family's religious background was Jewish. Mrs. Tobin's family of origin lived out of state. Her closest relatives were 4 hours away. Therefore, her immediate support system was her friends in the community.

The School

Our school is a very large building of nearly 800 students ranging in grades from preschool through grade four. Due to the size of the student body and the layout of the physical plant, communication among staff members can be difficult. The large number of 50 or more staff results in staff meetings that are somewhat formal. The school seems like two small schools operating in one building, the primary school and the older primary school. A significant number of the staff live in the community and, as a result, many of their children either have been students or currently are students in the school.

The population of the student body is predominantly suburban, white, middle class. There is a minority of children of color who are Asian, Indian, and African American. Most of the families are Christian, but there is a significant number of Jewish families and a few Moslems. In general, the parents tend to be highly educated professionals who value the education of their children. Due to the economic climate of the area, many of the families have experienced a job loss for the first time in their work career or are worrying about their job security. There are a great number of two-parent families, larger than the national average, many of whom are very involved in school and community activities.

Problem Situation: Course of Illness

In the first days of Mrs. Tobin's absence due to illness her fellow staff members were not overly concerned. As the days extended into a week the adults asked about her status and her students started asking when she would be back. (Substitutes are hired after several days of absence and the children were now being taught by a substitute.) A couple of her closer colleagues reported that she had a bad intestinal virus. A couple of days later Mrs. Tobin returned to school for a half day, but left because she did not feel well.

Mrs. Tobin, who was 35 years old, entered the hospital the following day with what was reported to be pneumonia. Except for a few neighbors' children and a few of her daughter's friends, the children in school were not aware of the hospitalization. However, Mrs. Tobin's fellow staff members knew and some expressed concern and worry. However, there was no clear diagnosis. The adults speculated: "She has a bad virus, she's run down, she needs to take better care of herself, she's been under too much stress."

Mrs. Tobin returned home after a 2-day hospital stay, but was rushed back to the hospital 2 days later with what appeared to be a worsening of an infection. That same day she went into a coma. The next day her family informed the school principal that her illness was quite serious and very possibly life-threatening. She remained in a coma for the next 4 days, until her death.

All were confused and shocked. It appeared as if Mrs. Tobin got a virus one week and died the next. Some adults worried whether this was a contagious condition; others worried whether there was something in the building that made her sick; many questioned the quality of her medical care. It was not until 3 days after her memorial service that the staff learned the cause of her death. The autopsy revealed a fast-spreading cancer.

Counselors' Involvement and Goals

Our primary concern was the impact of the undiagnosed illness and subsequent death of Mrs. Tobin on all the children and staff in the school. Our responsibility to act quickly and promptly, in an emergency situation, was paramount. We needed to help children understand and provide the opportunity for them to grieve successfully and healthily within the school setting and, thereby, empower all the children to cope with the loss.

As counselors, we viewed our role as guiding the administrators, staff, and students through a healthy and appropriate grieving process. Fortunately, our principal understood the importance of the process of grieving, supported us, and gave us free rein to do whatever we felt was necessary. We were aware of the importance of aligning ourselves with the needs of the family in order to validate their needs as well as those of the staff.

We were concerned about the most vulnerable children who might be in need of support and guidance. We saw these children as those who (1) had been directly serviced by Mrs. Tobin, (2) were in class with her daughter, (3) had experienced prior losses, (4) had a negative or ambivalent relationship with Mrs. Tobin, (5) had a weak support system (i.e., those whose families had difficulties or those who had a poor relationship with their classroom teacher), (6) had already been identified as having psychological problems, and (7) were not a part of the initial process because they were absent the day after she died.

We wanted to help educate the parents to the grieving process so that they could better support their children and, also, to provide advice upon the request from parents.

Interventions before Death

Verify and Share Information

Our first step was to address staff concerns. The principal held lunchtime informational meetings for staff during the 4-day period when Mrs. Tobin was in a coma. Some staff members were communicating with Mrs. Tobin's family and close friends directly, and the information that was shared was confusing. A friend of Mrs. Tobin told a staff member that her condition was terminal. However, Mrs. Tobin's family was not ready to give up hope and did not describe her illness as terminal.

A teacher is in a very public position. Her life touches the lives of her students and their families. In addition, Mrs. Tobin was a mother and fellow parent in the community. There was a great deal of discussion and thought about what information should be public and what should be private. We wanted to respect the family's privacy, but we also wanted to do what was best for the children. In addition, we did not want to give any information to the children or their parents unless we knew Mrs. Tobin's daughter already had been informed, nor did we want to give inaccurate information.

Once we knew that her condition was terminal, we had to prepare the children for the fact that Mrs. Tobin would not return, that her condition was serious, and that she would die. This required that a school counselor speak directly with a member of Mrs. Tobin's family to get permission to publicly discuss this. Although the family still held out hope, they were willing to do what was best for the children. Next, the hospital social worker was contacted so that we could get accurate information. The social worker confirmed the rareness of the disease and the fact that her condition was terminal, and tried to offer as much information as she could. However, no diagnosis was given to us.

Intervention Plan

When we learned that Mrs. Tobin was not going to live and that she would soon die, we quickly established a crisis team consisting of the director of pupil services, the principal and assistant principal, the school psychologist, and the two counselors. Our goal was to establish a plan of action. We focused on how best to help the children and staff. We discussed what we knew about Mrs. Tobin's medical condition, what more we needed to know, what we needed to do immediately, what we needed to do when Mrs. Tobin died, and what the sequence of providing information should be. Mrs. Tobin's daughter should be the first to know, her fellow colleagues in the Reading Room next, and finally the entire staff. Then we focused our efforts on actual task allocation, breaking the tasks into administrative and counseling.

Death Education Workshop: Education and Support for Staff

Arrangements were made to engage a consultant experienced in death education to speak to the full staff. The goals were to provide emotional support to the staff and to educate them on children's perceptions of death and how to talk to the children about death. We felt an outside person would be more objective, would not be emotionally involved, was experienced, and could lend expertise to our group of educators.

Meeting with the Crisis Team and Consultant

The consultant first met with the crisis team for 1½ hours. We told her about the lack of information regarding Mrs. Tobin's illness and the reactions of the staff to her terminal illness. We shared with her interventions that we had already implemented. She helped us to focus on what was necessary to help the staff and the children grieve healthily.

Mandatory Meeting with the Staff and Consultant

The meeting with the staff, 1½ hours long, occurred less than 24 hours before Mrs. Tobin died. The principal made an announcement on the public address system during the "morning news": "A meeting for all staff will be held this afternoon at 3:30 in the intermediate library. All staff are expected to attend." Emotions were high at this time and there was a feeling of impending doom. All during the day the staff was speculating about what the meeting was going to address and why it was mandatory. Everyone knew the focus of the meeting was Mrs. Tobin.

The consultant introduced herself as a former teacher, quickly aligning herself with the staff. Initially, her presentation took an educational approach and covered a review of the developmental stages of children and how they perceive and understand death at each stage of development. She talked about the four tasks that children must accomplish when a death occurs in order to have "good" grief. She emphasized the importance of talking to the children. The first part of her presentation was focused on the needs of the children.

The focus then shifted into a more experiential, interactive mode in which she referred to our specific situation, encouraging teachers to share their feelings, worries, and concerns. "What do you know about Mrs. Tobin's illness?" "All we know is she has pneumonia." "She's in a coma." Teachers shared what they knew and from whom they had learned it. They shared their worry and fear that they too were at risk and felt vulnerable. The consultant said, "It must be difficult for you, not knowing what's wrong." Many agreed. "Not having a clear diagnosis, or at least a hint of a diagnosis leads to confusion, which leads to more anxiety and makes people feel out of control." Many staff shared their feelings of disbelief, sadness, anxiety, and guilt. They shared their pain and talked about their worries about what was going to happen next. They learned that grief gets competitive and this is not helpful. Everyone grieves differently and that is okay. The meeting provided an important opportunity for the staff to bond as a group. Staff left feeling that they were not alone in this situation or in their grief, and that they could and would support each other at this very difficult time.

Interventions after Death

Notifying the Staff of Death

A family member called one of the counselors as soon as Mrs. Tobin died. This was shortly before noon. Our first concern was to keep this information confidential until Mrs. Tobin's family could come to the school to pick up Mrs. Tobin's daughter, Ruth, and tell her. Until this could happen, she spent time with her counselor.

Once Ruth had left school, a small meeting occurred with the remedial reading staff, the director of pupil services, the principal, the school psychologist, and the counselors. The principal informed the staff that Mrs. Tobin had died. A brief discussion centered around how the family was doing and plans for a memorial service. People cried and spoke about Mrs. Tobin as a colleague and as a parent. "Her poor children. What will happen to them?" This group was asked *not* to share this information with fellow staff members. The crisis team decided that since it was an hour before school closing, it was best to allow the teachers to hear this information after their students had left the building. Also, it was important for the full staff to be together as a group when they were told and to hear the same information. The remedial reading staff left the building to be together and to grieve, and to help plan the memorial service and reception.

At the end of the school day the principal announced over the public address system that there would be a brief staff meeting immediately after school which everyone should attend. The staff had been "on alert" all week so people instinctively knew that this meeting would be an update about Mrs. Tobin's serious condition and that probably she had died.

The room filled up quickly with all the staff, along with the members of the crisis team. The principal informed the staff of Mrs. Tobin's death. The staff had a variety of reactions. Some cried immediately, while others were stoic. Once again, people wanted to know about Mrs. Tobin's daughter. It was important for all of the staff to know who had told her, what she had been told, and how she was doing. The staff then focused on plans for the memorial service to be held the following day and plans for speaking with their students. It was agreed that all teachers would tell their students at the beginning of the school day. Briefly, the staff reminded themselves of the important themes presented by the consultant on the previous day.

Notifying Parents of Death

A letter signed by the principal, the superintendent of schools, and the director of pupil services was sent to all parents. The key points covered in the letter were as follows:

1. The announcement of the death
2. The cause of death
3. The actions taken by the school
4. The reactions that can be expected from children
5. The importance of talking to children about the death
6. The availability of school personnel, including counselors, if needed

Notifying Students of Death

The children were told of Mrs. Tobin's death by their classroom teachers at the beginning of the school day. The teachers used what they had learned 2 days before at the consultant's presentation to help them talk about death with their students. Some classroom teachers requested the presence of a counselor to help them facilitate the discussion. Both counselors and the school psychologist helped facilitate a discussion in Mrs. Tobin's daughter's classroom. One of the counselors helped the teacher of a small, substantially separate class of developmentally delayed students facilitate a discussion.

Meeting with Day-Care Program Children and Staff

The day-care program is available, for a fee, to all families in the community. It provides supervision for children before and after school in a community center near our school. The director of the day-care program requested that one of the school counselors talk to the children about Mrs. Tobin's death because Mrs. Tobin's daughter, Ruth, regularly attended. All of the children knew Mrs. Tobin as Ruth's mother, while some knew her as a teacher in our school.

The day-care program staff, with the help of the counselor, gathered the children together in a corner, on the floor of a large activity room. They sat in a double circle with the staff interspersed among them. The children ranged in age from 5 to 10 years.

Content of Session	Analysis and Feelings
COUNSELOR (Mrs. M): Good morning. As you know, I am the "feelings" or "helper" teacher. I am sure you are wondering why I am here today. We have some very sad news to tell you. You all know that Mrs. Tobin has been very sick. You have seen Ruth here more often and you have probably noticed that her mother has not been dropping her off. As you all know, Mrs. Tobin has been in the hospital for a few weeks. The doctors and nurses have been trying to help her get better but they haven't been able to and she died yesterday. (*I pause and look at the children and see very serious blank stares, very focused but dazed.*) That means that her body stopped working, her heart stopped beating, and she stopped breathing. (*No one moves, very serious looking, quiet children.*) I'm feeling really sad right now and I can see some of you are feeling sad, too. It's	I begin with the children's experiences, hoping that they would not deny their feelings and thoughts.

Children at this age are concrete thinkers and take things literally; I need to be clear and precise. |

really hard. I can see some of you are really thinking. I wonder if you have any questions?

STUDENT: When did she die?

C: Yesterday morning, we think about 11 o'clock.

S2: Was she alone when she died?

C: No, she wasn't. All of her family were with her, her mother and father, her brothers, and her children.

S3: How did she die?

C: We're not really sure. The doctors are trying to find that out. We do know that she was very, very sick and the doctors could not help her get well.

S4: My daddy said she had brain cancer.

C: I'm not sure that's true. I don't think the doctors know why she died.

S5: I heard she died of a cracked rib.

C: I don't think so, people don't usually die from broken bones. It's really confusing when we don't know why Mrs. Tobin died. What we do know is, it's very unusual for someone to die so young, usually people die when they're old.

Emphasizing the reality. Not having concrete information causes confusion.

Speaking to the unasked question, will my mother die?

DAY-CARE TEACHER: My grandmother died recently.

S6: How old was she?

DT: She was 92.

C: She was really old and lived a long time and that's usually when people die. (*Several children tell about the death of a grandparent. I encourage a brief discussion about how this made them feel. They share feeling sad, wishing their grandparent hadn't died and missing them.*) I wonder if you're feeling sad now? (*Eyes drop and a few children respond, "yeah."*)

S7: What's going to happen to Ruth? Who will she live with?

Children worry about who will take care of them.

C: Her grandparents are here now taking care of the children and I'm sure they will stay here for a while. (*A few others wipe tears from their faces, one little girl hides her face in the lap of a staff member.*) How do you think Ruth might be feeling?

S6: She's feeling sad. (*Many students nod in agreement.*)

C: What can we do to make Ruth feel better?

S8: Be nice to her.

S9: Be a good friend.

S10: We could have a party!

> I do not think that this is appropriate, but am not exactly sure how to respond.

C: I'm not sure this is a good time for a party, but maybe you could have a breakfast together, since you're here so early. (*There is an enthusiastic response from the children and staff.*) So, maybe you can think more about that and plan something really special. What else could you do?

S11: We could write letters to Ruth.

S12: We could write notes.

C: You've shared some really good ideas. You've thought of lots of things you can do that will help Ruth and yourselves feel better. (*Pause.*)

> I need to put closure on the dialogue because we have run out of time.

S13: Where will she be buried?

> Still needing more information.

C: We're not sure, her parents are from another state, so she might be buried a long way from here. There will be a service after school today so her family and friends can say good-bye to her.

> I am uncomfortable with the abruptness of the closure and would prefer more time to continue the discussion.

C: I think we have talked about a lot this morning, and it's time to stop for now. If any of you want to talk to me during the day just stop by my office, stop me in the hall or leave me a note. (*The children are already late for school, so the meeting ends fairly abruptly and quickly. They jump right up and noisily get their book bags and quickly go off to class.*)

> Some children might need more time with the counselor, I want them to know I am available should they want me.
>
> I am feeling really drained and very sad; they run off as if nothing has happened!

Meeting with Mrs. Tobin's Students

Mrs. Tobin's students heard of her death for the first time from the classroom teacher, unless their parents had already shared the information with them the previous evening. These students participated in their classroom discussion, but we, as counselors, felt it was important for them to get together as a group to discuss the loss.

The classroom teachers told Mrs. Tobin's students that there would be a meeting where all of Mrs. Tobin's students would get together with the counselors to discuss her death. The majority of children were comfortable coming to this meeting. Two third-graders from the same classroom were very anxious and told their teacher they were fearful of attending. Upon learning this, one of the counselors visited the classroom and explained what would happen at the meeting. They were told that no one would be forced to speak at this meeting. Also, they were told they would watch a videotape about death. This frightened them, but when it was further explained that the video was one with puppets their minds were eased. (One can only imagine what these children thought the tape would be about. This points out that such explanations need to be clear, concrete, and nonthreatening.)

One second-grader, Bobby, flatly refused to attend. He told his teacher he was not interested and he made comments like, "I'm not going to that stupid thing" and "I don't care." His counselor spoke to him and told him that although the meeting was not mandatory his presence would be very helpful to the other children. He was told he did not have to speak at the meeting and he was also given a clear and concrete explanation about the meeting. He acted as if he were not interested, but later that day he showed up promptly. (It was important that the meeting was not mandatory. Instead, the children could make an educated choice to attend or not.)

Scheduling the meeting was difficult because of the size of the school, the difference in schedules for different grade levels, and the children's tight schedules due to the academic demands at the school. Scheduling such a meeting, therefore, required the support of the school principal who told the teachers that it should take precedence over anything else. (The support of an administrator was essential because just as the children were ambivalent about attending, some of their teachers were equally ambivalent about sending them. On the one hand they wanted their students to get support, but on the other hand they felt protective of them and may have felt that *they* could best support their students through such a crisis.)

We coordinated a 30-minute time period at the very end of the day when all the children could attend. Our plan was to gather the children together, have a short introductory discussion, show a videotape which focused on the four tasks necessary for healthy grieving, then have a short group discussion. Our goal was to give the children an opportunity to be among other children who worked closely with Mrs. Tobin. Our secondary goal was to assess how the children were doing with the loss of their teacher.

The day was extremely hectic and emotionally intense for both counselors. Our time was completely booked with requests from students, parents, and administrators. We worked nonstop doing crisis counseling with individual children or with large and small groups. In between these child contacts we met with our peers and answered phone calls from parents. Also, Mrs. Tobin's daughter required a lot of time with her counselor.

The teachers sent the children at the appointed time. The counselors led the children into the room and a few of the older children sat in the chairs while the rest of the children sat on the floor in front of the television. There were four adults in the room: two counselors, the school nurse, and Mrs. Tobin's replacement teacher, Mrs. Smith.

Content of Session	Analysis and Feelings
COUNSELOR (Ms. D): We felt it was important for us to bring you all together because, except for Ruth, you are the children who were most special to Mrs. Tobin because you were her students. (*This seems to help a number of children individually. Several faces show some ease.*) We're going to show a puppet video which will help us to understand death and then we will talk as a group.	We are trying to establish a commonality. We expect this group to be cohesive and easily trusting of each other.

What we witnessed was very different from what we expected. The children were edgy and uncomfortable. There were several small groups within the large group, but this collection of children seemed to visibly lack the connection for which we had hoped. A few of the second-graders sat on the chairs in the back of the room. These children seemed very serious and they seemed to want us to say something to help them feel better. Two or three fourth-graders sat on the floor in front of their chairs. They acted as if they were waiting for a math lesson. They knew they needed to participate, but they were not too keen about this. In front of them sat a collection of third-graders. There seemed to be two groups within a group. These children sat very close together, as if their shoulder-to-shoulder arrangement would protect them from what they were about to experience. Two second-graders sat right up front. These girls were inseparable friends and they seemed eager to hear what we had to say and equally wanted adult attention. (These children were not a cohesive group because they were never seen by Mrs. Tobin as a whole group. Instead, they were seen individually or in small groups.)

One third-grader, Jared, sat on the periphery. He was smiling a lot and intermittently pushed himself into the other children's space. He laughingly pushed or shoved other children and then retreated. His smile seemed plastered on his face. The third-grade children who knew him saw him as entertaining, but some of the older children found him to be irritating.

We showed the children a short videotape entitled *The Death of a Friend: Helping Children Cope with Grief and Loss* (on loan from The Good Grief Program at Judge Baker Guidance Center). This tape uses puppetry to demonstrate the range of feelings children have when they lose a friend to death. It shows the children that it is natural to feel sad, guilty, angry, and wish for your friend's return. It emphasizes that it is okay to cry, but also okay to play and have fun. The video recommends that it helps children to talk about their feelings.

The third-graders who were sitting on the floor laughed frequently during the video, as did some of the second-graders. Their laughter seemed contagious and they required verbal limits to calm them down. They giggled at the funny voices of the puppets, and the puppet's comments such as, "You mean it's not my fault that my friend died?" At one point the children became so noisy that we questioned turning off the video, but they were able to respond to our strong reassurances. We told them, "We know that it is difficult to sit and watch the tape, but we will have time to talk when it is finished." The children quieted down and were able to listen, except for Jared.

After the video, we had a group discussion. The children were encouraged to bring up any questions, concerns, or feelings about Mrs. Tobin's death. We encouraged them to talk honestly.

Content of Session	Analysis and Feelings
COUNSELOR 2 (Ms. D): What kind of teacher was Mrs. Tobin?	
STUDENT 1: She was really nice.	
S2: She made you work hard. (*Several children enthusiastically agree.*)	
S3: I feel bad because I owed her some time.	
C2: Does anyone have a suggestion for Tommy [Student 3] to help him with these feelings?	

S4: He could do the time for Mrs. Smith.

S5: (*Beaming.*) You could think about Mrs. Tobin for that amount of time.

C1 (Mrs. M): Are there other feelings people want to share?

Relieved that the children are interested in talking and supporting one another.

S6: I feel bad for Mrs. Tobin because she died before she could see spring. (*Several of the children stoically sit in silence. Jared continues to be moderately disruptive throughout the video and discussion. C1 moves next to Jared hoping to contain his behavior and give him some support.*)

Jared is really having a hard time with this. He's disrupting the group. What should we do?

JARED: Yeah! She's dead! (*Loudly and enthusiastically.*)

Bothered by this remark even though we know that this is Jared's way of coping with loss.

DEREK: (*Angrily.*) Don't say that! She was a good person.

J: (*Tauntingly and pushing into other children's space.*) She's dead! She's dead!

D: (*Visibly angry and clenching his fist.*) You'd better stop that or else!

Would like to have explored this with Jared, but we are very concerned that Derek will lash out physically.

C2: Jared, you need to take a time out. We'd like to have you as part of the meeting, but you are getting into other children's space and it looks like you need a break. (*C1 escorts him out of the room.*)

We better stop Jared!

How does this make Jared feel? Is Jared trying to get himself hurt or rejected?

We reviewed the major themes of the videotape. Unfortunately, due to time constraints we had to end the meeting abruptly. All the children went back to their classes except for Bobby and Sarah. Bobby sat quietly, then began to sob as soon as the other children were gone, saying, "I don't know what to do. This never happened to me before. I can't believe she's dead." He cried for a few minutes and required reassurance that over time the sad feelings would begin to dissipate. Bobby agreed to address these issues with his counselor. Concurrent with this interchange, the other counselor slowly walked a sad and weepy Sarah back to her classroom, explaining to her teacher that she was feeling very sad. Sarah shared her guilt: "I feel like I gave her a headache and made her die." As her teacher picked her up and put her on her lap, she reassured her that this was not true. With gentle understanding and reassurance from both her teacher and her counselor, Sarah gained control of herself and readied herself to go home for the day. (A call was subsequently made to Sarah's mother alerting her of her daughter's difficulties.)

Counseling of Individual Students

Several children who were especially upset by Mrs. Tobin's death were referred to the counselors by their teachers or parents, or came to us spontaneously. This demonstrates the important role of the counselor in meeting the needs of individual children who respond to the death according to their own unique needs.

One of these was a child who had been having previous difficulties with his academic work and social relationships. He had been in frequent contact with Mrs. Tobin for help with his reading. This child was not working at grade level and he felt insecure about his abilities. He did not read well and believed that he had continually "let Mrs. Tobin down." This was the *child's* perception; he felt that Mrs. Tobin expected more of him that he could deliver.

Following Mrs. Tobin's death, this boy was very confused and anxious. He was glad to be free of what he perceived to be his teacher's "excessive demands," but was afraid that his anger toward Mrs. Tobin had contributed to her death. Of course, the child did not verbalize this directly. In situations like this, children "act out" through misbehaving, resulting in being punished.

In several play therapy sessions, many months after Mrs. Tobin's death, this child ventilated, through the mouths of two puppets, some of his feelings. While this boy will require ongoing intervention, the availability of the counselor/school social worker immediately after the death served an important function in diffusing some of this child's guilt and confusion about the teacher's sudden death.

Another child was worried about her grandmother's death which had occurred several months prior to Mrs. Tobin's. This girl did not even know Mrs. Tobin, yet the atmosphere in the school following the teacher's death had evidently stirred up feelings in this child about her previous personal loss. She came to the counselor, accompanied by a friend. During the meeting this child cried and acknowledged for the first time that, in fact, her grandmother had died. The availability of the counselor permitted the child's delayed, but important, expression of grief.

The counselor had contact with another child who saw Mrs. Tobin on a very regular basis. She valued her time and relationship with Mrs. Tobin. This child strongly believed that Mrs. Tobin had died from drinking too much coffee. Counseling gave this child the opportunity to understand the true cause of Mrs. Tobin's death and grieve the loss of a very important adult.

Commemoration

A memorial service, planned by the family, was held at a local temple the day after Mrs. Tobin died. The majority of the school staff attended as well as a handful of children. All of Mrs. Tobin's remedial reading colleagues participated as speakers in the service, as did one of her sisters. Because it was so soon after her death, there was a sense of denial for some and sadness for others. Many people were in the stage of disbelief, having only learned about her death that day. The service brought together many people who were important in her life: her family, her colleagues, her friends, her children's friends, and some of her students. It was the very beginning of the grief process for most people who attended. A reception followed the service which many staff attended. This was a time for sharing the memories of Mrs. Tobin and the feelings of sadness and grief.

Bulletin Board: In Loving Memory of Mrs. Tobin

In the midst of an annual Art Fair we commemorated Mrs. Tobin by placing an enlarged photograph of her on a bulletin board outside the Reading Room where she did most of her teaching. Under the photograph the title appeared: "In Loving Memory of Mrs. Tobin." Children drew portraits of Mrs. Tobin and wrote letters to her children. They drew pictures of their own feelings, of crying faces and of smiling faces, but mostly pictures with lots of tears. At a later date, all the pictures were put in a scrapbook and given to Mrs. Tobin's daughter, Ruth, for her to share with her siblings.

Staff Dedication

A small group of Mrs. Tobin's closest colleagues chose to dedicate a painting as an appropriate way to commemorate Mrs. Tobin in the school. A dedication ceremony was held in the hall outside of the Reading Room where Mrs. Tobin worked. A few of Mrs. Tobin's colleagues spoke briefly and then the lighted picture, which will hang permanently outside the Reading Room, was unveiled. This will provide a lasting reminder of Mrs. Tobin.

Student Commemoration

The counselors are currently in the process of offering the children an opportunity to commemorate Mrs. Tobin. We wrote the following letter of introduction to the parents:

> Dear Parents:
>
> Many children still have questions and concerns about Mrs. Tobin's death. This is not unusual even though many months have passed. As a way of responding to the children's needs, we will be offering them an opportunity to participate in a group project to commemorate Mrs. Tobin. This will give the children an opportunity to affirm the life of Mrs. Tobin and to grieve more completely.
>
> Their participation will be voluntary. It will be their decision to be involved or not and their decision will be respected. Different decisions will be right for different children.
>
> Those children who do choose to be a part of this project will work together to decide how they would like to commemorate Mrs. Tobin. We know that remembering, in a tangible way, someone who has died helps children to move on and we believe that this project will be helpful to the children.
>
> Please call us with any questions.
>
> > Sincerely,
> >
> > Caroline McElroy, L.I.C.S.W.
> > Gail Doster, L.I.C.S.W.
> > School Counselors

Ideally the commemoration should have occurred closer to the time of Mrs. Tobin's death. We do feel, however, that is it not too late and we look forward to helping children through the process. We will meet with them, brainstorm ideas, come to a consensus, and work on implementing their idea. We anticipate perhaps having a school fund raising activity such as a bake sale, as a way of funding the commemoration.

CONCLUDING REMARKS

The death of a teacher creates a crisis for the staff, children, and parents in the school community. Those who have grieved a loved one know that no amount of preparation takes away the pain when a death occurs. The following summary reviews the interventions that we found useful in helping the school community cope with the loss of a teacher:

1. Using a consultant who was knowledgeable in the areas of death education, childhood grief, and school systems was important. The consultant provided support to both the crisis team and the full staff at a time when it was most needed, immediately prior to Mrs. Tobin's death. It was important that this consultant take an educational approach with the staff as she presented information on the grieving child and discussing death with children. All the staff were given the same information at a critical time. This meeting empowered the teaching staff to feel secure when talking with their students and, also, gave them a chance to get in touch with their own feelings and the feelings of their colleagues.

2. Utilizing the pre-existing working relationship between one of the school counselors and the consultant prior to the teacher's death eliminated the tasks of searching for and building a new relationship at a time of crisis when so many other tasks required immediate attention. Schools are advised to prepare in advance by establishing working relationships with consultants who can be engaged in times of need.

3. Working within the framework of the school administration was necessary. The death of a staff member may exacerbate staff conflicts and some staff may differ about what is right and proper. It is the role of the crisis team to formulate decisions that are clinically sound and to implement them with the support of the school principal.

4. Providing mutual support within the counseling staff was helpful. The fact that the two counselors could share the work load and also share their own feelings of sadness made the stressful experience of dealing with this crisis more tolerable for both.

5. Maintaining realistic expectations about our work as counselors was valuable. The counselors needed to remind themselves and other crisis team members that no matter how well planned their interventions, a level of discomfort prevailed because of the crisis/grief factors. We could not take away the pain, no matter how hard we tried.

6. Meeting with groups of children to discuss Mrs. Tobin's death and the impact it had on them, within the school setting itself, was an invaluable part of helping the children understand and grieve.

In a school setting, a counselor/school social worker manages a high volume of counseling services and crises. After the initial phase of crisis intervention other types of crises emerged and regularly scheduled counseling services resumed. As a result, some of the steps of the grief process were overlooked due to the clinical "hustle and bustle" at school. The following are a few examples of additional interventions or adjustments that would have been helpful:

1. It would have been beneficial to more children had we planned the children's commemoration prior to the end of the school year in which Mrs. Tobin died, rather than waiting until the following fall. Because

of the delay, a whole grade level of students missed the opportunity to plan and participate in a commemoration since they moved on to the middle school at the end of the year.

2. It would have been helpful to offer a few follow-up sessions to the group of students serviced by Mrs. Tobin. This would have offered them further opportunity to share common concerns and to receive support from peers who had a closer relationship with Mrs. Tobin than other children in the school. Most of these children were, however, seen by their counselor individually or in small groups at school and several were referred for outside therapy.

3. The children contributed art work, letters, and poems to Mrs. Tobin's family by leaving them on a table below her picture in the hall. This picture was taken down earlier than planned at the request of Mrs. Tobin's daughter, Ruth. The art works and writings were gathered into a notebook and given to all three of Mrs. Tobin's children. Unfortunately, we did not make a copy for the school. The drawings and written materials were wonderfully expressive and could have been useful in the future.

4. Ideally, it would have been optimal had we had more time to check in with more children on an individual or small group basis or to facilitate further discussions within the classrooms. However, due to the general demand for our counseling services for all kinds of problems, we had to target for follow-up only those children who were obviously grieving or exhibiting changes in behavior. Those children who appeared to be coping well were not offered continued interventions. Some children had a delayed reaction to Mrs. Tobin's death. They appeared to be coping at the time of her death, but after their return to school in the fall or after an additional loss they required services.

In summary, the hardest part of dealing with the death of a teacher is the number of people that the death impacts and the varying needs of those who are affected. It creates a crisis for all and, as such, needs to be acted upon quickly. A school setting does, however, provide a perfect forum for helping children grieve. With the cooperation and help of the entire school community, with education and planned interventions, with a willingness to work hard in the best interests of the children, they can be offered an opportunity to grow from the experience of losing a teacher by death.

DISCUSSION QUESTIONS

1. The role of the counselor/school social worker is multifaceted because of the range of responsibilities and expectations to provide collaboration and meet direct service needs. Comment on the pressures implicit in this

role and evaluate the work of these "counselors/social workers" in meeting the needs of their school community.

2. Consider the dilemma of the sharing of "public" and "private" information in a situation of terminal illness when the family has not yet accepted the reality of the impending death. How can the counselor/school social worker balance the needs of the school community for accurate information with the needs of the family for privacy?

3. Comment on the meeting with Mrs. Tobin's students. Discuss the pros and cons of assembling a group of second- to fourth-graders for the purpose of discussing their feelings about their remedial reading teacher's death.

4. Discuss the impact of a teacher's death on children who have experienced other deaths. What is the appropriate role of the counselor/school social worker in identifying and helping such children?

REFERENCES

Bowlby, J. (1980). *Attachment and loss: Vol. III. Loss; Sadness and depression.* New York: Basic Books.

Brooks, R. (1991). *The self-esteem teacher.* Circle Pines, MN: American Guidance Service.

Carroll, D. (1985). *Living with dying:* New York: McGraw-Hill.

Fox, S. S. (1988). *Good grief: Helping groups of children when a friend dies.* Boston, MA: New England Associations of the Education of Young Children.

Grollman, E. A. (Ed.). (1967). *Explaining death to children.* Boston, MA: Beacon Press.

Grollman, E. A. (1990). *Talking about death.* Boston, MA: Beacon Press.

Nagy, M. (1948). The child's theories concerning death. *Journal of Genetic Psychology, 73,* 3–27.

CHAPTER THIRTEEN

Death of a Counselor
A Bereavement Group for
Junior High School Students

LUCY OPPENHEIMER HICKEY

A previously planned children's bereavement support group in a small rural community was begun 6 weeks after the death of the local drug education police officer. This group, for junior high school students from the town, also drew participants from surrounding areas, consistent with the format of regularly offered groups sponsored by the Bereavement Program of the area's Home Health Care Agency.

Officer Warner, the Drug and Alcohol Resistance Education (DARE) arm of the local police department, was a young man in his early 40s who had been involved with the junior high school students since their third-grade year in elementary school. The DARE project targets different schools and grades each year, providing an intense semester-long program. Officer Warner was also a parent, a softball coach, and a Sunday school teacher. He had touched the lives of most of the junior high school students in town. Many of the students who participated in this support group were deeply affected by his sudden, untimely death caused by a heart attack.

THE BEREAVEMENT SUPPORT PROGRAM

The Bereavement Program provides two after-school support groups per year for children on a rotating-age basis for the purpose of providing support and education to children who have experienced the death of an important person. The Hawaiian tradition of "talking story" is based on the fact that everyone has a story to tell, and there is healing value in

239

the telling and in being heard. Our support groups rely heavily on the retelling of each of our stories—orally, in writing, and in pictures—to others in the group who listen, who understand, and who through their attention give validity to our feelings.

Art, writing, brainstorming, and written exercises all help elicit feelings, identify issues, and assist in resolving confused feelings and perceptions. Creating a piece of art expressing intangible and unformed feelings externalizes and helps to give form to those feelings. The process helps to reduce the negative power of emotions, and allows the individual to gain mastery over those feelings (Rubin, 1984). Sharing personal creations in the group gives validity to the feelings underlying the art, while also providing support to the individual (Zambelli, Clark, & Heegaard, 1989).

Group Leadership

The groups are led by a social group worker and a counselor trained as an art therapist. The marriage of bereavement specialist and art therapist provides a unique blend of skills. The group worker brings an understanding of the grieving process at different developmental levels, of the universal themes associated with grieving, and a respect for individual responses to loss; the art therapist brings knowledge of the healing power of creating a work of art, and a sensitivity about the symbolic communication of children's art work.

A college student whose brother died of cancer when she was 16 years old provides volunteer assistance to the group. She is closer to the age of the children in the groups, and her own experiences create a bond of commonality which participants appreciate.

Group Structure

The group sessions are held in the art room of the local junior high school during after-school hours. The groups meet for 1½ hours, 1 day a week, for 8 to 10 weeks, depending on school vacation schedules. Participants come from our centrally located town and surrounding towns and villages. Information about the group, referrals, and invitations to participate are usually channeled through school guidance counselors. Referrals also come through the Home Health Care Agency's ongoing adult-support group, through hospice contacts, by the Bereavement Program's in-school elementary-level grief education program, and by word of mouth. All parents and students receive a letter outlining the purpose of the group, and a personal reminder about the first meeting.

The group under consideration here was begun in the fall of the year, encompassing the Thanksgiving holiday and ending just prior to Christmas. The types of losses experienced by participants ranged from parental death to loss of a family friend, and, as previously noted, many participants had been affected by the recent death of Officer Warner.

Collaboration with Parents and School Personnel

Throughout the course of the group sessions, the group facilitators maintain contact with school personnel and parents. Two meetings are held with parents to distribute general information on children's grief, to share parental concerns and questions, and to advise parents about what they may expect as a result of their child's participation in the group.

It is normal for children dealing with difficult and confusing feelings of grief to carry these feelings into their behavior outside of the group. Parents and teachers need to be aware that this may occur, and that group facilitators can provide extra support to families and teachers when this happens. This aspect of grieving is also addressed within the group, and the participants know that while no personal issues raised in the group are discussed without prior consultation with the student, we discuss these general concepts with their parents and guidance counselors or teachers. Facilitators also maintain informal contact with parents and school personnel throughout the duration of the group sessions, according to specific needs.

Group Format

For the group discussed in this chapter, each session was structured with introductory and check-in activities at the start (including snacks); several thematic art or writing activities during the bulk of the meeting, providing the focus for discussion; and a closing segment of time for review, preview, and closure.

Each week during snacks, we discussed everyone's previous week and we identified issues that needed to be addressed. We took time to share memories or personal mementos, pictures, and items that belonged to or had been given to the children by the person who had died, and we talked about favorite shared activities or stories. We also encouraged the children to read and report back to the group about the books on dying and grief which are part of the Agency's library, and which were circulated through the group.

The progression of themes addressed during the nine sessions was designed to move from identifying grief and the ways it can affect us, through the telling of our stories in detail, and, finally, moving on toward healing, coping, and living our lives. The activities employed were varied, working from impersonal, nonthreatening but participatory projects like brainstorming to more intensely personal, individual ventures like "My grief feels like. . . . " This balance gave general information about children's grief, and also allowed each child to explore his/her own feelings and issues.

The closing of each group included eliciting unanswered questions, sharing important things the participants learned in a session, and expectations about the issues we would explore the following week. This decompression time allowed participants to pull back from the often painful and intense feelings dealt with in the group, and to regain the safety of a more intellectual and general group-focused activity before going back into the everyday world.

Before discussing the details of group membership and process I will review briefly the normal developmental conflicts of the preadolescent youngster and the typical understanding and response to death among students of junior high school age.

DEVELOPMENTAL CHARACTERISTICS OF PREADOLESCENCE

Normal development during the junior high school years reflects a time of transition marked by pivotal cognitive, physiological, and psychological changes. The pubertal youngster between ages 11 and 14 is no longer a "child" and not yet a full-blown adolescent. The increased flow of hormones stimulates uncomfortable affects and a sense of vulnerability. Sarnoff states that "almost universally puberty is a time of inner turmoil as a result of psychological factors and internal sensations derived from bodily changes" (1987, p. 11). These drastic changes in the body bring about an increased sense of narcissism and fear of unfavorable comparisons or rejections by peers.

The ability of the preadolescent to think abstractly, however, increases his/her ability to communicate verbally and to understand the motivations of others. The opinions and behaviors of peers often help the youngster forge an identity separate from his/her nuclear family. Indeed, identity formation looms as the major task of adolescence (Erikson, 1968).

Understanding and Response to Death

As discussed in Chapter 1, the prepubertal child (ages 9–12) has a realistic perception of the finality and irreversibility of death. Lonetto's work with children of this age, however, reveals that despite their correct *understanding* about death they *believe* it is in "the domain of the aged" (1980, p. 157). Sarnoff concurs with Lonetto, stating as follows:

> Direct contact with dying is rare in this age group. When a fellow teenager dies, the effect is massive. Tears, monuments, poems spring up as if creativity could erase doom. The reinforcement of the sense of one's mortality and vulnerability intensifies fears, triggers depression, and intensifies the impact of the impending separation from the family that jobs and colleges away from home imply. . . . Part of the mastery of separation and growth is a preoccupation with and working through of death. (1987, pp. 141–142)

Separation, thus, is the bottom line both in death and in adolescent identity formation. Its occurrence in the life of the preadolescent threatens both internal and external stability.

Implications for Peer Bereavement Support Groups

The previous discussion highlights the vulnerable state of the preadolescent youngster buffeted by hormonal waves and desperately trying to maintain some sense of self, congruent with that of his/her peers. The occurrence of a death in his/her family automatically distinguishes the student from peers who continue their regular school and extracurricular activities. The pubertal preadolescent young person, already under great stress, may feel unable to respond when a death occurs.

A group approach serves a very important purpose to help such a youngster deal with bereavement in the company of peers who are similarly bereaved. The "common ground of group support" (Schwartz & Zalba, 1971) eliminates feelings of embarrassment or "difference" that otherwise might dominate in a situation in which a youngster might withdraw in solitary grief. St. Exupéry expressed the feelings of union and acceptance implicit in support groups in the statement, "I am of the group, and the group is of me" (1948, p. 118).

THE GROUP

Group Membership

Participants in the Bereavement Support Group included the following:

Nina: The 11-year-old sixth-grade daughter of Officer Warner. A town resident with extended family in the area, she lived with her mother and older brother, who would graduate from high school the following June.

Debra: Nina's best friend, age 12, and a seventh-grader. She and her family were the Warners' closest family friends. Debra attended the group as a support person for Nina, but also to deal with her own sense of loss over Officer Warner's death.

Jody: A sixth-grader, age 11, from a neighboring town. Her older sister, a high school freshman, had died suddenly 1 year previously while at school. Jody's close extended family lived primarily out of state, with the exception of one family that lived in the same village. Her oldest sister was to graduate from high school in June. Her mother provided Jody with many opportunities to discuss her sister's death and to share feelings and memories, but her father was unable to talk about it. The family lives next to the cemetery where her sister is buried, and her parents visited the cemetery daily.

Michelle: Jody's seventh-grade cousin, age 12, who lived almost next door. Her only sibling was also due to graduate from high school in June; neither he nor his father could talk about the cousin's death.

Heather: A quiet 12-year-old seventh-grader from town whose grandmother had died 1 year previously. Her grandmother had been the primary day-care provider since Heather's birth. Heather, herself, had an undiagnosed, episodic, life-threatening illness. Her older sister was about to marry and move out of state, and her older brother was due to graduate from high school the following June. Heather frequently expressed a desire to join her grandmother, but had been resistant to individual counseling or therapy in the past.

Steve: An eighth-grader, age 13, whose father had died when he was 3. Steve lived with his mother and maternal grandmother, and had limited contact with his father's family, most of whom lived out of state. His mother was unable to talk with him about his father. He was quiet, with little affect, and it was often difficult to engage him in the group.

Greg: A seventh-grader, age 12, who had participated in a previous Bereavement Support Group, and who was dealing with the abandonment by his father, the death by cancer of his stepfather, and the loss of his stepgrandparents with whom his family shared a house: The house burned, his stepgrandparents then moved out of state, and the grandfather then died. Greg had been close to Officer Warner and he was still dealing with issues of anger and episodes of rage resulting from his previous loss experiences.

Mark: An 11-year-old sixth-grader from another town whose father had died of cancer when he was 4 months old. He maintained close contact with his father's family, aided by his mother. He had some discomfort with his stepfather and had questions about his place in his family of two half-brothers and parents.

Adam: A 14-year-old eighth-grader from another town who was dealing with the death of the grandfather who had been his primary male relationship. His grandmother had died in the spring, and his grandfather in September.

Tracy: A seventh-grade girl, age 13, from a village some distance away. Tracy's mother died when she was 8 years old, leaving her to care for a 5-year-old brother. Her father was involved in a relationship which relieved Tracy of many of her maternal responsibilities, but also brought other young children into the home. A history of abuse and neglect in the family and the illness of her maternal grandmother made Tracy's participation in the group extremely important, providing her with an anchor and a safe place.

All of the children attended the group because of parental or school recommendation, or at their own request. Several came tentatively, agreeing to attend the first two sessions to see what the group was like. Nina and Debra, and Jody and Michelle came in pairs to provide mutual support, as well as to deal with their own losses.

A summary/overview of the group follows:

Name	Age	Grade	Person who died	How long ago
Nina	11	6th	Father	6 wks.
Debra	12	7th	Family friend	6 wks.
Jody	11	6th	Sister	11 mos.
Michelle	12	7th	Cousin	11 mos.
Heather	12	7th	Grandmother	1 yr.
Steve	13	8th	Father	10 yrs.
Greg	12	7th	Stepfather	4 yrs.
			Stepgrandfather	2 yrs.
Mark	11	6th	Father	11 yrs.
Adam	14	8th	Grandfather	1 mo.
			Grandmother	4 mos.
Tracy	13	7th	Mother	5 yrs.
			Grandmother	During group

Session 1

Activities/Goals	*Responses*
Introductory activities	Bustle and busy work create a level of comfort.
• Name tags	
• Interest inventory (Table 13.1)	Blind walk breaks down many barriers and produces a lot of giggles.
• Blind walk	
• Set ground rules	

TABLE 13.1. Interest Inventory

What grade are you in, and where do you go to school?
What is your favorite thing to eat?
What are your favorite television shows?
What do you like to do in your spare time (hobbies/sports)?
If you had one thousand dollars, what would you spend it on?
What was the happiest day of your life so far?
What was the saddest day of your life so far?
What do you look forward to in the future?

Goals
• To build trust and a sense of safety
• To set ground rules and build a sense of
  group identity
• To acknowledge our purpose and the
  courage it took to attend

Self-portraits (paper in thirds)
• Self now (center)
• As a baby (left)
• When old (right)

Goals
• To recognize change and loss as part of
  life
• To introduce talk of feelings

Beginning discussions of loss
• Change as a part of life
• Recognizing smaller losses of
  childhood
• Recognizing large changes,
  losses in their lives now
• How long would you like to
  live if you could choose?
• Several say they would not
  want to be old and sick, in
  pain or unable to be active.
• How did they act when they
  lost something important
  when younger? Denial?
  Anger? Cried? Replaced it?
• Facilitators reinforce that
  these are all "normal"
  reactions to loss.

    Facilitators explained the purpose of the group as a combination of
sharing stories and learning about grief. Although acknowledging that
the participants themselves were the "experts" about their own feelings,
we also stressed that we were all dealing with losses that had deeply affected us. The recognition of a common base that also allows for individual
ownership of feelings provided an accepting and nonthreatening atmosphere. Adam participated guardedly, Steve very little, and Heather
showed some hesitancy when it came to sharing her story but not her

response to the exercises. The fact that Tracy and Greg had participated in previous groups helped to start discussions: They were used to the facilitators and the process. Jody's, Michelle's, and Mark's natural loquaciousness and desire to have a place to talk about their losses also helped to open discussions. It was an unusually open and vivacious first meeting.

Session 2

Activities/Goals

Feelings in the body
Placement and size of feelings

Goals
• To recognize that a relationship exists between feelings and our bodies
• To give information and to look at our own feelings

Brainstorm: Feelings of grief
Initial list kept open, added to for next three sessions.

Responses

Recognition that each of us is different

Michelle: Level of fear relative to all other feelings; location of anxiety (Figure 13.1)

Jody: Level of anxiety; across the board, hands all red (Figure 13.2)

(Table 13.2)

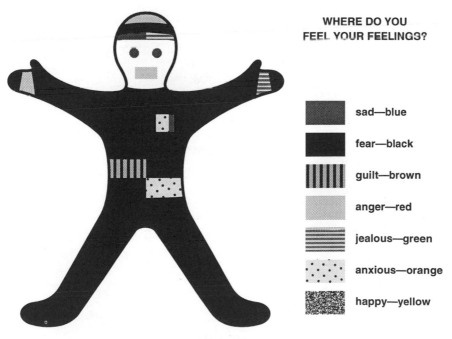

WHERE DO YOU FEEL YOUR FEELINGS?

sad—blue

fear—black

guilt—brown

anger—red

jealous—green

anxious—orange

happy—yellow

FIGURE 13.1.

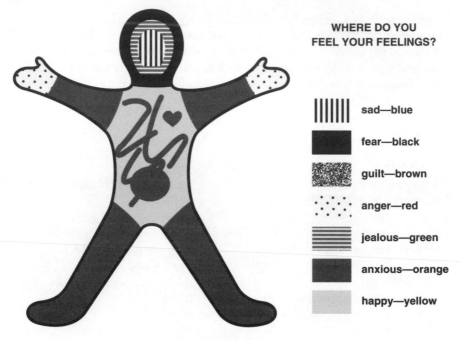

**WHERE DO YOU
FEEL YOUR FEELINGS?**

sad—blue

fear—black

guilt—brown

anger—red

jealous—green

anxious—orange

happy—yellow

FIGURE 13.2.

TABLE 13.2. Grieving Feels Like . . .

sadness	*Added during third discussion*
hurting all over	upset
lonely	disconnected
wondering why person died	numb/insulated
mad at self	miserable
guilty for what didn't do	left alone
feel like crazy	angry at person who died
okay	angry at God, at disease
self-conscious/different	wonder if same thing will happen to me
responsible	feel small
whole life gone down the tube	sick
pretend not really happened	confused
not believe	hate
expecting person to return	
don't have any more friends	*Added during fourth discussion*
	jealous (of families who are together)
Added during second discussion	
less self-esteem	
blame self	
nothing	
vulnerable	
empty	
easily hurt	

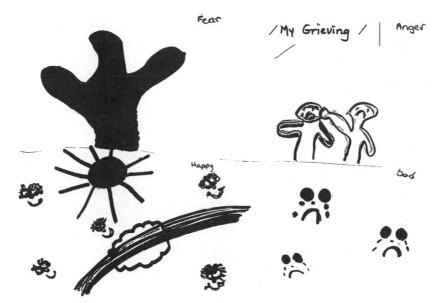

FIGURE 13.3.

Goals
- To focus on feelings in a nonthreatening way
- To recognize the range of feelings associated with grief; that everyone grieves differently; that feelings may change over time

Draw own grieving feelings
- Relate general activity to each person

Personal contributions about *feelings* blended with ideas about how people would respond in hypothetical situations

(Figure 13.3)

Group discussion
- Regarding the *differences* between individuals in the group
- Questions about how invidual reactions reflected personalities
- Recognition that "being happy" is also okay

The nature of the material covered in this session required that participants take greater risks than in our introductory meeting. Accordingly, most of the students were more hesitant to share and more reluctant to volunteer information. The notable exception was Nina whose loss was recent and whose feelings were intense; her need to tell her story was almost palpable. In general, this session had a subdued tone.

Session 3

Activities/Goals

Additions to "feeling list"
• Sharing mementos
• Weekly check-in

Goals
• To keep in touch with the feelings generated by the group
• To initiate discussion of the role of guilt, magical thinking of childhood that we carry with us through life

Brainstorm: "Grief looks like"
• Make *"My own grief looks like"* list or picture.
• Personal feeling lists give ownership and validity to feelings and individual differences.

Goals
• To give information about behaviors associated with grieving
• To focus on individual behaviors and their relationship to grief and loss
• To begin to focus on coping skills

Self-esteem circles
• To explain the relationship between loss and self-esteem; to help participants understand why many of them have lowered self-esteem, or do not feel whole
• To recognize how long it takes to fill out the holes left by a loss, and to feel whole again
• To recognize that that "new" self will be different: one will not be the same again

Responses

Tracy: Guilt regarding mother's death, not making her mother take her medications, take better care of herself, anger at her mother

Heather: Guilt regarding not being able to visit grandmother in the hospital because of her own hospital phobias, at not being able to attend the funeral due to her own illness, at not being with her grandmother now

Discussion of feelings of suicide, "life not worth living" without the person. It is normal to feel that way, even though people do not usually act on it. It is also normal to have difficulty sleeping, concentrating, or thinking about anything else, to be cranky, have temper tantrums over little things, have headaches, or want to forget the whole thing ever happened. It is scary to have feelings and/or behaviors be out of control; we are not the same person we are used to being.

(Table 13.3)

Jody: Feeling different, conspicuous, how little of her was left whole

Powerful impact on several of the girls to recognize visually something they had been sensing but could not put into words; recognition of loss of confidence in relationships and friendships, feelings of being not liked, of being different

(Figures 13.4 and 13.5)

TABLE 13.3. My Grief

sadness	want to do everything and not take
burning eyes	a break
stomach ache	think that everyone is going to hate
lonely	or stare at you
chest aches	keep thinking why it happened
can't sleep	feeling blue
can't consintrate [*sic*]	think that there [*sic*] whole life is gone
everything aches	down the tube
don't know what to do or say	in shock
go crazy	thinking it's my fault
pretend your [*sic*] feeling fine	
don't want to talk or do anything	
dream a lot	

Session 4

Activities/Goals	Responses
Where were you when you first heard about the death/recognized the loss? (Draw or write.) • What happened? • What did you do? • How did you feel?	Nina: Went next door and stayed there; overwhelmed by strange activities, rescue squads, strangers in her home; chose to distance herself, as it felt safer.

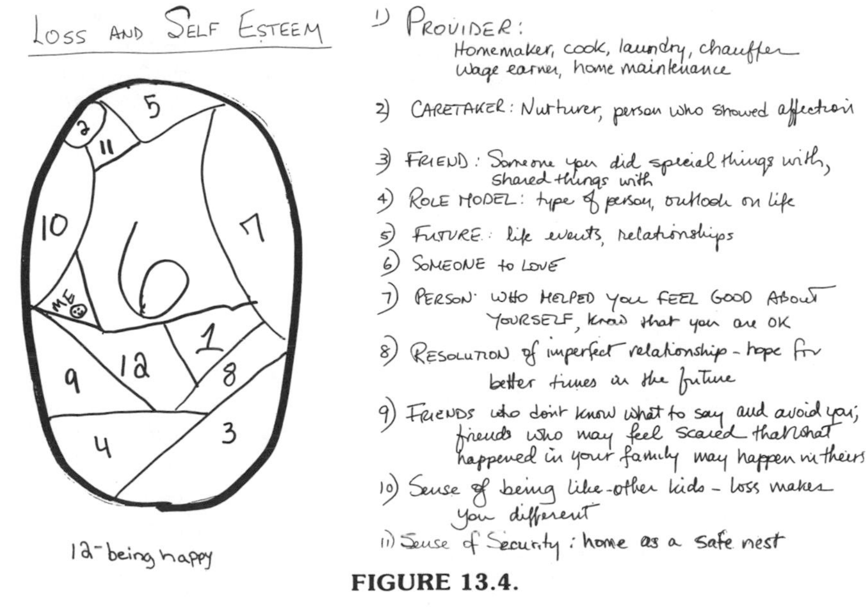

LOSS AND SELF ESTEEM

12 - being happy

1) PROVIDER: Homemaker, cook, laundry, chauffer, wage earner, home maintenance

2) CARETAKER: Nurturer, person who showed affection

3) FRIEND: Someone you did special things with, shared things with

4) ROLE MODEL: type of person, outlook on life

5) FUTURE: life events, relationships

6) SOMEONE to LOVE

7) PERSON: WHO HELPED YOU FEEL GOOD ABOUT YOURSELF, know that you are OK

8) RESOLUTION of imperfect relationship - hope for better times in the future

9) FRIENDS who don't know what to say and avoid you; friends who may feel scared that what happened in your family may happen in theirs

10) Sense of being like other kids - loss makes you different

11) Sense of Security: home as a safe nest

FIGURE 13.4.

LOSS AND SELF ESTEEM

1) PROVIDER: Homemaker, cook, laundry, chauffer, wage earner, home maintenance

2) CARETAKER: Nurturer, person who showed affection

3) FRIEND: Someone you did special things with, shared things with

4) ROLE MODEL: type of person, outlook on life

5) FUTURE: life events, relationships

6) SOMEONE to LOVE

7) PERSON WHO HELPED YOU FEEL GOOD ABOUT YOURSELF. knew that you are OK

8) RESOLUTION of imperfect relationship - hope for better times in the future

9) FRIENDS who don't know what to say and avoid you; friends who may feel scared that what happened in your family may happen in their

10) Sense of being like other kids - loss makes you different

11) Sense of Security: home as a Safe nest

12. Self esteem ● Feel like everyone I love is leaving me

FIGURE 13.5.

Goals
- To recognize the healing value of telling the story, externalizing the horror
- To test understanding of the death and cause of death
- To help to face the reality of the death
- To elaborate on the differences between the ways children and adults may act or feel when they grieve
- To take closer look at shock behaviors and the role of denial as protection

Funerals
- What was it like for you?
- What would you have changed?
- Did you attend?
- Who made the decision?

Goals
- To heal through storytelling and focusing on their involvement, family decision-making
- To be able or unable to say good-bye

Agenda of issues
- Value of funerals and mourning rituals
- Permission to be kids, to be safe

Jody, Michelle: Sense of being included in the whole process, which helped with the feeling of disbelief

Nina, Jody, Michelle, and college student: Issues of sharing their personal losses because they were also public deaths or public figures; resentments at having to share; difficulties and hurt when others claim their share of the grief

Greg: Sent off to neighbors when stepfather died; grandparents had moved when grandfather died; strong sense of exclusion and anger over it; anger exacerbated by loss of all stepfather's belongings in fire

Heather: Deep regrets over parental refusal to allow her to read her poem to her grandmother at the funeral, and the

FIGURE 13.6.

subsequent illness which prevented her attendance at the funeral

Adam: Forced to be a pall-bearer; unable to talk about the experience, or do more than describe the picture (Figure 13.6)

Nina: Family conflicts acted out at the funeral horrified her (Table 13.4)

TABLE 13.4. The Funeral

I didn't like not having anything to put in her casket and I didn't like that when I touched her she was cold. She looked sad and she didn't really look like herself. I didn't want to cry because I needed to be alone and it was impossible to be alone if you were crying because there was a lot of relatives who didn't want me to be sad and wanted to help me understand what happened. I felt like I was helpless because there was nothing I could do to bring her back. I knew I would never see her again. I hadn't realized exactly how much I loved her.

Questionnaire/interview

• For children whose parent died before conscious memory

Goals

• To help children find ways to connect with the part of themselves and their families represented by the absent parent
• To give the boys permission to ask questions of a reluctant parent or another relative

Mark, Steve: One facilitator works with these boys to focus on questions they have about their fathers, to identify people they would be comfortable talking to.

(Table 13.5)

Session 5

Activities/Goals

Where do you think the person is now? (Draw or write.)

Responses

Mark: Reveals he has seen shadows that look like his father at various times in his house; wonders if he is crazy, if anyone else has experienced this.

General discussion about normalcy of seeing, hearing, smelling, feeling presence of someone who has died

Greg: Stepfather is in heaven driving racing cars, which he loved to do.

(Figure 13.7)

TABLE 13.5. Questionnaire/Interview

What was he like when he was a kid?
What did he like to do?
Was he quiet?   serious?   joking?
How did my parents meet?
Do I look like my Dad?
Do I do things like my Dad did? Am I like my Dad in any way? How?
What did he like to do with me?
What did my Dad do for a living?

Where She is Now: In The hearts of the people who loved her.

FIGURE 13.7.

Brainstorm: Difficulty of not having opportunity to say good-bye.
- What would you like to have said?
- Difficulty of saying good-bye to someone you love
- Recognition that it is difficult never to have known a parent—a different kind of pain, a different kind of hole

Discussion of talking to person who has died
- It is not crazy; you are not crazy.
- It is a way to stay connected.
- We do not stop loving someone because he is no longer with us.

Mark: Open about questions he has about his father and the people who can help answer them, his mother's efforts to help him find answers, the constraints that exist because he is careful of his stepfather's presence

Steve: Unable to do more than acknowledge that the difficult feelings exist

Goal

- To begin to focus on healing and on ways to compensate for things undone

Ways to say good-bye

- Letter or special memento in coffin
- Visiting cemetery
- Writing feelings, thoughts
- Memories, sharing stories

"Dear _____": Write a letter to the person who has died; tell him/her the things you wanted to say but never had the chance. Tell what you miss about him/her and what you do not miss, too.

Powerful experience. Done in private in the room, but not shared. Tears and hugs *are* shared.

Facilitators regretted that Adam was not present at this session as we wished to explore further with him the issues raised in his picture related to his grandfather's funeral. Because both Adam and Tracy had been absent from one previous session, it was not immediately evident or recognized that they had dropped out permanently. Facilitators felt some frustration—yet little surprise—that neither Steve nor Mark had followed through on the family/interviews about their fathers. For Mark it may not have been necessary as he has information about his Dad; we felt the exercise was helpful to him in focusing his search for identity and that the formal interview format was not really necessary. For Steve, the exercise may have helped him focus his feelings and questions, but we also had hoped that the format and our "assignment" would enable him to have access to information he was otherwise denied.

Session 6

Activities/Goals

Sharing and subsequent discussion

- Recognition that the group stirs up sad feelings, and deals with things we would rather not think about
- Any behavioral changes noted?

Responses

Nina: Reads a lengthy poem she has written after the previous session as a way of saying goodbye to her cousin.

Greg: Temper, fights at school; inability to tolerate when things do not go his way; feelings related to loss come out in other arenas

Discussion: That these are connected; feeling cheated in life leads to frustration when other things do not go his way.

General: Acknowledgment of inability to pay attention at school, daydreaming, crankiness with other friends and family; discussion of issues; each does his/her own "time line."

Adolescent/grief waves

• Recognition of the emotional roller-coaster of adolescence
• Difficulty of grief and overlying of waves of feeling

Recognition: That it is confusing when the waves and peaks go in opposite directions (Figure 13.8)

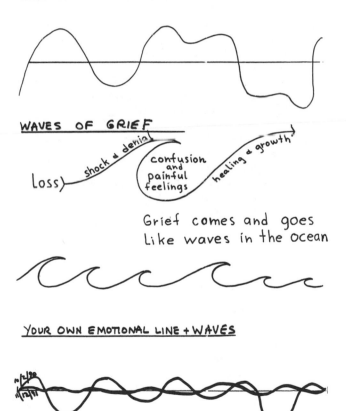

FIGURE 13.8.

TABLE 13.6. Signs of Stress Checklist

Rarely	Often		
____	____	1.	Headaches
____	____	2.	Stomach problems—diarrhea, constipation, nausea, heartburn, urinating often
____	____	3.	High blood pressure or heart pounding
____	____	4.	Pain in neck, lower back, shoulders, jaw
____	____	5.	Muscle jerks or tics
____	____	6.	Eating problems—no appetite, constant eating, full feeling without eating
____	____	7.	Sleeping problems—unable to fall asleep, wake up in middle of the night, nightmares
____	____	8.	Fainting
____	____	9.	General feeling of tiredness
____	____	10.	Shortness of breath
____	____	11.	Dry throat or mouth
____	____	12.	Unable to sit still—too much energy
____	____	13.	Teeth grinding
____	____	14.	Stuttering
____	____	15.	Uncontrollable crying or not being able to cry
____	____	16.	Smoking
____	____	17.	Use of excessive alcohol
____	____	18.	Use drugs
____	____	19.	Increased use of medication—aspirin, tranquilizers, etc.
____	____	20.	General anxiety, nervous feelings, or tenseness
____	____	21.	Dizziness and weakness
____	____	22.	Irritable and easily set off
____	____	23.	Depressed
____	____	24.	Accident prone
____	____	25.	Feeling angry in general
____	____	26.	Feeling overwhelmed and unable to cope—want to run away, cry, or end it all
____	____	27.	Doing weird things without thinking
____	____	28.	Nervous laughter, easily startled, jumpy
____	____	29.	Always concerned about disease and death
____	____	30.	Bored with life
____	____	31.	Always worried about money
____	____	32.	Afraid of weekends or vacations
____	____	33.	Feeling that you can't discuss problems with anyone else
____	____	34.	Afraid of heights or closed spaces
____	____	35.	Feeling rejected all the time, especially by your family
____	____	36.	Unable to concentrate or finish things you start
____	____	37.	Never laugh
____	____	38.	Allergies
____	____	39.	Always in a hurry
____	____	40.	Don't have friends and may not care about being with other people
____	____	41.	Don't do your assignments
____	____	42.	Can do one thing well and most of your time is spent on it

Grieving often shows up in physical symptoms and stress.

Stress inventory (Table 13.6)
• Recognition of several relationships between loss and stress, as well as individual responses to stress and potential consequences for health

Discussion of coping with holidays, anniversaries, weddings
• Supposedly happy occasions
• Ways to start new traditions
• Ways to incorporate remembrances of the person who died into the holiday

Discussion: Reveal new insights into their own stress levels, recognition for many (Nina, Steve, Mark) that grieving may have more impact on their lives than realized

Traditions and celebrations (of Thanksgiving and Christmas)
• Will not be the same
• Look at family plans for the holidays
• How things will be different, what different plans, how they feel about differences
• Sharing, by those who have been through one or more holiday seasons, with those in the group who are facing these occasions for the first time since a death; may also involve new losses

Jody, Nina, Michelle: Facing sibling high school graduations, leaving home

Heather: Facing sibling graduation and wedding and moving

Group members and facilitators were moved by Nina's poem and the intense emotions expressed in it, creating a very mellow yet emotional session. The group reached a new level of cohesion also having to do with the absence of Adam. Because his participation in the discussion had been minimal he was something of an uncomfortable unknown presence in the group, which we did not recognize until he was no longer present.

Session 7

Activities/Goals

Masks (out of paper plates)
Front: The side we show to the world
Back: The way we feel inside

Goals
• To recognize that we often wear masks as protection, as a coping mechanism, as escape, to fit in socially

Responses

It does not always feel okay to be so different inside and out, but it does often serve a purpose

• To not have to talk about problems/issues if you do not want to
• To keep self together; fear of

Different grieving patterns in families
• To reinforce the idea of individual differences
• To recognize that children may not grieve as continuously as adults, that we all need time to escape the pain

losing control if a crack opens in the facade

Discussion
• Of differences, patterns
• Recognition that people may be grieving, feeling the pain, even if they do not show it or can not talk about it (Figure 13.9)
• Of loss of control in life already out of control
• What is the worst that can happen?
• Scenarios discussed

Family changes
Changed alliances, roles, members (new additions); use clay to represent family members in relation to each other

Discussion
• How this is different
• How it has changed
• Scenarios discussed

Changes noted
• More time alone
• More responsibilities at home
• Moving
• Parents dating/stepparents and siblings
• Some other adult to talk to and share feelings with

FIGURE 13.9.

The "family changes" exercise was not effective with this group. Facilitators acknowledged that many of the losses had been too recent or were too far in the past for changes to be evident.

Session 8

Activities/Goals

Discussion
- Look to the future; it is okay to move on with your own life.
- What happens when it is hard to move on, to accept life without the person
- Recognition that future losses will activate feelings and maybe behaviors associated with old losses
- Recognition of what we still have that is important to us; what feels connected to what gives us pleasure, satisfaction, what has helped to fill the hole created by the death (draw or write).

Closure
Anticipating termination of the group
- Any special ways to say good-bye?

Responses

Brainstorm/discussion
- Physically ill
- Feeling suicidal
- Risk-taking behaviors
- Dwell on death—focal point of life
- Build walls to protect self from pain and to keep people out, especially with multiple losses, isolating
- Temper out of control
- Feels scary, painful, angry
- Feels like betrayal of the person if you are happy

(Figure 13.10)

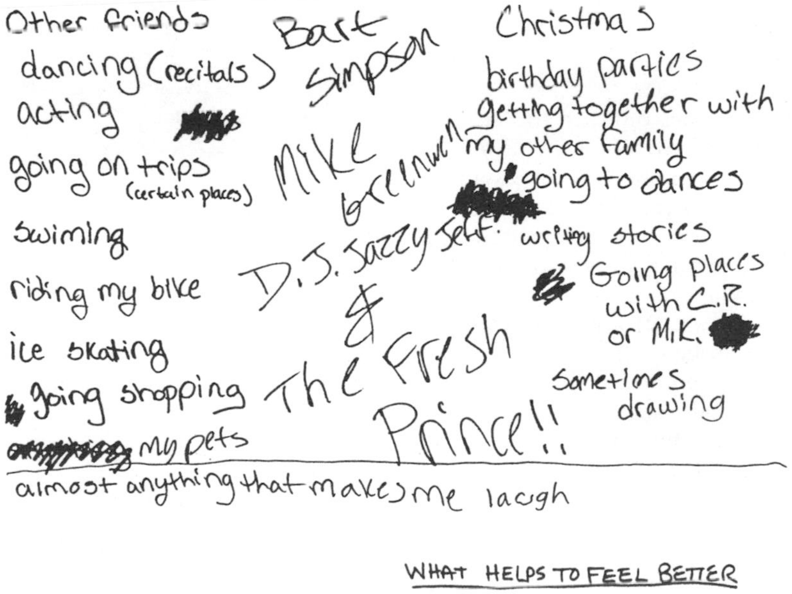

Other friends
dancing (recitals)
acting
going on trips (certain places)
swiming
riding my bike
ice skating
going shopping
my pets
almost anything that makes me laugh

Bart Simpson

MIKE BREUNMAN

D.J. Jazzy Self

The Fresh Prince!!

Christmas
birthday parties
getting together with my other family
going to dances
writing stories
Going places with C.R. or M.K.
Sometimes drawing

WHAT HELPS TO FEEL BETTER

FIGURE 13.10.

Discussion
- Sharing is both upbeat and poignant.
- Reminders that it *is* okay to go on with life
- We do not stop loving people when they die.
- Memories, pictures, telling stories help to keep us connected to people we love.

Session 9

Activities/Goals

Responses

Closure
Snacks and check-in time are occupied by a pizza party, setting the atmosphere of festivity yet marking the close of the group.

Draft of letter is read and some changes are requested by group members. Seen as a safe way to have parents "participate" at a distance.

Letter to parents
This is the way the group chooses to inform their parents about the group's content, without impinging on their ownership and confidentiality.

Activities
- Memory books are made. All written materials are returned to the individuals. Decorated covers are made and books put together. Books seen as a tangible moment of the group but also as a continuing source of information about grief and communication with families about the child's loss.
- Origami cranes are made with messages inside to be used as Christmas ornaments. Seen as tangible mementos of the group and link to the person who died.
- Cards are made for each other, with individual messages.
- Individual conferences are held with one of the facilitators.

These activities are going on simultaneously.

Goal
- To share any concerns the facilitators had

Mark: Okay to tell his mother of his ambivalence about his stepfather trying to replace his father, but only if she does not discuss it with Mark.

- To find out if the child had questions or unanswered concerns
- To get permission to pass on any information the child wants his/her parent to have but is not comfortable discussing him/herself

Candle ceremony

In a circle, each person lights a candle in memory, and passes the light around the circle.

Candles, memory books, cranes, cards provide:
- Group closure
- Tangible mementos of the group
- Links to the person who died
- Tools and information for future use— support, a way of opening communication with parents or about the person who died.

Heather: Tell Mother that special afternoon a week with each other is important, and not to let it slide in the flurry of wedding and graduation. Tell Mother that she wants to be able to visit cemetery "alone," but with her mother nearby.

Michelle: Ask parents not to get angry at her when she is being silly. She needs a change from all the sad times

Steve: Would like to have more access to people who knew his Dad and can talk about what his Dad was like and how he died. It is okay that his Mom cannot do this, but he wants her to help him have access to someone who can.

Parents are invited in to stand around the group.

This was a very satisfying meeting for all of us. There were a lot of expressions of sadness about the termination of the group, yet everyone recognized that it was all right to be saying good-bye.

The facilitators met informally after each session to process the content, to adjust plans for subsequent sessions, and to determine necessary interventions or school contacts. As previously noted, several avenues built into the life span of the group provide for facilitators' contact with parents and school personnel.

Evaluations

The composition of this group worked well but we realized once the group had begun that the experience had potential value for Mark and Steve, primarily because they shared similar experiences of loss. We did not consciously recognize how different the issues were for a child who had no conscious memory of a parent and would pay more attention to this circumstance when forming future groups. As it was, Mark and Steve connected for the first time in their lives with another youngster who shared this experience and the impact was considerable on both of them.

Adam and Tracy dropped out of the group due to transportation problems that could have been solved had facilitators been notified. Neither family could be contacted by phone. Their guidance counselor later related that Adam did not want to return, but that Tracy wished she had been able to continue. We made contact with both children through the school guidance counselor, returning their materials to them and expressing our regrets that they were no longer in the group. With Adam's permission, facilitators conveyed their concern to the guidance counselor related to the issue of his enforced pallbearing at his grandfather's funeral, and they worked together at school around this issue.

Participants filled out a form detailing their assessment of the group's helpfulness to them during the final session, and parents were requested to return their evaluations by mail. Informal feedback about the group's impact on participants also emerged from the facilitators' contacts with area guidance counselors, parent participation in the adult bereavement support group, and smalltown networking.

Group participants felt that talking about feelings and the deaths in their lives was the most helpful aspect of the group. One student commented that "it was helpful to understand it was not my fault." When asked what was the most important thing that they learned, responses validated what we know about support groups: "I learned that I wasn't the only one my age that was missing a parent," "that it's okay to be upset," and "talking about it makes it better." All participants said that they would recommend the group to a friend who had had a death in the family "because it was helpful to me" and "I learned how to cope with my feelings."

The parental evaluations were also extremely positive. Evaluations and personal contacts with many of those who did not return the forms indicated that most parents felt that their children had benefited from the group and were very sad to see the group ending. Steve's mother felt that the group had had an enormous impact on her son; she reported that he was more outgoing and had much more self-confidence. Although there were still concerns about Greg's handling of his anger, he seemed to exhibit fewer incidents of explosive, aggressive behaviors by the end of the school year. A year later, Heather's parents reported that she was in counseling and that her own illness seemed to be under control, and, "best of all, she was able to cope with and even visit her other grandmother in the hospital when we thought she was dying. I'm sure it was because of the help she got in your group."

One of the advantages of this kind of group is that diverse needs, different "stages" of grieving, and various learning styles can be accommodated. The benefits for Nina derived from being able to "talk story" about her disbelief and shock at her father's recent death, and her horror at the subsequent family dynamics at a time when she did not appear able to do this with her family. Still in the very early days of shock and adjusting to the reality of her father's sudden death, Nina will have information about grief available to her in her memory book, even though she may not have been able to absorb much of that information during the course of the group. The group provided a safe place to "talk story," and a community of people who let her know she was not alone in her experiences, which is what she needed at the time.

Others in the group who were farther along on their journey through grief benefited from the exposure to information and the sharing of pain that follows the numbness of shock.

The variety of activities and options for executing them recognized and permitted the differences in the way individuals receive and process information. This became dramatically clear to the facilitators with the feedback from both Steve and his mother. Our perceptions of his limited participation in the group and his flat affect would have led us to believe he was not engaged in the group to a meaningful degree. Yet his mother and school personnel reported dramatic changes in his affect and behavior once the group ended. Steve himself gave us the clue to the benefits the group held for him when he reported that "writing things down on paper" was the most helpful aspect of the group for him.

DISCUSSION QUESTIONS

1. What are some considerations with regard to group membership in a bereavement group for preadolescents? How important are age and gender characteristics of the participants, and how do you evaluate the appropriateness of combining recently bereaved with those whose loss was more remote?

2. Discuss the responsibilities of the group leader when group members drop out prematurely, as in session 5. How should this be handled in the group?

3. What characteristics distinguish the normal grief reactions of junior high

school youth from that of latency-age children? What are the implications of these differences in planning bereavement support groups?

4. What are your ideas about the advisability of follow-up meetings of time-limited bereavement groups such as described here. If you believe that such follow-up might be included, how long after termination would you implement this, and how would you structure this session?

REFERENCES

Erikson, E. H. (1968). *Identity: Youth and crisis.* New York: Norton.

Lonetto, R. (1980). *Children's conceptions of death.* New York: Springer.

Rubin, J. A. (1984). *Child art therapy* (2nd ed.). New York: Van Nostrand Reinhold.

Sarnoff, C. A. (1987). *Psychotherapeutic strategies in late latency through early adolescence.* Northvale, NJ: Jason Aronson.

Schwartz, W., & Zalba, S. (1971). *The practice of group work.* New York: Columbia University Press.

St. Exupéry, A. de (1942). *Flight to Arras.* New York: Harcourt, Brace and World.

Zambelli, G., Clark, E., & Heegaard, M. (1989). Art therapy for bereaved children. In H. Wadeson, J. Durkin, & D. Perach (Eds.), *Advances in art therapy* (pp. 60–80). New York: Wiley.

CHAPTER FOURTEEN

School-Based Intervention following Violent Death in a Classmate's Family

MARY MUNSCH

The death of a child is always a tragedy, but when the death occurs because a mother shoots her own child, the tragedy is compounded by horror and disbelief. Elementary school children need to feel safe and protected by their parents. Although they may witness violence on television, most do not realize that the televised violence can happen to someone in their own circle of family and friends.

This chapter deals with the harsh reality of a mother's murder of her 1-year-old child and the serious wounding of her 7-year-old daughter. The school implemented an immediate crisis intervention to help the second-grade classmates of the wounded child and to assist the school staff and parents with the aftermath of this tragedy.

This incident occurred over a weekend. When the children returned to school on Monday morning, some of them had details of the tragedy from the neighborhood or from the television or newspaper accounts, while others knew nothing of what happened. Consequently, when they met on the playground that morning, the conversation about what had happened included both accurate and inaccurate information, while some students and faculty still had no knowledge of the incident.

CRISIS INTERVENTION PLAN

This tragic event had tremendous implications for the student who survived the attack, but my focus as a school counselor was directed toward the school community. A crisis intervention plan had to be enacted immediately to deal with the impact of such an horrific event on that community. The immediate task of the intervention worker was to meet with the school principal to ascertain correct information regarding the tragedy. A second concern was to identify students who would be adversely affected by this event and to develop a potential strategy for intervention (Humphrey & Harper, 1991). This was a small elementary school, kindergarten through eighth grade, with frequent interactions between grade levels. Because of this, we decided that intervention had to include the entire student body.

Prior to intervening with the children, however, the faculty and staff had to receive correct information about what had occurred. It was also necessary to get their perception of what the immediate effect was on the school community (Humphrey & Harper, 1991). Parents, too, had to be included in the intervention strategy (Humphrey & Harper, 1991). They, like the faculty, staff, and children, needed to know the correct information about what had happened and, in addition, they needed help to understand how they could participate in the intervention plan, since the families' responses to the death and early crisis would strongly influence the responses of the children (Haran, 1988). Time was a pressing factor since the tragedy was very public, and faculty, parents, and children had already begun to pass misinformation. There was also the real likelihood of media presence at the school. All of these factors necessitated that the intervention proceed without delay. A threefold intervention plan was enacted immediately, consisting of the following:

1. Meetings with each individual class in the school
2. A general parent meeting followed by meetings with parents in smaller class groupings
3. A meeting with the faculty

A crisis team of seven social workers was convened to staff these meetings, working in teams of two.

REACTIONS OF SECOND-GRADERS TO DEATH

The primary focus of this chapter will be the work with the second-grade classmates of the student who was directly involved in the tragedy, and their parents, since these students were the ones most affected because of their personal contact with her.

The children in this second grade were 7 or 8 years old, in the latency period of development. The child in latency is becoming less egocentric and more able to view the world from an external point of view.

It is during this time that the child develops the capacity for feeling guilty for events that have happened or might happen (superego development). In this case it was common for some of the children to react with feelings of responsibility for what happened to their classmate and feelings of guilt because they did not prevent it. It is also during latency that the child's concept of death develops, depending on the influence of the family, religion, and the child's own life experiences (Haran, 1991). The horror of this tragedy was that it was caused by the mother of the children. Although this was a Christian school where there was a strong belief that people who die go to heaven and are happy forever, no belief could compensate for the fact that a mother seriously hurt one of her children and killed another.

Children in latency often believe that death is a punishment for wrong-doing (McIntire, Angle, & Struppler, 1972). The children in this second grade struggled long and hard to find a reason for the tragedy, hoping that their classmate did nothing to provoke her mother's reaction.

Latency children also begin to understand that death is not reversible and that it can happen to anyone, including themselves (Haran, 1991). Children at this age may begin to experience sleep disturbances, somatic complaints, and concerns for their own and others' safety as they begin to think of the possibility that they too might die as the victim of a violent crime. Children at this age are very curious about the body in general and about what happens after death when it stops working. In an attempt to master the concept of death they will ask repetitive questions, many having to do with the mechanics of the body and the circumstances surrounding the death. In a violent tragedy such as this, it is common for the children to ask for many details about the violence and the actual cause of death. They may respond to the trauma by needing to tell and retell the story in all of its horror.

FIRST GROUP MEETING WITH THE CHILDREN

Many of the above mentioned concerns were voiced by the children in the second grade during the first group session following the tragedy. In this session there was clearly a beginning, middle, and end, each with a specific focus. In the beginning, I was introduced to the class as the school counselor by the principal. He explained that I had come to the class today to talk about some very serious information with them. The principal was well known and liked by these children; his alliance with me made it easy for them to trust me. The middle phase of the session was devoted to allowing the children a time to clarify what they had heard about the tragedy, to correct any misinformation, and to vent their feelings about the situation. Part of my function was to assess the impact of the event on each individual to determine if the tragedy had precipitated a state of crisis for certain students, based on the significance of the event in each student's life (Dixon, 1987). The group was brought to closure by giving the students an opportunity to make cards for their hospitalized classmate. This helped bridge the transition back-to-school work and gave the children some control over the situation. It gave them something that they could do, besides feeling helpless (Roberts, 1990). After the classroom session, the children who appeared to be especially affected by the tragedy, due to their personal experiences, received individual follow-up contacts to assess further their need for more intense crisis intervention. Some were referred for ongoing therapy. Repeat visits to the classroom were held on the next day and every few days for about 2 weeks, at which time it was determined that the children as a group were able to resume their school functioning without ongoing intervention.

THE CASE: SAMANTHA, AGE 7

Family Information

Samantha Miller was a 7-year-old second-grader who lived with her mother and 1-year-old sister, Sarah. The mother had been in psychiatric treatment for postpartum depression on and off since the birth of the baby. The father of the children had been absent from the family since he became aware of his wife's pregnancy. The family was supported by public assistance and the children were cared for by Mrs. Miller's sister in her absence. Beginning shortly after her sister's birth, Samantha had been worried about her mother's illness and shared this openly with her classmates. The family were Christians with a strong belief in God.

Presenting Problem

Early one Sunday morning, the mother awakened and heard voices that told her that her children would be happier if they could be in heaven with Jesus. She listened to these voices and shot both children and then herself. Neighbors heard the shots and called the police. Samantha survived, as did her mother; however, the younger child was dead when the police arrived. The story aired on the evening news Sunday night and was reported in the papers on Monday morning. All of the horror was depicted, including pictures of the bloodied apartment. When the second-graders came to school on Monday morning, it was evident that they had not for the most part seen the news or the papers but had heard rumors that someone in the school had been shot. Some connected it with Samantha, others did not.

Session 1: Second-Grade Class

I was accompanied to the classroom by the principal whom the children knew and liked. We hoped that his presence would help to create a climate of trust between the children and myself. The classroom teacher remained in the room, also to facilitate trust and so that I could model for her the essential skills to enable her to talk to the children about this event after I had gone.

After the principal and I entered the room, his first task was to introduce me to the children as a counselor, whose job it was to come and talk to children when they might be worried about something that had happened to them. They responded to me by saying "Good morning," but clearly they had no idea about what I did. The following section reconstructs details from this meeting.

Content of Session	*Analysis and Feelings*
COUNSELOR: Good morning.	
CHILDREN: (*In unison.*) Good morning.	
C: I have something very important to talk to you about today, so could you please clear off your desks and give me your best attention?	As I begin, I am very apprehensive as to how the children will respond to this terrible news.
CH: (*They buzz a little as they move to put books away and give me attention.*)	
C: Are we ready? (*They nod yes.*) Mr. Smith [principal] tells me that Samantha is absent today. (*Some respond by putting their heads down, others cry silently, others look around to see if she is really absent.*) Does anyone know where she is?	Obviously there is a big difference in the information that various children have.
CH: I think that she is in the hospital.	
C: That's right, she's in the hospital. Does anyone know why she's in the hospital?	
CH: I think that she has the chicken pox. (*Children who obviously know what has happened are angered by the response.*)	Confirmation that they all do not know.

C: No, she doesn't have the chicken pox.
Has anyone heard anything else?

CH: Yes, she got hurt. (*This child is cry-ing and very solemn.*)

C: Yes, you're right, she was hurt and
hurt very badly. I'm here to tell you about
it and to answer your questions. (*Almost
spontaneously, many children ask, "How
was she hurt?"*) She was shot with a gun.
(*Many children are now crying—the
teacher, principal, and I are moving
through the room offering comfort.*)

CH: Is she going to die?

C: She was hurt badly but the doctors
think that she will get better, but it will
take a while. I have spoken to her uncle
who saw her and he said that she is
awake and talking but she hurts.

CH: Where was she shot?

C: In her back and arm. (*There are gasps
from some of the children.*)

CH: Who did this to her?

C: This is going to be very hard to un-derstand so listen carefully. Samantha's
mom has been sick (*some nod agreement*)
and because of her sickness, she was the
one who shot Samantha. (*Children begin
to cry loudly. Many of the children are
asking why? Others are saying, "I knew
it, I saw it in the paper"; other are say-ing, "I didn't believe the kids who told me
that this morning."*) It's very important to
understand that Samantha's mom did this
because she was sick. I know that she
loved Samantha very much and would
never hurt her if she was okay, but she
wasn't.

CH: Did she have cancer?

C: No, she had a sickness called depres-sion. Do you know what that means?

CH: It's when you feel sad.

Further clarifying my role.

It is impossible not to be af-fected by their grief. It is
almost overwhelming for the
adults in the room.

I start to feel like I cannot
continue.

At this point it becomes very
hard to continue as I
empathize with their pain.

It is really *hard* to accept that
a mother could do this to her
own child!

It is important to give infor-mation so children won't con-fuse "sick" with killing.

C: Right, but it's not an ordinary sad feeling like you might have when you can't go someplace that you want to go. The *sickness* depression means that you are sad that you don't *ever* feel happy— *nothing* makes you smile.

CH: Can you take medicine?

C: Yes you can and, as a matter of fact, Samantha's mother was taking medicine but she stopped taking it, and she felt so terrible that she thought there was no good reason for *anyone* to go on living, not even her children.

CH: What about her baby sister? Did her mom hurt her too?

This is very difficult. I am not sure how much more they can hear.

C: This is very hard to hear but, yes, her mom hurt the baby too and she was hurt much worse than Samantha. She won't get better; she died. (*More crying, sobbing, and questions why—we adults are again moving around the room comforting children.*)

It takes up to this point to get the information out. Rather than present the information all at once, I let it evolve in bits from the children's questions.

CH: But where is her sister now?

C: She's in heaven.

Consistent with the children's religious instruction.

CH: (*Crying.*) My father's in heaven too, and now we are moving and he won't know where to find us.

Death of the baby brought back feelings about the father's death. This child may need further intervention.

C: Up in heaven your dad can look down on you and he will always know where you are and how you're doing.

CH: That's what my teacher said. Will Samantha's sister know where she is?

Evidence of consistency with religious teaching.

C: I think so. (*At this point there is more discussion about what heaven is like.*)

CH: (*Sobbing.*) I could have stopped it.

C: What do you mean?

CH: I was supposed to sleep over at Samantha's house and if I was there that night I could have stopped her mother from doing that. It's my fault. I was her best friend.

Another child who will need further help based on her feelings of guilt and responsibility for what happened.

C: I know Samantha was your best friend and that you loved her a lot, but I'm afraid that you might never have been able to stop her mom—kids are just too small to stop adults. (*Other children to this girl: "If you were there you might have been hurt too. Good thing that you weren't there."*) I'm really glad that you're okay. Samantha is going to need a good friend to help her when she comes home. (*Child goes on to say what she will do for Samantha when she comes home. We encourage this.*)

Trying to reassure this child.

CH: My mother has depression—I hope she doesn't hurt me (*crying*).

Another child for further help.

C: How do you know that?

CH: She's supposed to take medicine but sometimes she doesn't. Once the ambulances had to get her. She yells a lot now.

C: Has she ever tried to hurt you?

CH: No, never; but now I'm afraid.

ANOTHER CHILD: My mom would never hurt me, she's too tired from my birthday party.

A real break in the heavy mood—children are laughing. Good example of the fact that they are all at different places.

C: (*Back to child with the depressed mother.*) I think that you and I should meet a little later in private to talk about mom. Would you like that?

CH: Yes.

C: As a matter of fact there are some other people in the room I would like to meet in private (*I identify them*). Would that be okay? (*They respond yes.*)

CHILD NOT SO IDENTIFIED: Can I come too?

What is going on? Is this attention or crisis?

C: Sure you can. As a matter of fact any of you can. I will ask your teacher to make a list of any children who want to talk in private. Okay. (*Smiles.*) This was a *very* hard day. How are we doing now? (*There is soft crying—some answer for the class that they are sad—they don't want to do anything.*) I have a great idea! Why don't we spend some time making get-well cards for Samantha. We can let her know that we want her to get better and that we are praying for her. (*This is met with enthusiasm from the group and we distribute materials and proceed with the task.*)

Further screening is necessary for children who have not spoken up.

Comment on the Session

By the time I was ready to leave the room, the children were very absorbed in the card making. They were each trying to make a "best card." I felt confident that they were all right for the moment, but I was totally drained. Explaining the tragedy to the children had a tremendous impact on me. I was almost overwhelmed with the horror of the situation. I needed to meet with a colleague to vent my own feelings of grief and horror. The principal and I did just that. It took some time for me to "regroup" before I was ready to begin to see individual students or to meet with faculty.

Session 2: Second-Grade Class

I went into the room on the next day to ask how they were doing. I had a report from the hospital that Samantha was progressing and was able to give them that information. There were many questions on that day about the incident. Some of the questions were very graphic as to where she was shot, how much blood had she lost, and so forth. Many more of the children had seen the newspaper by now and had seen pictures of the bloodied walls in the apartment. This prompted more specific questions. In addition to these, there were many concerns about Sarah, Samantha's little sister—specifically about where her body was, what it looked like, when it would get buried, and what happens when it gets buried.

Many more children spoke of relatives who had died and about going to funerals and cemeteries. They wanted to know about a funeral for Sarah, and we still had no information about this.

Another issue for the children concerned their safety. They wanted to know what to do if an adult was threatening them. I inquired about sleep disturbances and found that many had not slept well the night before. I tried to normalize this and we discussed what to do if they woke up in the middle of the night.

Comment on the Session

In general, this session was much less emotional with the children asking more questions. The hardest questions were about the mother's depression. It was hard for them to conceive of a sickness that would make a mother hurt her children. I struggled with this, but never got to the point where I felt that they could really understand.

Meeting with Second-Grade Parents

On the evening of the first session with the children I met with the parents of the second-graders. My purpose was to inform them as to what had been done with their children during the classroom session, to allow them to express their fears and concerns relative to their children, and to identify for them some behaviors that their children might be demonstrating as a response to the tragedy. Among these behaviors were the following: generalized fear, insomnia, nightmares, excessive clinging to parents, and regressive symptoms such as bed-wetting or thumb-sucking. As I had done with the children, I wanted to normalize these reactions (Roberts, 1990, p. 67). I also indicated to the parents that if these symptoms persisted for several weeks, further professional help might be indicated.

A major concern for many parents was how to speak to their children about the tragedy. I encouraged them to take their lead from the children, responding as honestly as possible to questions raised in response to what they had heard or seen on television, or to worries they might have. I also encouraged the parents to be very supportive to the child who required extra attention, especially around bedtime. It might be a time for bending rules about bedtime behavior. As an example, some children had already asked their parent(s) to lie down with them for a while before they fell asleep. I suggested that this was a normal reaction to such a tragedy and predicted that the need for this reassurance would be transitory.

This meeting seemed to allay many of the parents' fears. The information presented gave them a handle on how to approach their children. Having some idea of what to expect from their children and having been given language with which to answer their children's questions gave the parents more control over the situation and removed some of their feelings of powerlessness.

INDIVIDUAL CASE EXAMPLES

As a result of the classroom meetings with the second-graders, certain children were identified as requiring further intervention. Among the children so identified were John, the child who related the death to his father's; Karen, Samantha's best friend; and Lauren, the child whose mother also suffered from depression.

John, Age 7

Identifying Data

John was a 7-year-old second-grader, the youngest of four children. His father had died suddenly of a heart attack the previous year. John lived with his mother and three siblings and they were planning to move within the next month to a new home across the country so that they could be closed to their extended family.

Presenting Problem

John had already been upset by the anticipated move. At first he said that he did not want to leave school and friends. Some time later he expressed to his mother that his real fear was that his father (in heaven) would not be able to find him in the new home. John and his father were very close and he was devastated by his death. The impending family move exacerbated his feelings of grief as did the discussion of the death of Samantha's sister.

Initial Contact

At my initiation, based on John's reaction during the first classroom session, John came to see me in my office in the school. Initially, he appeared to be very comfortable with me and expressed being happy that I had chosen him to come to see me all by himself. His mood changed dramatically when I mentioned his father.

Content of Session   *Analysis and Feelings*

COUNSELOR: John, I remember that when
I was in your classroom, you told me that
your daddy had died.

JOHN: (*Begins to cry.*) He had a heart at-   I reach out to take his hand
tack when I was in first grade, and I miss   and he climbs up on my lap.
him a lot.

C: It must still hurt so much.

J: It does, because my daddy did lots of
stuff with me and I miss him. (*Cries harder, his head on my shoulder.*)

C: (*I hold him but continue speaking.*)   My attempts to comfort him.
It's okay to cry. I know you miss your
dad very much.

J: (*Nods.*)

C: John tell me a little about Daddy.   I want to talk about the posi-
What did he do with you?   tive relationship he had with
                                                    his father to move toward the
                                                    significance of the move for
                                                    him.

J: We used to play, go to the store, and
he helped me with my homework.

C: (*At this point I get him to elaborate
more about what they did; he gets off my
lap and talks while moving around the
room.*) Your daddy sure loved you a lot!

J: And I love him!   He uses present tense.

C: Do you think that your daddy can still
love you from heaven?

J: Of course he can, because he knows
everything I do. (*Mood becomes somber.*)
But when we move, he won't know where
to find me.

C: He won't know where to find you?

J: Who would tell him?

C: I think you could.   I see his confusion.

J: I could?

C: Sure you could. If Daddy knows
everything that you do, then he must be
able to hear you.

J: How?

C: I'm not sure but I really believe that people in heaven who love us can hear us when we talk to them.

J: You do.

C: I really do. As a matter of fact, my mom is in heaven and I talk to her and I believe that she can hear me.

J: Wow!

C: Pretty neat, huh? (*He nods.*) Do you know what you call it when you talk to people in heaven?

J: No, what?

C: It's called praying.

J: Oh, yeah, right! I remember, like when you talk to God, it's a prayer.

C: You got it!

This becomes difficult because we are in the area of belief, yet, I know that this child has been taught this concept.

He is obviously thrilled by this news.

We continued the session with some discussion of what heaven must be like. I asked him to draw me a picture of his father in heaven. He drew a man sitting on clouds looking down on a little boy. Both the man and the boy were smiling. He took this picture home to hang in his room to remind himself that his father knew where he would be.

On John's last day in our school he came to my office to say good-bye. During this brief session he asked me if I could please tell his dad that they were moving tomorrow and mention the address, just in case he had not heard him. I promised that I would and I could see relief on his face. He left my office happy.

Assessment

John came from a very loving and supportive family who were sensitive to his feelings of loss exacerbated by the move. Their belief system supported the concept that his father would always know where he was and this provided him with some sense of security. His mother would be alert to signs that he was not adjusting well to the move and would seek help for him.

Karen, Age 7

Identifying Data

Karen was Samantha's best friend. She had been asked repeatedly by Samantha to sleep over at her house. For one reason or another this had never happened. Karen was starting to feel that she could have prevented the attack on Samantha and the death of Sarah, her sister, had she been sleeping over the night of the attack.

Presenting Problem

In the days following the tragedy, Karen's mother approached me for help because Karen was having nightmares and crying excessively. As she had expressed in the classroom, Karen expressed her feelings of guilt and helplessness to her mother about not being able to prevent the tragedy. She kept coming back to the point that if she had been at the Miller home on the night of the tragedy, she could have prevented the horror. I had already planned to see Karen but was further concerned after learning about her mother's concerns.

Initial Contact

Karen appeared sullen when she came into my office. I explained that I had wanted to see how she was doing because I knew that Samantha was her best friend and that she had been very upset by the tragedy. She acknowledged my concern but let me know again that she could have stopped Mrs. Miller if she had been at the house that night. It was a long and hard session, during which I tried to have her explain to me just what she might have done, all the while gently pointing out that as a kid she might not have been strong enough to stop Mrs. Miller and, in fact, could have been hurt also. She seemed to reach some understanding of this. I then switched the focus of the session on to what she could do for Samantha now. She wanted to visit the hospital; however, this was not yet possible. We settled on an immediate task of making another get-well card for Samantha and enclosing a letter with it. We did this together in session. In the letter she reassured Samantha that she was still her best friend and wanted her to get better soon. Karen left this session with the card and letter in hand and was going to get her mother's help in mailing it. I knew that she was relieved for the moment, but I was very concerned for her long-term well being.

Assessment

I felt that Karen would require ongoing therapy. Her grief was complicated by the fact that she felt somehow responsible for what happened.

Having her do the card and letter gave her some control over the situation and helped to relieve her feelings of powerlessness. Her recovery would be further complicated by the fact that when Samantha recovered, she would move to live with relatives and would be attending a new school, far from the old neighborhood. This loss of her best friend was for Karen very severe and only made her future adjustment more problematic. I referred Karen for therapy outside of the school setting.

Lauren, Age 7

Identifying Data

Lauren was the little girl in the class who said that her mother also suffered from depression. She lived with both parents and her 4-year-old sister. She also expressed a fear that her mother would try to hurt her like Samantha's mother did. I had asked her in the class if she would like to come to talk to me about this and she replied yes.

Presenting Problem

Lauren identified her mother with Samantha's mother and was very afraid that she could be hurt the way Samantha and her sister were hurt. Although she had stated in the classroom that her mother had never tried to hurt her before, I was very concerned that this incident would cause her to fear her mother.

Initial Contact

I saw Lauren very shortly after the classroom meeting. She came into my office knowing that I wanted to ask her about her mother's depression. She began by describing a time when her mother was real bad and the police had to come with an ambulance and take her to the hospital. She described being very scared by the police and being afraid that her mother would not come home. I asked her if she knew why her mother had to go to the hospital and she replied that her mother was yelling and screaming and trying to hurt her father. At this point, I was not sure what was wrong with Lauren's mother but was more concerned with uncovering her fear.

Content of Session	Analysis and Feelings
COUNSELOR: Lauren, you must have been very scared by all of that.	
LAUREN: I thought that my mom was being arrested.	

C: That must have been awful.

L: Yes, and I was afraid that Mommy would hurt Daddy.

I am losing the connection to depression.

C: Were you ever afraid that Mommy would hurt you, too?

L: No, I go into my room.

C: You go to your room, when?

L: When Daddy and Mommy fight.

I am confused as to what is going on.

C: Do you get afraid when they fight?

L: Yes, but I'm safe in my room.

C: They can't hurt you in your room.

L: No, but . . . (*She begins to cry, more confusion.*)

C: (*I reach out for her hand.*) But what Lauren?

L: (*She continues to cry and mumbles something about Daddy hurting Mommy.*)

At this point, she would no longer speak. She could not tell me what happened, and so I asked her if she could draw me a picture of what happened when Mommy got hurt. She took the markers and drew a picture of herself, her sister, her parents, and her aunt. All of the figures were in black, except her mother who was in red, with red blood on her face where she was hit by her father. She showed herself hiding in a circle (her room) and her sister in bed (see Figure 14.1). I had an impression that there was a lot of family violence in this home. No one in the school had suspected this up until this point. My concern at that point was to ascertain the safety of the children in this household.

As the session progressed, I tried to get an idea of how often the parents were violent with each other and what recourse there was for this child when it happened. She told me that Grandma knew that it happened and told her to call whenever she got afraid. Indeed, Lauren had called Grandma on a number of occasions and Grandma had come to pick her up. She left the session somewhat relieved and with the promise that we would talk again.

Assessment

After this first meeting, I was still uncertain as to why Lauren had connected the depression of Samantha's mother with her own mother. Fam-

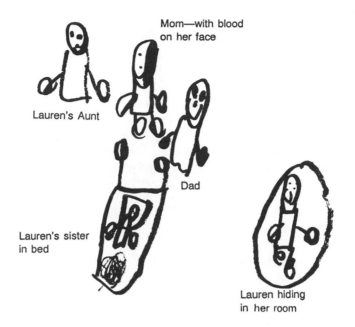

Mom—with blood on her face

Lauren's Aunt

Dad

Lauren's sister in bed

Lauren hiding in her room

FIGURE 14.1. Lauren's drawing of what happened when Mommy got hurt.

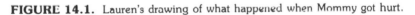

ily violence seemed to be the connecting factor for me. Further investigation did reveal that Lauren's mother had indeed been suffering from depression at the time she was removed from their home. She was also being medicated for the condition. Lauren had connected the violence with the disease.

Some sort of family intervention was necessary for this family. I did call a meeting with Lauren's parents and presented them with her fears for them and for herself. They admitted to being very physical with each other, but they thought that Lauren was unaware of their problems. After some conversation with them, I told them that I felt they could best help their child by trying to work out their difficulties. They said that they had tried counseling and found it to be useless and there was really no hope for their marriage. I then expressed my concern for Lauren and for her safety. I asked for permission to continue working with her to allay her fears and to monitor the situation. They were in agreement. Lauren has continued in therapy. Many of our sessions revolve around playing with dolls to play out the family tension and, thus, serve to relieve her anxieties.

CONCLUDING COMMENTS

This chapter outlined the immediate crisis intervention plan enacted with a second-grade class when a member of that class was seriously wounded and her sister was killed by the action of their mother. My primary goal was to help these children through the crisis and to identify those for whom ongoing help would be necessary in the aftermath of this tragedy. Immediate *work with the class* involved clarifying the information, allowing them to vent their feelings, reassuring them of their own safety, helping them to understand that their feelings were normal reactions to the tragedy, and helping them to understand that each would react differently. An important goal was to *identify individual students* who, because of their personal histories, needed ongoing intervention to return to normal functioning after the tragedy.

Intervention with the parents of all children in the school focused on helping them to understand their children's reactions to the tragedy. They needed encouragement and guidance about discussing the tragedy with the children rather than avoiding such discussion because of the discomfort it generated.

Although not presented in this chapter, the crisis intervention team also *worked with school personnel,* similar to the intervention with the parents. Emphasis was on helping them to facilitate the children's healing process.

The bright light at the end of this tragedy was that Samantha was able to come and visit her class before she moved away. The children were delighted to see her and her presence gave them the concrete assurance that she was okay. They exchanged addresses and many continue to write to her. After a period of approximately a month, the majority of the students in that second grade were able to return to their level of functioning prior to the tragedy.

DISCUSSION QUESTIONS

1. Consider how religious teachings can help or hinder a latency-age child's acceptance of the finality of death. Critique the counselor's responses to various children's questions about heaven and suggest some alternate responses.

2. Discuss the pressures on the school counselor, whose role requires both group and individual intervention following a traumatic death. What can the counselor do to avoid "secondary traumatazation" associated with feelings of horror and helplessness about such tragic deaths?

3. How do you understand Lauren's anxieties about her mother? What im-

pact can the school counselor effect on parents who admit to a failed marriage, and have given up on therapy?

4. Describe some play therapy interventions that can be utilized in a group format with children experiencing traumatic grief. What is the value of using some nonverbal approaches with latency-age children?

REFERENCES

Dixon, S. L. (1987). *Working with people in crisis* (2nd ed.). Columbus, OH: Merrill.

Haran, J. (1988). Use of group work to help children cope with the violent death of a classmate. In J. Haran (Ed.), *Violence: Prevention and treatment in groups* (pp. 79–92). New York: Haworth Press.

Humphrey, G., & Harper, C. (1991). Interventions in schools and communities after the violent death of a student. *The Forum, May/June,* 3–15.

McIntire, A., Angle, C., & Struppler, L. (1972) The concept of death in Midwestern children and youth. *American Journal of Diseases in Children, 123,* 527–532.

Roberts, A. (1990). *Crisis intervention handbook: Assessment, treatment and research.* Belmont, CA: Wadsworth.

APPENDIX

Training Programs and Certifications

PLAY THERAPY

A comprehensive directory of play therapy training programs may be obtained for a fee from the Center for Play Therapy, Denton, TX 76203. The programs listed here represent a small selection in different parts of the country.

Boston University
Postgraduate Certificate Program in Advanced Child
and Adolescent Psychotherapy
School of Social Work
1 University Road
Boston, MA 02215
(617) 353-3756

California School of Professional Psychology
Dr. Kevin O'Connor
1350 "M" Street
Fresno, CA 93721
(209) 486-8420

Center for Play Therapy
Dr. Gary Landreth, Director
University of North Texas
Denton, TX 76203
(817) 565-2909

Fairleigh Dickinson University
Psychological Services Department
Dr. Charles Schaefer
139 Temple Avenue
Hackensack, NJ 07601
(201) 692-2649

Pennsylvania State University
Human Development and Family Studies
Dr. Louise Guerney
University Park, PA 16802
(814) 865-1751

Postmaster's Certificate Program in Child and Adolescent Therapy
Dr. Nancy Boyd Webb, Director
Fordham University
Graduate School of Social Service
Tarrytown, New York 10591
(914) 332-6000

Reiss–Davis Child Study Center
Color Silbergeld, Director of Social Work
3200 Motor Avenue
Los Angeles, CA 90034
(213) 204-1666, x349

The Therapy Institute
180 North Michigan Avenue, Suite 1100A
Chicago, IL 60601
(312) 332-1260

GRIEF COUNSELING

Association for Death Education and Counseling
638 Prospect Avenue
Hartford, CT 06105-4298
(203) 232-4825

Certification courses for grief counselors and death educators. Offered during the 2 days preceding the annual National Conference in March of each year. Contact ADEC Central Office for details.

National Center for Death Education
Mount Ida College
777 Dedham Street
Newton Centre, MA 02159
(617) 969-7000, x249

Offers 1-day workshops (spring) and week-long institutes (summer) to train professional caregivers. A Certificate of Thanatology will be awarded following completion of necessary requirements.

TRAUMA/CRISIS COUNSELING

American Association of Suicidology
2459 South Ash Street
Denver, CO 80222
(303) 692-0985

Conducts an examination for Crisis Worker Certification prior to the annual meetings in April. Course work and relevant counseling experience must be verified to determine eligibility to take the exam.

International Association of Trauma Counselors
4131 Spicewood Spring Road, Suite G-6
Austin, TX 78759
(512) 795-0051

Endorses training programs to certify persons engaged in the field of trauma counseling. For further information, contact the IATC office.

Resources

SUPPLIERS OF PLAY MATERIALS

Chaselle, Inc.
New England School Supply
P.O. Box 1581
Springfield, MA 01101
1-800-628-8608

Childcraft, Inc.
20 Kilmer Road
Edison, NJ 08818
1-800-631-5657

Childswork Childsplay
Center for Applied Psychology, 3rd floor
331 N. 5th Street
Philadelphia, PA 19123
1-800-962-1141

Constructive Playthings
1227 East 119th Street
Grandview, MO 64030
1-800-225-6124

Kidsrights
10100 Park Cedar Drive
Charlotte, NC 28210
1-800-892-KIDS

Learn & Play
Troll Associates
100 Corporate Drive
Mahwah, NJ 07498
1-800-247-6106

Toys for Psychotherapy with Children
Play Therapy Associates
1603 9th Street, Suite 400
Greeley, CO 80631
1-800-542-9723

Toys to Grow On
P.O. Box 17
Long Beach, CA 90801
1-800-542-8338

Western Psychological Services
12031 Wilshire Boulevard
Los Angeles, CA 92005-1251
1-800-648-8857

BEREAVEMENT RESOURCES

The Rainbow Collection Catalog
477 Hannah Branch Road
Burnsville, NC 28714
(704) 675-5909

Lists books, films, and tapes for purchase related to bereavement in general, including many focused on children.

The Good Grief Program
Judge Baker Children's Center
295 Longwood Avenue
Boston, MA 02115
(617) 232-8390

Offers consultation to schools and community groups to help children when friend is terminally ill or dies. Maintains a resource library of films, books, and materials that may be borrowed or purchased.

National Center for Death Education Library
Mount Ida College
777 Dedham Street
Newton Centre, MA 02159
(617) 969-7000, x249

Maintains a collection of print and audiovisual materials on all aspects of dying, death, and bereavement. Some may be borrowed on interlibrary loan. For information, contact coordinator of Resources.

BIBLIOGRAPHIES

The following books contain listing of books, films, and tapes related to bereaved children.

Fox, S. S. (1985) *Good grief: Helping groups of children when a friend dies.* Boston: New England Association for the Education of Young Children.

Chapter 7 includes a list of selected books and films for children and a list of selected articles and books for adults.

Rando, T. A. (1991). *How to go on living when someone you love dies.* New York: Bantam (Original work published 1988)

A list of references on grief, categorized according to type of grief (i.e., pet loss, suicide, murder, chronic and terminal illness; not focused especially on children, but many references apply).

Wolfelt, A. (1983). *Helping children cope with grief.* Muncie, IN: Accelerated Development.

Includes separate reference lists of children's literature concerning death, readings for parents, teachers, and counselors, and general texts focusing on death and dying.

References on Religious/ Cultural/Ethnic Practices Related to Death

Berger, A., Badham, P., Kutscher, A. H., Berger, J., Perry, M., & Beloff, J. (1989). (Eds.). *Perspectives on death and dying: Cross cultural and multidisciplinary view*. Philadelphia: Charles Press.

Coles, R. (1990). *The spiritual life of children* (Christian salvation, pp. 202–224; Islamic surrender, pp. 225–248; Jewish righteousness, pp. 249–276). Boston: Houghton Mifflin.

Grollman, E. A. (1967). (Ed.). *Explaining death to children*. Boston: Beacon Press.

Johnson, C. J., & McGee, M. G. (1991). (Eds.). *How different religions view death and afterlife*. Philadelphia: Charles Press.

Ryan, J. A. (1986). *Ethnic, cultural and religious observances at the time of death and dying*. Boston: The Good Grief Program.

McGoldrick, M., Almeida, R., Hines, P. M., Garcia-Preto, N., Rosen, E., & Lee, E. (1991). Mourning in different cultures. In F. Walsh & M. McGoldrick (Eds.), *Living beyond loss: Death in the family* (pp. 176–206). New York: Norton.

Note: A list of references at the end of this chapter cites additional sources related to the following cultural religious groups: Irish, Indian, African American, Jewish, and Puerto Rican.

Index